BREAKTHROUGH MOMENTS IN ARTS-BASED PSYCHOTHERAPY

BREAKTHROUGH
MOMENTS IN ARTS-BASED
PSYCHOTHERAPY

Aileen Webber

KARNAC

First published in 2017 by
Karnac Books Ltd
118 Finchley Road
London NW3 5HT

British Library Cataloguing in Publication Data

A C.I.P. for this book is available from the British Library

ISBN-13: 978-1-78220-306-3

Typeset by V Publishing Solutions Pvt Ltd., Chennai, India

Printed in Great Britain by TJ International Ltd, Padstow, Cornwall

www.karnacbooks.com

This book is dedicated to Petruska

CONTENTS

ACKNOWLEDGEMENTS

My son, James Webber, the editor for this book provided me with patience, advice and support throughout its creation. Without him the book would never have been written and I am full of gratitude.

I would also like to thank my courageous clients, who have provided the rich inspiration and substance for this book and who have so generously given me their permission to include their stories. I would particularly like to acknowledge the work of my supervisor Jocelyne Quennell and my therapist colleague Sophia Condaris who have both been right by me side throughout the whole process. I am also grateful to Professor Volker Heine FRS a theoretical physicist (Cavendish Laboratory, University of Cambridge) for generously giving me feedback on the scientific aspects of the book. I am also thankful to my family (particularly Jonathan Webber and Kate Webber) and to my friends Suzanne Little and Mary Hart and to the many other friends and colleagues who have helped me overtly and unknowingly in my research and the writing of the book.

Many of my ideas have been inspired by the words of others. I would like to make particular mention of Petruska Clarkson, who I believe desired to write a book that drew upon the scientific concepts that I have included in my book. Whilst I have been working on this book

I have sensed her presence on many occasions. I would also like to pay tribute to Daniel Stern, who sadly died during the writing of this work and who was pivotal to my research. Were Petruska Clarkson and Daniel Stern still with us I would have asked them to write a preface to this book. In their absence I pay homage to their influence in the philosophies that underpin the book and hope that I have in some way "Dreamed the Dream On" …

Finally I would like to thank my granddaughter Anya Webber for always reminding me how to play.

Client permissions

The client stories presented in this book are based on actual therapy sessions with my own clients. Names and details have been altered to ensure anonymity. The clients involved have given written permission for the way their stories are presented. A few are composites of more than one client, and more than one therapeutic experience. I have aimed in all cases to ensure the essence of the stories is authentic.

ABOUT THE AUTHOR

Aileen Webber is a gestalt and integrative arts psychotherapist who provides therapy for adults and children and also supervises the work of other therapists. She has a private arts-based psychotherapy practice in Cambridge. Her work has been inspired by four years of gestalt psychotherapy training with Helen McLean in Cambridge and four years training at the Institute for Arts in Therapy and Education in London. Prior to working as a psychotherapist she worked as a teacher of children with physical, emotional and learning difficulties and as an adviser and consultant to others working with children.

The story begins …

Ben's Story

"I feel pathetic!"

This was the first thing Ben told me when he came for a therapy session at the higher education counselling service where I was working. He said he was desperate to stop being so "clingy" around his girlfriend. This self-assured young man sitting opposite me in the practice-room certainly did not strike me as being the clingy type.

He said that he was managing to "hold it together" so far in his new relationship but recognised the increasing fear of becoming "clingy" and was wary of it. This was a quality he felt had led to the demise of all his past relationships. He feared it would not be long before he was checking up on his new girlfriend's every move. He would become angry and tearful every time she left the house and would be thinking the relationship was over every time she became deeply absorbed in her work or a television programme. Ben told me that he only had this one counselling session with me to fix the problem. He wanted to try and work out what was going on because the following week he would be moving away from the area.

What could I do to help this distressed young man? And how could we identify his problem with just one session? I am an arts-based psychotherapist so this gave me several options. I work through arts media that include gestalt experimentation, puppets and drama, music and sound, visual and mental imagery, painting and drawing, sand trays and miniatures, rituals and enactments, poetry and clay. At this time I was still in training, but from my limited experience I had learned that looking at pictures can sometimes help a client encapsulate a feeling or problem in a creative and non-literal way. So I handed Ben a large pile of postcards (containing visual images) and suggested he turn them over one by one.

I asked him to select any cards that he felt represented his relationship or resonated with him in a way that could throw light on his dilemma. I recommended that he go with his gut instinct and not think about it too logically. Ben turned over card after card, discarding each one—the butterfly with translucent wings, the bleak blue landscape, the child crying in a vat of freezing water ... the whole time I watched intently. He paused at the image of a voluptuous woman in a towel but this too was eventually passed over. I was beginning to think that none of the images would resonate with him and I felt a stab of disappointment. Was I disappointed with myself or with what was going on for Ben here in this room? Was it a projection of what was happening in his life and relationship or a surfacing of my own sense of wanting to help him but not being able to?

I was musing on these possibilities when suddenly Ben stopped in his tracks, arrested by a particular postcard he had stumbled upon. Slowly and carefully he placed it on the floor between us. It contained the image of a mother orangutan and her baby (see image on next page).

Ben seemed to have slipped into a trance-like state as he and I focused our attention on the striking image in front of us. For some reason we were both spellbound. Ben was also clearly shocked, and after what felt like a very long time he spoke, in a voice choked with emotion.

"I don't know why I'm so upset," he said. He continued to gaze at the image. I looked across at him then down at the floor to the orangutan picture. It felt as though time was standing still and a moment laden with potential stretched out between us.

Given my own inexperience at the time, I felt unsure whether to break the silence or not. After a long pause I finally said softly, "The baby in the picture looks very 'clingy' to me, like he's clinging onto his mother in desperation".

Ben's mother and baby orangutan.

"Yes," Ben replied, still gazing at the picture, before adding breath-lessly, "and the mother orangutan looks depressed".

"And what about *your* mother?" I asked him.

I was acting entirely on my instinct here as I had only just met this young man and had no idea of his family circumstances, relationships or any proper context for the situation he had described. But I saw clearly from his face a sudden, powerful flash of understanding. In fact, it felt as if we both experienced this astonishing insight at the same moment. It seemed to come prior to all intellectual understanding; it had resonated somehow with a deeper understanding Ben did not yet have of the unique circumstances that had created this life dilemma and brought him to therapy with me. It was a breakthrough moment—all the more extraordinary for seeming to arrive out of nowhere.

"My mum was depressed when I was young," he said after a while, with tears in his eyes.

I felt an intensification of the connection between us as we each absorbed the significance of what he had said. For the remainder of our single session together there was a dramatic shift in his emotions and understanding as we spoke about this "clingy" behaviour with his girl-friends. We talked about how Ben might be recreating the feelings he had had as a little boy, desperately trying to reach his depressed mother. He told me he had lived alone with his mother in a dilapidated flat on the outskirts of the city. I could imagine him as a little boy, desperately trying to connect with the only person who was there for him in his lonely world.

We spoke at length about Ben's breakthrough moment, when every-thing in the room had seemed to change. The orangutan image had provoked deep feelings of sadness, and a powerful new insight that instantly threw light on an issue he had not previously recognised. It also seemed significant that he was aware I understood his feelings and the connection between his relationship with his mother and him being "clingy" with his girlfriends.

* * *

So much of how Ben understood himself seemed to change or reorganise itself in that intense moment. It was as if he suddenly recognised new aspects of himself and understood and accepted them in a deeply emo-tional way. He seemed to realise for the first time that his adult, intimate relationships were triggering feelings of desperation he had as a little boy about his inaccessible mother. From this moment onwards, every-thing about Ben's understanding of himself, his relationship with his girlfriend and his way of viewing the world seemed to be transformed. The discovery of one, seemingly random image had facilitated a cross-roads, a turning point, a tipping point and a breakthrough that brought about the potential for change.

PART I

SETTING THE SCENE

CHAPTER ONE

The first breakthrough

I was seven years old and sat at the kitchen table by myself eating breakfast. I was staring absentmindedly at the cartoon image on the back of a cereal box and perhaps daydreaming about the day ahead, when suddenly I was arrested by something about the image I hadn't noticed at first. The image was of Mickey Mouse holding a bucket and spade, which was not sufficient in itself to halt the wandering attention of a seven year old, but I now noticed something else about it: on the bucket that Mickey was holding there was a smaller version of the same image of Mickey Mouse holding a bucket, and on that bucket there, again, was the image of Mickey Mouse holding a bucket, and so on and so on, smaller and smaller, as far as my eye could see.

It was my first vivid encounter with the recursive phenomenon of *mise en abyme*—a formal technique from Western art history in which a given image contains a smaller copy of itself, in a sequence that appears to recur infinitely. My seven-year-old imagination was enchanted and bewildered by the mind-boggling effect. Mickey and his bucket were getting smaller and smaller until they were so small I could see nothing at all. And yet still I imagined him going on and on.

Even now, some six decades later, I can recall how radically and dramatically my way of viewing the world seemed to shift in that moment.

I was awestruck, confused, excited ... breakfast was abandoned. I had stumbled upon the single most important thought I had ever had and with it came endless new questions: Do these Mickey Mouse images go on forever? What is forever? And if an image seems to go on forever then where does it end? What would the end of forever look like? I did not have the vocabulary for concepts such as infinity or eternity. My mind hurt with trying to think about all these things, and I became aware for the first time of another person awakening within me. A deeply questioning person. In fact, this was so far beyond my usual experience that I felt as if I was an entirely different person to the one who had sat down to breakfast. I mentioned it to my parents, to my brother, to my friends and teachers, but no one seemed to share my wonderment.

When people ask me when my fascination began with breakthrough moments in therapy, I always come back to this striking moment my young mind was blown open by a seemingly infinite series of Mickey Mouses. It was my first clear memory of thinking about the unthinkable, which was to become a lifelong obsession. Ever since that moment I have yearned to increase my understanding and satisfy my curiosity about existential mysteries. I recall thinking in my seven-year-old mind that this was something vitally important and that seeing as other people didn't share my conviction it must be up to me to pursue it.

This is a book about breakthrough moments in arts-based psychotherapy. In this first chapter I look at how I first became fascinated by charged moments in therapeutic relationships and how they led me to train and practise as an integrative arts psychotherapist. I will present a number of examples of the sorts of moments I am referring to, from the perspective of both client and therapist. I will explain how I came to understand and classify them as breakthrough moments and how I ultimately chose the research methodology for this book.

My Mickey Mouse experience was a turning point. My seven-year-old self was forever changed in a single moment. I had a new, previously unformed belief that there is infinitely more to this world than we can ever know, and that the most fascinating and compelling way to live one's life is to question the things we take to be commonplace. From this point onwards, one part of me carried on with mundane everyday existence while another part got lost in impossibly big questions: Why are we here? How did we get here? What does it mean to be alive? Where do we go when we die? What is my purpose in life? Thanks to that cereal box I have had a continual dialogue with myself about these existential questions for many years now. These questions challenge me, possess me and often unsettle me, but most surprisingly perhaps, they are comforting. They remind me there is far more to this life than first appears and that our journey on this earth is wonderfully steeped in mystery.

Becoming a therapist

As I emerged from childhood to adolescence I dabbled with different religions and schools of philosophy but none were ever able to present what felt like satisfactory answers to the recurring questions that haunted me. One of the biggest of these questions was always: what is my purpose in life? I kept changing my mind as to what might be the answer. I became a teacher of children with disabilities, an advisory teacher for children with special needs; I studied the disciplines of philosophy and psychology. I even dabbled in art, creating my own paintings and drawings. And I had two children of my own. And for a while this felt enough.

But when my three-year-old son started grappling with big existential questions of his own I felt ill-equipped to satisfactorily answer him: "What is beyond the stars?" he would ask me, or "Where does the universe end?" One day he said simply, "Why am I me and not someone else?" I did not want to be intellectually dishonest with him and felt compelled each time to answer, "I don't know". As an adult himself now, my son assures me that the fact I never ended his stream of "why?" questions with a false answer or a "because I said so" was deeply important to the development of his own inquisitive mind. He recalls that together we would revel in mutual wonderment about the fact we simply didn't know and that this ultimately led him on a life-long quest of his own to pursue the impossible answers for himself.

It was seeing the same burning questions begin to arise in my son's mind that strongly reawakened them in my own. I decided to find a fulfilling new career—one in which I could acknowledge and somehow live among these existential questions. I wanted to help people engage with how to live their lives in the most satisfying way possible. And so—alongside no doubt many other unconscious motivators—I found myself embarking on training to work with children and adults as a gestalt psychotherapist.

Gestalt therapy is a humanistic-existential therapy concerned with a client's awareness of what they feel (about their issues, lives, and behaviour) in the present moment. Intellectual explanations and interpretations (from client or therapist) are generally considered less relevant. One of the first requirements of this training was to find a gestalt therapist to work with me, as well as an experienced trainer. I was fortunate enough to find two of the most exceptional practitioners, and the trajectory of my four required years of weekly therapy was extraordinary and life-changing. It took me to places and emotions I had never experienced. It enabled me to delve deeply into my unconscious and begin to understand how much of my past was still there, in my present. But as amazing as all of this was, it was not the thing that astounded me most.

What arrested me most about the work was the mystifying arrival of sudden and unexpected moments within a therapy session—moments in which the ground beneath me seemed to shift and the therapist and I were transported to another realm of experience, much like Ben's experience with the orangutan postcard. These profound moments, which occurred time after time, had the power to bring about new realisations that changed everything I thought I knew about myself and my way of being in the world. There were many such moments; one that I remember particularly vividly involved the acting out of a dream I had had in which I was carrying my red bicycle up a spiral staircase. In the dream I was trying to manage the contortions I had to put my body through to carry out such a difficult feat. Whilst I was engaged in acting out this impossible task, I looked up and caught the eye of my therapist. We both spontaneously burst into laughter and seemed to meet each other in a new way.

The humorous side of the moment was just one aspect of the experience. It was also the first time I had viscerally felt how the contortions in my life (at that time) were being physically and analogously represented by the contortions I was putting my body through as I attempted to carry my bicycle up the spiral staircase. I realised my dream was a powerful metaphor that seemed to contain the message: why do you make your life more complicated than it needs to be? Within this new, *felt* understanding was the genesis of what would later become a profound change for me. It felt like a genuine moment of transformation.

This pivotal moment with my gestalt therapist stayed with me. Every time I felt life twisting me up in knots, I remembered that ascent up the spiral staircase. It would make me laugh and I would look anew at whatever was the current set of circumstances. Time after time, as a result of this realisation, I would metaphorically put down my bike and just climb up the staircase. It was as if thinking about leaving my bike at the "bottom of the stairs" allowed me to leave unnecessary details and difficulties of a situation behind and just get on with it.

In short, this one, dramatically potent moment ultimately led me to change my entire habit of overcomplicating my life. The end result being that I was irrevocably changed in a way I was extremely grateful for and continually surprised about. But what was it about this initial moment that had brought about such a profound change in me? I can remember feeling a buzzing in my head and the sensation of being in a dream or trance. This was accompanied by a sudden and powerful moment of clarity. It felt like an overturning of my previous thoughts, feelings, and ways of behaving. At the same time it held the potential for change and the possibility of a new way of encountering and deal-ing with problems. Like the best possible kind of eureka moment, it felt as though I could never not know this fundamental truth about myself again.

Once I had discovered firsthand this powerful way in which therapy can assist a client to change, I was sold. I had intuitively believed ther-apy could help a person, but this moment and others like it had shown me it could have a profound, mysterious power to heal beyond any-thing I had previously imagined. I became very excited. If I could steer my own clients to (and through) such profound moments, I felt sure it could make a difference to their lives in deeply significant ways. But here was the problem. How could I ever hope to enable my clients to experience similarly resonant and mysterious breakthrough moments when in truth I had no idea how my own had really occurred? Perhaps only experienced therapists were able to provide a setting in which such moments could occur. Perhaps they knew some special trick or technique that made them arise.

No amount of pondering on the subject gave me an answer and I began to sense that my own clients might never experience something akin to my bicycle-staircase moment. I felt deeply disappointed. If moments like these were the most important and transformative part of my own personal therapy, it would be a sad lack if my clients never had the chance to have similar experiences of their own. Just as I was begin-ning to feel that such a moment would never arise for one of my own clients, on an otherwise ordinary working day, a small but promising example occurred that helped me reassess my opinion.

Jade's story

Jade was trying to explain to me how desperate she was feeling one day. This young female client of thirteen years said that a fury had erupted in her when she was told to take her jacket off in class. The only way she could feel safe enough to be in the classroom was if she wore her jacket with the hood up. Why couldn't her teacher understand that? She was becoming visibly exasperated as she recounted the experience (despite the fact that she was wearing the jacket in question at the time, her face half hidden by its large hood). I was understanding of her point of view and deliberately did not present any opposition. In fact, I found myself thinking the jacket was indeed necessary for her, as it was a form of defence against what she experienced as total vulnerability, both in her classroom environment and now here with me, in her therapy session.

I asked if Jade could describe what it had felt like to be told to remove her coat. She thought about it for a while and then, hesitatingly, said it was as though there was a volcano hidden inside her jacket. I asked if she could describe it further and she began telling me about the colours, the noise, the rumbling and the eruption of the volcano. As she did so, she seemed to be going through some of the stages of the actual experience. I could see this in her body but made no comment as I did not want to break the spell of what was happening for her. "People always annoy me!" she said petulantly but then, sitting back in her chair with a triumphant air, she seemed suddenly to arrive at a new realisation. A breakthrough. She looked at me and it felt as though our eyes, our minds and our hearts met in a profoundly connected moment. In fact, this feeling between us was so profound that Jade quickly looked away. Loudly and in one big rush she suddenly said, all hesitation having vanished, "It's like there is this fire inside me. All these people keep getting at me. In class the other day, it built up and up and the stupid teacher said 'take off your jacket Jade!'" Her colour was reddening. "That was the final straw that ignited the whole volcano and then it erupted!"

I found myself picturing poor Jade disintegrating in a massive explosion—I had an alarmingly vivid picture of this *actually* happening. I was unsure what she needed from me, her therapist, and I rather inadequately said, "Wow! No wonder you felt as though you might explode!" Fortunately, it didn't matter what I had said. The experience had already been so profound and her realisation so filled with new, visceral understanding that Jade did not require much from me. She needed me only to empathically attune to the magnitude of her feeling and accept her belief that the volcanic eruption of anger could not have been prevented. Up until now she had not been able to properly understand why being asked to take her jacket off had resulted in her screaming and swearing at the teacher. Now she saw it vividly. She had shown herself, through the use of the metaphorical imagery of a volcano, what had been taking place within her at this time. Her breakthrough was the realisation that it was a build-up of all the previous times she had been told what to do that had led to her explosion. Her teacher's command to "take your coat off, Jade"—which was after all just a reminder of the school rule about not wearing coats indoors—was the final straw in a long line of previous demands made upon her.

* * *

Jade's breakthrough moment was the first that I witnessed as a therapist. It had slipped magically into the session and in truth I had done very little to encourage its arrival. I found myself wondering if moments like this just wondrously arose in all therapy. It wasn't long afterwards however that another such moment occurred, one that was even more strikingly transformative for the client involved, and one that changed my thinking yet again.

Discovering the arts

Samuel's story

At the time, I was working at a secondary school that included children with physical disabilities, many of whom had no speech and had to use alternative means of communication. One of these children was twelve-year-old Samuel. On this particular afternoon Samuel, who was intellectually able but physically disabled, spelled out for me on his alphabet board that he felt as though he was in "a pit of despair". I invited him to tell me more about this pit and he spelled out that it was "big, black and bleak" and that he felt "trapped in it forever".

I almost recoiled at the power of his metaphor. I imagined what it must feel like to be trapped in a body and life that require so much dependence on others. Samuel had little ability to shape his own destiny. Surprisingly, he asked me to draw a picture of this empty pit for him. I started to draw it and he asked me to include further details— a few extra lines here and there and some boulders. Many weeks of our work together went by in which Samuel and I would sit together in his emotional pit of despair, my illustration always on the floor in front of us. And then all of a sudden during one session he spelled out the unexpectedly moving sentence, "I am just beginning to climb out of the pit".

I repeated the words out loud to confirm I had received them correctly. For a while they hung palpably in the air between us. Samuel looked at me and broke into a gentle, knowing smile. There was a tangible sensation of something profoundly important having just taken place for him. I felt it viscerally and could sense that he felt it too. I found myself asking what kind of shoes he had been wearing as he climbed out of his pit of despair. He told me climbing boots and with great excitement spelled out a request for me to draw him climbing out of the pit. I quickly drew a big black climbing boot, cut it out and stuck it onto my illustration of the pit, thus creating a new image (see Figure 1.1). It seemed that having a visual image for his feelings helped Samuel to feel more understood. The metaphor he used for climbing out of his pit of despair may have been inspired by the view he could see from his bedroom window, of snow-capped mountains and craggy ravines. I imagined he had spent much of his young life looking out at this awe-inspiring scene, perhaps dreaming what it would be like to climb the rugged terrain for real. Samuel

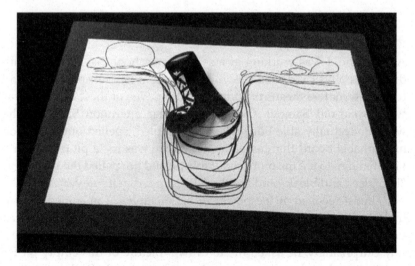

Figure 1.1. Samuel's pit of despair.

had cerebral palsy quadriplegia and was never going to be able to walk.

* * *

I have reflected often upon this session with Samuel over the subsequent years. It was clear that he experienced one of the same profound, transformational moments I had experienced as a client—one of those very moments I had been longing for my clients to experience. And yet this time it had arrived in another new and mysterious way. It seemed the illustration of the pit had somehow made it possible for Samuel to show me how he felt. But how? The drawing of the pit of despair had helped him see his problem in a new light and the climbing boot appeared to symbolise his belief that he was starting to climb out of the impasse. But how had a drawing enabled him to heal in such a transformative way, particularly when all else had failed?

So important was this session with Samuel and so hungry was I to chase and understand these kinds of pivotal moments, I decided to undergo some further training. Seeing as it was a drawing that had played the key role in leading Samuel to his breakthrough, I decided to expand my therapeutic training to include the use of integrative arts with my clients, in the hope that this might bring me closer to my goal. The new training would enable me to extend the use of drama and experiential exercises from my gestalt qualification to include the visual arts, the use of sand trays and miniature objects, and various other arts media. Having a powerful visual metaphor had helped Jade understand her disruptive behaviour; having a drawing of his predicament had helped Samuel show me how he felt; and seeing an image of Mickey Mouse had helped the seven-year-old me begin a lifelong obsession with vast, existential questions. The use of images was clearly able to bring about key moments when everything seemed to change forever. I felt I owed it to myself and to my clients to see what would happen if I specifically incorporated the use of these images into my therapeutic work.

I began training as an integrative arts psychotherapist, and as the training went on and I began to include art and art materials in sessions with my clients, it was extraordinary how many more of the transformative moments I had been chasing seemed to arise. And they always came suddenly. They appeared to herald both subtle and profound changes for my clients. And they came enveloped each time in the same heightened, mysterious atmosphere. For the first time, I decided to try and cast a net over these moments and really identify what they were.

Breakthrough moments

I knew what I meant when I thought about these moments but I also found myself referring to them in various different ways. I came across references to what might be considered such moments in the work of other writers. The descriptions I found included variously: tipping points, turning points, pivotal moments, change moments, profound moments, "a-ha" moments, eureka moments, crossroads moments, transformational moments, intersecting pathways, significant moments, key moments, critical moments, "I–Thou" moments, seminal moments, extraordinary moments, dramatic moments of change, moments of transformation, sparkling moments, metamorphoses, "no-boundary moments", light bulb moments, magical moments, cognitive snaps, epiphanies, hot present moments, charged moments, and transitional moments …

It was impossible to know if all or any of these descriptions were referring to the exact moments I had in mind, particularly when what I had in my mind was so specific. I was interested in moments of profound insight that arrive *suddenly*, without appearing to go through any incremental stages. It seemed beneficial to choose my own term and at least be sure then that my understanding of these moments could not be confused with any other. I tried out various ideas and at first nothing felt quite satisfactory. I wanted to encapsulate the transformative quality of these moments, the essence of which seems to provide a spontaneous breakthrough for a client to another level of insight, emotion, or connection.

A breakthrough has variously been defined as an advancement, step or leap forward; an innovation, revolution, or headway. Each of these seemed apt when applied to the moments Ben, Jade, Samuel and I had experienced in our therapeutic work. So I decided to settle on the term breakthrough moments. Now that I had a specific term for these moments, my thinking about them clarified. I could begin to discuss them with others and have a conceptual framework within which to increase my own understanding at the same time.

What does a breakthrough moment feel like?

A breakthrough moment always arrives suddenly. The atmosphere in the room appears to change in an instant. The accompanying feeling can be described as astonishing, profound, deep or mysterious for the client who experiences it (and often also for the therapist); it can feel transformational—beyond the usual experience of a therapy session. It can hold the intense possibility for a client that something deeply significant is about to happen. Sometimes it feels as though time is standing still or that there is no time at all, when in reality the moment is over in seconds—perhaps this is because the flow of all internal thoughts and mindless chatter has been halted.

There is a real intensification of the connection between therapist and client in these moments and it often feels as though they have each experienced the same insight at the exact same moment. In the wake of these magical, abstruse moments the whole relationship seems to change and become more intense. The client may enter a trance-like state and become mesmerised or spellbound. It may feel like a buzzing in their head. There may be a sudden rush of emotion or a flash of new understanding. It can feel like the best possible kind of eureka moment. A spotlight is shone on something not previously recognised and the client understands for the first time something she did not know she knew, something that can never then be forgotten. How a client understands their own self can also change or reorganise itself at this time in new and deeply emotional ways: a breakthrough moment seems to hold the potential for change and the possibility for a new way of looking at problems. From that moment onwards everything seems to shift and the way a client views the world seems to change and be transformed.

Once I had introduced the use of art and art materials into my practice, there was a marked increase in the number of breakthrough moments that arose with my clients. When I first began training in this integrative arts-based methodology it seemed strange to be introducing a box filled with sand to my clients. Why should that be helpful? But once I had gained firsthand experience as a client of making images in a sand tray, I understood the transformative potential of this approach. My therapist would ask me to choose objects (or figures) from a box that I felt symbolised different aspects, situations and people in my life, and to place them in a wooden tray filled with sand. Once placed in the sand tray these objects seemed to take on a life of their own and begin to tell me things I did not know I knew.

Now, many years after having completed my integrative arts training, I have my own box of objects—although in truth, this box has expanded to several dozen boxes, baskets, and packed shelves. One shelf displays, for example, a giraffe, a box of sheep, a two-headed monster, a mermaid, a scorpion, a witch's cauldron, a box of jewels, a dragon, a blue elephant, a miniature mask, a pack of Dalmatian dogs, and some miniature trees. A basket of painted stones sits on the floor (see title page). I now invite my own clients to select something to represent the issue they wish to work through. A family problem, for example, might be represented by a client choosing a group of elephants, a pile of stones or shells, different sized crystals, or a Russian doll family.

The integrative arts approach does not just involve sand trays and objects. My practice-room also contains masks, puppets, and musical instruments, as well as various art materials for making drawings, paintings etc. Other media may be selected by the client to create their images—chalks and charcoal, paints, or wax crayons. Situations from the past can be dramatically re-enacted in a number of ways. Images, symbols, metaphors and the different forms of arts media can be used separately or in combinations within the therapy. Day in, day out, my practice-room is thus peopled with events and characters from each client's past and present, brought to life in myriad imaginative and theatrical ways. The client and I can each see and relate to these creations and they in turn can support the telling of the client's story in a new and surprising way.

I am fascinated by dramatic and pivotal breakthrough moments, but I should point out that there are other important occasions and experiences in a therapy session that can be significant in a less dramatic way. Every image a client creates or selects brings something new to the work and they all lead somewhere unexpected. But there is something about breakthrough moments that stands out from the crowd. It is clear these moments help clients in a deeper and more profound way than any other aspect of the therapy. In this book I wish to ask *why.*

I will attempt to answer some of the dizzying questions that haunt me about these mysterious moments: What is happening in a breakthrough moment? How significant are these moments? Is it possible to know they are coming? Can the therapist do anything in particular to ensure they will arrive? How do they assist the client and the therapy? Do these moments always lead to change for a client, and is this a lasting change? What even is change in the context of psychotherapy? How can it be measured? These questions and more have provided the backdrop to my life as an arts-based therapist and supervisor, and here they will provide the backbone to this book. However much I scoured the literature, attended lectures and asked colleagues and psychologists,

I could not seem to find satisfactory answers to any of them. I was going to have to uncover the answers for myself.

Martin's story

I wasn't quite sure how to begin my investigation into breakthrough moments, but while I was busy wondering, a particular session with one of my clients led me to think differently about them again.

Martin was an anxious young man who had been studying art at college for two years. He had chosen to come for arts-based psychotherapy in the hope of finding out more about himself through the artworks he had been creating. Although he had been attending sessions with me for a while, his work had not yet presented any dramatic moments. Instead he would sit quietly for most of each session, sketching a succession of black and white images, all of which contained claws of some description (see Figure 1.2).

Martin would create further images of these claws in between sessions and arrive each week with a handful of new drawings. The whole time he seemingly had no idea what these claws might symbolise. They seemed always to be leading the way to something of vast significance and emotional magnitude for him, which never arrived. Would the significance of these claws arrive suddenly in a breakthrough moment? Or would they reveal their meaning more slowly and gradually? I was left feeling that the images were teasing us. I wondered if this sensation

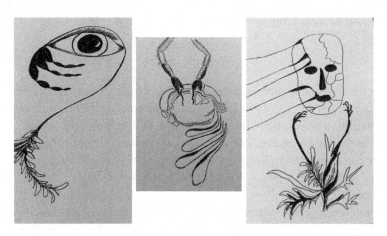

Figure 1.2. Martin's claws.

contained a hidden message for me about how Martin led his life. I felt almost seduced by the claws—pulled in and caught up in something I could not understand. I also felt *cautious*—I wondered if I might be attacked by the claws somehow if I did not tread carefully enough.

Around this time I had a dream that Martin was walking in the park with a tiger on a leash while I watched them both from the safety of a nearby tree. In the dream I felt nervous. It was clear that Martin was not able to properly control the animal as it strained and tugged against the insubstantial leash. Upon waking, I wondered if the dream illustrated an unconscious concern I had about Martin and his yet-to-be-revealed emotions—emotions that were perhaps difficult for him to control. The claws in Martin's drawings were unexpected and seemed to pave the way for future change, but why was he never able to access this? Were the claws somehow *denied* emotions nudging their way to the front of his consciousness? Did they contain feelings he had been told were unacceptable and should not be expressed or talked about—emotions such as anger, fear, and frustration? Either way, it was powerfully clear that his sketches were trying to tell him something.

* * *

We didn't find out what it was until much later in his therapy and Martin's experience left me with a new set of questions. There was no breakthrough moment in this instance, no single eureka moment of insight. Instead, it felt more like an extended journey of experience, filled with unexpected creativity, potential insight and hidden emotions that spanned several months of therapy.

Susan's story

Shortly after these developments with Martin, my client Susan arrived for her fourth therapy session. Nothing about her demeanour on this particular day seemed different to any of her previous visits, until suddenly she tipped an entire basket of stones out onto the floor. As their heavy clatter broke the silence, she said with a hint of defiance, "*These* are all the Susans—so who do you want to talk to today?" (See Figure 1.3).

I felt a tingle of excitement. This seemed more real and unexpected than the articulate and well-presented Susan I had met in each of her three previous sessions. We stared at the stones on the floor. I found

Figure 1.3. Susan's stones.

myself feeling challenged. Clearly Susan was defiantly expecting
something from me. But equally the moment seemed to hold an intense
possibility for something significant to happen (or indeed be lost)
depending on the appropriateness of my response.

There was a long silence in which it felt as though we were at a cross-
roads. Which way would we go? The potential of the moment was palpable. It felt like the *ah ... ah ... ah ...* build-up to a sneeze. It could
lead to something real, new and important or remain in the swell of
general possibilities. I found myself gazing intently at the stones as if
I were seeing them for the first time. They were painted with different colours and designs; some contained creatures and faces; all were
different shapes, sizes, and textures. I remember thinking they quite
successfully appeared to represent the different aspects of Susan that I
yearned to learn more about. And it was this thought that eventually
led me to announce, directly to all the stones, "Hello Susans—you are
all welcome here!"

As soon as I had said this, Susan shot a look at me; she knew suddenly, or so it seemed, that I had seen her in all her complexity and she

no longer had to hide or pretend. The moment felt timeless. The flow of my internal thoughts came to a halt. It felt as though a numinous, transcendent quality had entered the room. In one seemingly arbitrary moment, Susan's secret pain of feeling fragmented and having parts of her personality hidden to herself had begun to be revealed. And yet, at the same time, her secrets were still being kept safely concealed within the metaphor of the stones. It was at this point our real therapeutic work began and it would never be the same again. One seemingly insignificant moment within Susan's therapy had become a profound, pivotal moment—a breakthrough moment—and everything between me and Susan had irrevocably changed. How was this possible? I was more determined than ever to find out.

* * *

My burning desire to find out more about breakthrough moments as well as to understand the powerful role that images seem to play became all-consuming. It was no longer sufficient to be merely engrossed by these moments; I wanted to find a way to understand them in a more rigorous manner. But I would frustratingly find that no sooner had I begun reflecting deeply on a particular breakthrough moment with one of my clients (such as Martin and his mysterious claws) when another such moment would arise with somebody else. It became hard to keep track of them all. It was as if by steeping myself in the minutiae of each new breakthrough moment I was forgetting what might be crucial details of the past ones. I hated the fact that some of these magical moments were slipping away from me, like dreams I could no longer quite remember. How could I capture the experience of these moments in a more satisfactory way? If I was going to move from mere fascination to gaining some sort of concrete understanding of their actual significance, I was going to have to change my approach.

After a month of indecisiveness about how to proceed, I woke up one otherwise ordinary Wednesday morning and discovered a momentous decision had seemingly been made for me while I was asleep: I would start systematically recording and collecting every single example of these moments as they arose with my clients. I would also document the images and artworks from my clients' therapeutic journeys. This may seem like a small, even *obvious*, decision to the reader, but to me at the time it was a momentous one.

My first step was to embark on a formal research programme. I sought the framework of a university within which to carry out my study. I was accepted at two institutions to undertake a PhD but the additional requirements involved in a purely academic approach felt unnecessarily confining. I decided instead to set off on my research adventure alone. This way I was free to follow the course of the research wherever it took me.

The heuristic approach

To begin with I immersed myself in possible research methodologies in order to decide which would be the most appropriate approach for my study. I chose a heuristic research path that I would undertake as a practitioner-researcher. Braud and Anderson have said of the heuristic approach that it allows for a "plurality of voices" (Braud & Anderson, 1998). By this they mean that it allows a researcher to simultaneously include a number of different perspectives on their chosen topic—one of which represents the researcher's own voice. This approach was beneficial to me because it meant that as well as asking questions about breakthrough moments as a researcher, I could present what it *feels* like to be a therapist in the room with a client at the time a breakthrough moment occurs. I could also include the vantage points of my clients themselves, as well as therapists whose work I supervise. Alongside these perspectives I could include "other ways of knowing"—images, art-experience, tacit understandings, intuition and dreams, and I would be able to include data generated from psychology and psychotherapeutic theory.

Braud and Anderson suggest that heuristic research can involve data about anything that illuminates the subject being researched, providing it "promises to contribute to a full and rich depiction of the studied topic" (ibid.). In the case of my own research, a heuristic methodology would allow me to include ideas from the new sciences and spiritual wisdoms, as well as from the world of the arts and arts therapy. Unlike almost all the other research approaches I considered, the heuristic approach would allow me to present my own thoughts and experiences. In my role as researcher I would be able to include my self-reflections and phenomenological self-discoveries as a therapist, a client, and a human being. These multiple perspectives would, of course, need to be carefully categorised and recorded.

Clark Moustakas' excellent study of the heuristic method describes such an approach as being self-directed and thus demonstrating a unique pathway for the researcher who adopts it (Moustakas, 1990). Moustakas says that such a method takes the researcher through a series of stages. The first he calls initial engagement; I had already embarked upon this stage without realising when I began compiling information about pivotal moments in my therapy sessions and deciding to call them breakthrough moments. The next stage he calls immersion; for me this stage would involve gathering theories, ideas and images from the existing literature. I would turn to the various worlds of psychology, psychotherapy, art therapy, neurobiology, chaos and complexity theory, quantum physics, and spirituality. There was no one ideal place to look for a perfect understanding of breakthrough moments. Rather, there was a host of possible worlds and disciplines that could all shed some light on them. Adopting a heuristic approach to my research would allow me to move variously between them all. It was time to get started.

CHAPTER TWO

Mapping the landscape

Christine's story

At precisely the moment my client Christine was wondering if there was anything that could help her solve the dark and seemingly impossible circumstances of her life, an answer came that felt like it was sent from heaven. In our session one day, she was busy creating the beautiful image of a stone hand holding a crystal ball when a sudden ray of light exquisitely emerged from between the hand and the orb (see Figure 2.1).

It took a few seconds for us to realise that this was because the sun had emerged from behind a cloud and a ray of sunlight was shining through the practice-room window and was suddenly reflected under the orb. But it *felt* as though some sort of magical, otherworldly light had suffused her image with a revelation. The arrival of this light invoked the presence of something far greater than just the two of us and the strange process we had been engaged in. Although we were both aware of the explanation for the dramatic appearance of this light, it nonetheless felt like a powerful metaphor.

Figure 2.1. Christine's orb.

Later, Christine would describe the experience as feeling as though our attention was drawn towards a golden elephant in the room. She said it was as though "something bigger than either of us came into the practice-room at that moment". Her comment was all the more surprising seeing as she was a very down-to-earth sort of person, who up until that moment had only spoken of practical things, such as problems with her finances, relationships and academic work. It was as though the ray of sunlight breaking through the clouds and illuminating Christine's orb had in that instant enabled her to feel a profound awareness of the bigger picture of life and its ineffable mysteries. For my own part, as her therapist, I felt strongly that a force of some kind, far greater than either of us, was participating in her therapy at that moment.

* * *

As part of the immersion phase of my heuristic approach to research, I turned to the existing work of writers, therapists and psychologists to see if any of it could assist me in my quest to understand what makes breakthrough moments like these so extraordinary. In this chapter, I present some of my earliest findings.

The power of a moment

Martin Boroson's discussion of the concept of a moment proved a useful starting point. Boroson reminds us of the Latin derivation of the word "moment" from "momentum" in referring to a moment as "a particle sufficient to turn the scale" (Boroson, 2007). He states that whether moments are big or small, happy or sad, trivially significant or life-changing, they can all remind us that "ordinary life has the possibility to be extraordinary". In a single instant, "ordinary life can crack open to reveal another reality that was inconceivable the moment before ... The next moment might change things a little—or totally and forever" (ibid.).

Boroson's description seemed apt for the sort of breakthrough moment that had taken place with my client Christine. Christine and I both felt as though ordinary life had cracked open to reveal another reality previously unimaginable. Boroson's thoughts also lent weight to the idea that if a moment feels significant to a client (and/or their therapist), that in itself can contribute to the possibility of precipitating life changes. Whenever I have reviewed with clients what they remember most about their therapeutic work, they almost always mention the heightened charge they feel during a breakthrough moment. This charged atmosphere frequently includes sudden flashes of images and/or rushes of emotion/insight.

I found several references to the numinous, spiritual quality of moments where a therapist and client meet in an intense way. Fritz Perls (1973), Martin Buber, and Hycner and Jacobs all write about the "I–Thou" quality of such profound moments of meeting in therapy. Buber describes them as moments of "illuminated meaning". He suggests that in such moments a client comes to know themselves and others and is thus able to recognise their humanity more fully (Buber, 1958). Hycner and Jacobs see the therapeutic relationship as a transcendental process that includes an awareness of "the higher reaches of existence" (Hycner & Jacobs, 1995). Such ideas certainly capture how it felt with my client Christine. We both experienced an "I–Thou" quality in a moment that had "illuminated meaning"—this was in a literal sense, with the light illuminating the orb in the room, but also in a metaphorical sense, as it illuminated our experience of feeling connected to the higher reaches of existence and each other in a compelling new way.

* * *

As my research progressed, I came across dozens of images, descriptions and metaphors of different kinds of transformative moments in therapeutic situations. Tomas Böhm provides the lovely image of a slow-turning ocean liner to describe the gradual changes experienced by a client in psychoanalysis. But he also identifies a more abrupt kind of turning point that can occur in the therapeutic relationship—one he describes as "a momentary sudden change in quality, depth and direction" (Böhm, 1992), as experienced by Christine, Ben, and Susan.

Another description of Böhm's that felt particularly resonant was his poetic metaphor for what it feels like when a transformative moment occurs. He writes that it is "as if a metaphorical new door to a new unexpected room is opened". When Susan threw a heap of stones on my practice-room floor and asked which of the Susans I wanted to talk to that day, it felt precisely as though a door to a new room had been flung open. It was as if we both stood at the threshold together, gazing in amazement at the unexpected landscape before us (in this case, a room full of Susans). Christine, too, seemed to see new possibilities of support in the wake of her own breakthrough moment, as though a new door had opened for her.

In my study of the existing literature, I also looked to disciplines outside the field of psychology for what might be happening at the time of a breakthrough moment. As we have seen, my heuristic approach expressly invited the study of a range of different disciplines and media that might assist me. I was delighted to find a wide variety of different contexts in which reference is made to moments precipitating change. For example, Malcolm Gladwell speaks about "tipping points" in the worlds of fashion, crime, and publishing. He uses the metaphor of a moment spreading like an epidemic virus that becomes more and more contagious as it grows and infects. Gladwell's image resonates with how I imagine a breakthrough moment arising in a therapy session—like the slow, steady build of a wave that swells to a breaking point and crashes onto the shore. Gladwell writes that in the instance of a tipping point, a small cause can have a very big effect. He says that such effects do not happen gradually but involve "one dramatic moment" (Gladwell, 2000). Susan, for example, appeared to have "tipped" into a new state of being when she physically tipped the basket of stones onto the floor.

There appears to be a moment immediately prior to a client's breakthrough when the therapy could go either way, like a looming sneeze. The moment almost seems to hover in suspension, waiting for direction to emerge. Sometimes the opportunity is missed and the therapy must continue as it did before the promise of this seminal moment arose. It was this way for some time in my sessions with Martin and his depictions of claws.

Martin's story (continued)

Martin continued to prolifically create his sketches at home and within our therapy sessions together and still they always contained claws somewhere in the image. We had drawn a blank about what these claws might signify. Then one afternoon he walked into the practice-room and said quietly that he'd begun working on a new image, one that felt different somehow. He placed the drawing in question on the floor between us. It was a sort of elaborate doodle that involved a series of spiralling shapes and lines (perhaps the roots of a plant of some description) and a fully formed bird. The drawing also contained, once again, a set of his signature claws (see Figure 2.2).

Figure 2.2. Martin's bird claw.

When he began creating the image, Martin hadn't thought there were going to be any claws this time. But he said that at the last minute "they managed to claw their way in". He seemed defeated about the fact that these claws kept invading his pictures.

We had been waiting patiently in our sessions for months to see what the claws might signify, but the work had so far drawn a blank. I noted that at times Martin seemed guarded about learning their significance. He also seemed bewildered. I felt confused too, but I had experience in the mysterious nature of the therapy process and trusted that the meaning would reveal itself in good time. On this rare occasion, however, my impatience got the better of me and I found myself speaking directly to the claws: "Oh, hello claws", I said rather absurdly, talking to the drawing on the floor, "Martin thought you weren't going to make an appearance today, but here you are. Good to see you!" There was an immediate shift in the atmosphere. Martin's neck reddened and he looked as though he was about to speak. It felt vividly as though a breakthrough moment was about to occur. I could almost *feel* it hovering between us. I held my breath … the seconds ticked by. Still nothing happened. Finally, Martin said, "Well *I* certainly don't welcome them, I'm fed up with them!"

The heightened atmosphere dissipated immediately. The swirling moment had collapsed, like a broken spell, and the swell of a wave that had been building for months once again receded back into the relative calm of the sea.

* * *

We would have to wait longer before we found out what emotions were behind Martin's claws and why they were always present in his drawings. But here is a clear example of the rise and fall of a seemingly impending breakthrough moment that fills the room with possibility and then recedes down to nothing. If I could understand breakthrough moments more successfully, perhaps I could learn how to encourage the swelling wave of these moments to break more routinely for my clients.

Moments in time

I organised my thoughts and discoveries about breakthrough moments into a series of research diaries, journals, and mind-maps. This helped me to systematically capture my evolving ideas. My research data included clinical examples of clients' breakthrough moments together with a record of the arts media and client-created images that had featured in those sessions. Whilst I was busy at work with all this, an extraordinary session took place with my client Hayley.

Hayley's story

Hayley, a plucky eighteen-year-old university student, had been visiting me for therapy for about a month, following the death of her close friend Carrie (who had died two months previously). She admitted that in addition to being shocked and upset about her friend's death, she was deeply curious about where exactly Carrie had gone. She told me in this particular session that she had recently had a vivid dream about her deceased friend. I suggested that Hayley recount the dream to me in the present tense—a technique I had learned from my gestalt training that can sometimes enable a client to recapture the *feel* of a dream more powerfully.

In the dream, Hayley and Carrie had been in a taxi on their way to a restaurant. A surreal and dreamlike element was that Carrie was actually dead but still able to speak and move. Hayley had to explain to the taxi driver that her friend was dead and that she needed him to keep an eye on her for a moment, while Hayley went ahead to check that the restaurant they were visiting had made the right preparations for their arrival. Climbing back into the taxi she told Carrie, "The restaurant is fine and you'll manage okay when we get there. But tell me, what's it like to be dead? Where are you spending your time these days?"

At this moment in her recollection, Hayley stopped abruptly and fell silent.

"What's happening?" I asked her.

"I am so frustrated," she said. "I woke up! *I woke up* before Carrie could tell me about being dead! And now I am *desperate* to know what she was going to say!"

"Perhaps you could imagine being Carrie in the dream and give Hayley an answer to your question?"

Hayley closed her eyes and tried to imagine being Carrie in the dream.

"What's it like to be *dead*, Carrie?" I asked her. "Where are you spending your time now?"

"I'll tell you when we get to the restaurant," she replied (in the role of Carrie, spontaneously and without hesitation).

This felt like a potential turning point. I needed to respond with something that kept Hayley's phenomenological memory of the dream alive and that did not shut down the emotional content contained within. After a while I asked her simply, "what might this restaurant symbolise, do you think?"

"... Heaven?" she asked hesitantly.

And there was the breakthrough.

Time seemed to stand still. The tears flowed freely from Hayley, and my eyes, too, were moist. Hayley's breakthrough moment had broken the dam of her pent-up emotions. She had been caught up in intellectual curiosity about the metaphysics of her friend's death, but in recalling this dream about the "restaurant", she had woken deep emotions and previously inaccessible grief.

* * *

Ken Wilber speaks poetically of moments like this one with Hayley as being "no-boundary moments"; moments that remain so far outside of time that the past and future melt into obscurity because an individual is "totally absorbed in the present moment" (Wilber, 2001). Time all but disappears in such instances. The ancient Greeks had two different words for time: *kronos* and *kairos*. Kronos referred to ordinary, objective, sequential time (which has since been shown to be relative (Einstein, 1905)). Kairos referred to opportune time, a period of indeterminate length in which something special happens. "In the midst of the ordinary time (kronos) extraordinary time (kairos) happens" (Freier, 2006). It seemed, for example, that Susan and I had entered kairos time in that breakthrough moment when she poured stones onto the practice-room floor. Kairos is the Greek god of fleeting moments, who represents the subjective experience of a passing moment. In my experience of breakthrough moments and how my clients describe them, time does indeed seem strikingly altered.

Art as catalyst

Lisa Haneberg has her own description for timeless, transformative moments. She calls them "a-ha moments"—moments when a person receives "an insight, aha, idea, cognitive snap (relative to the preceding period) or epiphany" (Haneberg, 2006). She suggests that such moments involve a discontinuous positive change or leap forward in thinking or action. The resulting change may be large or small but there is always an acceleration of progress or insight that is sudden and transformative, rather than incremental. Susan's revelation when she tipped the basket of stones felt like the a-ha of a new insight; an idea that arrived suddenly. It was transformative for me too in that it provided me with a new entrance to her internal world. in the case of my client Tina, this aspect of new insight was equally remarkable and seemed to be brought about by a lump of clay.

Tina's story

Tina was working with modelling clay in our session one day. She said she was making a sculpture of her mother. First she formed a rough outline of the main figure and then rolled out a longer, thinner piece of the clay, which she proceeded to coil around it. She told me she was not quite sure why she had done this but that it had something to do with her mother being caught up in "not very nice things" from which she had been unable to disentangle herself.

I observed that the object Tina was modelling had a rather phallic appearance. It led me to wonder about the nature of these "not very nice things". I commented on this aspect of her sculpture's appearance, but Tina said she could not see anything phallic about it at all. My interpretation was not helpful to her at this time. Several weeks later, however, Tina referred back to the sculpture she had made (I had kept it for her in a safe place). I took it out of the drawer and placed it on the floor between us. She fell silent and was transfixed. I experienced this moment to be pregnant with possibility. Something that had been latently contained within the clay sculpture, patiently waiting for the right moment to present itself, now seemed to be tantalisingly ready to emerge, like a butterfly from a chrysalis. The image she had made had taken us to the edge of an insight. And this time it broke ...

Suddenly and apparently without really knowing why, Tina began to talk about her mother's relationship history and the farm where Tina had grown up. She told me that her mother used to flaunt herself in front of the farmhands. This then led Tina to reveal that one of these farmhands had exposed himself to her and her friends when they were in their early teens. As she told me this, a rush of emotion came and she suddenly pushed the clay figure away saying, "It's disgusting! Ugh ... It looks like that farmhand exposing himself!" I silently acknowledged what she was saying as she looked at me with an expression of surprise and revelation. She had experienced a breakthrough moment.

It seems Tina had never told anyone about this incident with the farmhand, but she had nonetheless always yearned for her mother to pick up on the unspoken feelings and empathise with her. I felt that Tina had a need for some reparative work in our therapy, so later we found a safe place for her to take a hammer and smash the clay figure into tiny pieces as she sobbed and shouted her anger at the farmhand whilst I supported her with my own outrage at his behaviour. This deliberate act of destruction enabled her to go deeply into previously hidden feelings, and, in fact, several further breakthrough moments occurred over the following weeks.

* * *

The clay figure that Tina had made somehow seemed to contain within itself the latent potential for change—a potential that emerged more and more whenever we revisited the figure she had made. My hypothesis is that this historic event had been shut off from Tina's awareness and the clay enabled it to surface, thus precipitating a breakthrough moment. The clay had enabled the emergence of an unformed image that morphed seemingly unconsciously from a depiction of Tina's mother into a phallic representation. This fits with Naumburg's suggestion that an art therapist's aim is "to engage [their] clients in a creative process so as to elicit spontaneous images which may function as a kind of symbolic language" (Naumburg, 1966, quoted in Henley, 2002). The figure that emerged from Tina's modelling clay seemed to represent a message from her unconscious that there was something pressing to be resolved. In this sense it became a vehicle for her breakthrough moment to arise and, eventually, a vehicle for change—when she engaged in the cathartic expression of outrage, anger and shame as she smashed the phallic object.

In this breakthrough session with Tina I had provided empathy and understanding without really voicing much (prior, at least, to my audible outrage as she smashed the clay figure). But silence can be seen as making a meaningful contribution to these kinds of moments. O'Connell says that, "silent amplification nourishes and expands the container—there is meaning in the *not-saying*, in the conscious use of silent incubation, an inner witnessing" (O'Connell, 1986, my italics).

Thanks to her breakthrough with the clay figure, Tina was able to begin the process of reintegrating her disassociated memories and linking them with cognitive and affective neural networks across multiple pathways. This was further supported by the fact that after these sessions Tina felt able for the first time to talk to her mother and father about what had happened on the farm when she was a young girl. Her father apparently said, furiously, "If I had *known*, I would have sent the man away and ensured he never worked on a farm anywhere ever again!" This paternal response helped Tina to integrate her many difficult feelings surrounding the event.

The clay image *itself* seemed to be the catalyst for Tina's breakthrough. I trawled through the literature, periodicals and website articles to discover if there were any studies that specifically discuss the use of arts media at pivotal moments in therapy. I was surprised to find relatively few. I felt a mixture of disappointment and excitement—if I couldn't find what I was looking for in the existing literature then maybe my research was more unique than I had realised.

Daniel Stern has described transformative moments in therapy as being *key* for client change to occur (Stern, 2004). It seems strange, therefore, that he did not discuss the use of arts media to bring about transformative moments. Stern's research would, however, prove incredibly useful to me (as we shall see in Chapter Four), as his ideas are focused on non-verbal moments within therapy, which makes his work particularly relevant for therapy using the arts.

I did find a few direct references to transformative moments in arts-based therapies. Jim Duvall et al., for example, researched the power of working with story in their Brief and Narrative therapy work in Toronto. Duvall et al. studied pivotal moments, which they called "sparkling moments" (Duvall et al., 2007). Duvall et al. suggest that their dialogue and narrative approach to therapy creates tentativeness, ambiguity, and "not knowing". This they feel "provides fertile ground for curiosity" and enables clients to reconsider the effects of their life circumstances.

My client Ben showed much tentativeness, ambiguity and "not knowing" when he was looking through the pile of postcards. His sudden realisation (when he saw the orangutan mother and baby) seemed to provide a powerful shift that was pivotal to the success of his therapeutic work. I found that many of my other clients, too, would refer to the fact that such moments felt like turning points in their therapeutic process and that they seemed to provide a "powerful shift" in the way they related to me, their therapist.

Idell Natterson's article "Turning points and intersubjectivity" underlines the importance of the unconscious element in the transactional dynamic between client and therapist. Natterson also speaks of these "turning points" in the therapy as being "shifts in the patient's behaviours, attitudes and feelings". She believes these shifts are dependent on a special kind of interaction between therapist and client, one that may be the result of insight or of a client's emotional, affective experience in the therapy (Natterson, 1993).

The journey ahead

My heuristic research approach exposed me to many different images, ideas, theories and texts that inspired me to frame and forge the path of my quest to understand breakthrough moments. For the remainder of this chapter, I will touch briefly upon some of the ideas that will be explored later in this book.

The power of images

Images started to become an integral part of my research. The images created by my clients and myself within arts-based sessions had been central to my work as a therapist and supervisor for many years. But now I also began collecting all and *any* images that resonated somehow with my quest. We will see how some of these images influenced my thinking about breakthrough moments along the way.

Peering inside the brain

One of the images that inspired me was a beautiful digital representation of interconnected neural pathways within the brain (see Figure 2.3). This helped me decide that I would delve into the world of neurobiology and see if it could support my understanding of breakthrough moments.

In Joseph LeDoux's brilliant but unorthodox work *The Synaptic Self* (2002) he presents ideas about how a person's ways of experiencing

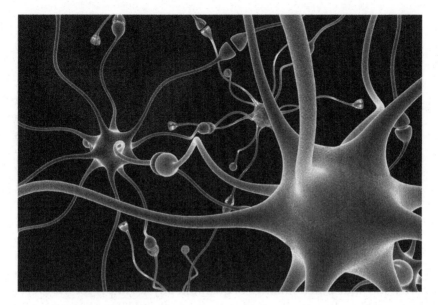

Figure 2.3. Neural pathways.

themselves (and relating to others) are linked to what is happening at the level of neural pathways inside their brain. LeDoux is interested in how we experience ourselves predominantly as a *self* rather than a multitude of ever-changing *selves*. He says the self is the totality of what an organism is—physically, biologically, psychologically, culturally, and spiritually, and that these aspects are made up of different neural systems that work separately and together. In this sense, he believes it is possible to experience oneself, at times, as separate *selves* even whilst one is experienced by others as a predominantly coherent *self*. The different neural systems pull together most of the time, which means an individual feels as though they have a relatively consistent personality, but at times the different systems can pull in different directions and act more like an "unruly mob" (ibid.).

Discovering LeDoux's theory led me to ask if perhaps the changes that took place in a therapy session were influencing different aspects of a client's self and thus the different systems. Could, for example, Susan's feelings of being a multitude of different Susans (some of whom no one had ever met) be explained by visualising these different Susans as different systems that were not fully linked together?

Dynamical systems theory and quantum physics

Ideas, notions and metaphors from the dynamical systems theory (Clarkson, 2002) also enabled me to view my question from a new angle. This is a relatively new science that describes how changes in complex, open systems are not linear but rather happen in a number of different ways simultaneously. The potential for a client to change seems to have a domino or ripple effect, far beyond that which can be predicted. This is neatly encapsulated in Sharon Salzberg's motivational quote: "Life is like an ever shifting kaleidoscope: a slight change and all patterns alter". The dynamical systems theory would open my eyes to what might be going on in my clients' breakthrough moments in new and exciting ways.

I discovered Lynne McTaggart's inspirational book *The Field* (2004), which introduced me to the world of quantum physics and "the interconnected holistic field" that exists at the subatomic level (ibid.). This turned my world upside down. The fact that there is no consensus as to what the undisputed findings of quantum physics imply for the everyday world fuelled my imagination even further. I became increasingly enraptured by the mind-altering ideas of this nebulous science. Might the key to my understanding of breakthrough moments lie in the hazy mysteries of this quantum world? And if so, how did I have a chance of penetrating them?

Visual images of the quantum realm were often beautiful and inspirational in themselves. I viewed them with awe and delight. In fact, it became something of a new obsession. The images seemed to expand my mind—not in a logical sense but rather in a new, intuitive pattern-making sense. These images demonstrated the importance of recurring patterns in nature (see Figure 2.4).

I discovered a number of writers who have made links between the self-repeating patterns of fractals and the patterns that manifest themselves in human nature. Terry Marks-Tarlow suggests in her fascinating book *The Psyche's Veil* (2008) that the fractal metaphor can illustrate repetitive dynamics occurring at different levels in an individual (see Figure 2.5). I found myself wondering if this metaphor contained any answers to my question about breakthrough moments.

Discovering *how* these images and ideas from the new sciences were going to throw light on what is going on in a therapy session proved challenging. Few texts have been written that make connections between these ideas, but I devoured all those that I found. I seemed to

Figure 2.4. Cauliflower fractal.

Figure 2.5. Mandelbrot fractal.

be wandering into territories that I had no idea previously existed, and frequently I felt completely lost. I was comforted by J. R. R. Tolkein's words that, "not all who wander are lost" (1954).

* * *

As my research for this book progressed, I found myself discovering that the new sciences (neurobiology, quantum theory, dynamical systems theory, and chaos and complexity theory) are filled with facts of mysterious imponderabilia that cannot be ignored, but equally cannot be rationally understood. And this holds a striking analogy with breakthrough moments. It is undeniable that such moments occur in therapeutic work and yet it is near impossible to logically understand them; art similarly addresses unspeakable and unknowable aspects of existence that make emotional sense to a spectator. The combination of art *and* therapeutic work together seemed to spark something extraordinary.

CHAPTER THREE

The power of using the arts

It was quite clear that using arts media within a therapy session could lead my clients to experience powerful breakthrough moments. Sometimes these moments would arise from the use of a single arts medium, such as Ben's selection of the orangutan postcard, or Christine's creation of the stone hand; other times it was a combination of various arts media that proved most effective. Varying the art objects and materials used in a session enables a client to see their life situation from a wide range of different vantage points and offers different metaphors, which can increase opportunities for insight and change. This was especially the case with my client Betty. Thanks to Betty's patient creativity and brave desire to explore her feelings, one strange afternoon we found ourselves sitting down to dinner with a cockerel.

Betty's story

Betty was an attractive young woman with a strong personality. She had recently begun a drama course in the city, many miles from her hometown and had been coming to see me in the hope of gaining perspective on difficulties she was experiencing with her training. In this particular session, she told me she had just returned from a weekend's visit home to see her parents. Whilst there Betty had become aware that she felt hyper-vigilant when back in the company of her family. She had felt this sensation when she was around them ever since she was a little girl. Hearing this prompted me, for some reason, to tell Betty that a cockerel stays permanently vigilant, watching out for signs of danger in the roost, which means the hens can peck for grain or rest peacefully, without needing to be on the lookout for predators. This information resonated deeply with her and she decided she would like to make a mask of a Vigilant Cockerel (see Figure 3.1).

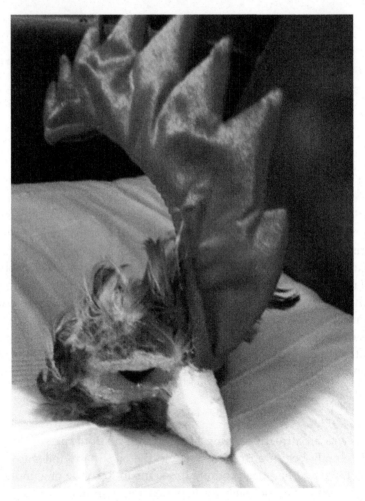

Figure 3.1. Betty's cockerel mask.

She worked carefully and diligently for many sessions making the beautiful mask. Once it was finished, Betty, with great ceremony, laid out cushions on the floor of the practice-room that were to represent her family sitting around the dinner table. She then proceeded to put on the mask and sit down alongside them. She sat very stiffly and unnaturally straight, glancing from time to time at the cushions that were arranged around her, as though she was indeed sitting with family members at an imaginary dinner table. The stark image of her sat there in such an arresting mask with its striking red cockscomb gave me goosebumps on the back of my neck. I felt viscerally as though we had been transported back to Betty's past, although my role was more of a bystander, watching Betty sat at the table with her "family".

She was bristling with nerves, every contour of her body taut as she watched fearfully for signs of the beginnings of conflict. She was vigilantly trying to catch the subtlest signs of danger that lurked amongst them. From the dramatic way her body language had changed I felt as though Betty had regressed to becoming a child once more and that I was witnessing a powerful enactment of her childhood experience. How many times had she sat at the meal table in this same way, waiting in terror for a violent storm she felt may arrive at any moment? But what was this storm?

In a subsequent session, Betty once again put on the Vigilant Cockerel mask and took up her watchful position at the table with her "family" (the cushions). This time, however, during her enactment of the meal, I asked what might happen if she took off the mask and put down her hyper-vigilance for a moment. At first Betty froze in horror at the idea, but then very tentatively began to take off the mask and look around the "dinner table". With a sudden wave of emotion, a breakthrough moment occurred. "I have to watch ..." she was busy saying, terribly flustered and scrambling to put the mask back on "... or he'll get violent and take me by surprise. I am only safe when I'm vigilantly watching! No one else can keep us safe!"

This was something new. It was suddenly clear to us both that Betty believed she held some sort of responsibility within her family dynamic for ensuring things remained calm and safe. In a later session when she was again wearing the mask, I suggested to Betty that she take it off once more. It seems she found it helpful being able to take the mask on and off while I was there to ensure she felt safe. I did this by reminding her she was in a therapy session and not in fact back at her family home.

I hoped Betty might be able to experience *how* the hyper-vigilance had affected her as a child, and still affected her now as an adult. When Betty took the mask off again another breakthrough moment occurred. It took us both by surprise when she suddenly screamed: "Where are the NSPCC? Why aren't they here? It's not safe for me in this family!" Following this outburst she sat and wept. Her plea for the National Society for Prevention of Cruelty to Children seemed to be an adult part of Betty finding a voice at last for the child who had so vigilantly checked on her family to ensure a violent scene would not erupt, or to be ready for it when it did.

When Betty and I spoke later about her experience of these sessions, she still vividly recalled the power of the work. It was clear to us both that the creation of the mask and its use in the re-enactment of her family drama (with myself as witness) had enabled her to gain a new perspective on her situation from an experiential vantage point. She had also gained a new awareness of how hyper-vigilant she *still* felt as an adult in so many life situations. As a child she had never had a voice to protest against what was happening. She was a cockerel after all, and birds cannot speak. Now as an adult she had begun to find her voice.

* * *

I had faith that using arts media with my clients brought with it an enhanced opportunity for them to experience breakthrough moments. But there are so many different arts media and each has something special and unique to offer. Did they all provide a gateway in the same way? In this chapter I will present some further examples of working with Betty and other clients using different arts media, and consider in each case how the art medium used was able to bring something unique to the work. I will also begin to ask what might be happening neurobiologically for my clients at these moments.

A client case study: understanding Betty

Betty's story shows us how several different forms of arts media and performance can work together in leading a client to breakthrough moments. She was first affected by the metaphor of the cockerel keeping watch over the roost; then she was affected by the process of making the mask and by the act of wearing it. In addition to these aspects, the enactment of being with her family at the meal table and the dramatisation of taking the mask on and off both helped her arrive at her breakthrough moments.

A taboo of silence around her "family secret" meant that Betty could not just speak about what had happened to her. Reawakening her childhood experience with drama and re-enactment enabled her to show me what she could not tell me. This intensified the experience for her, in a similar way to taking part in a psychodrama.

I turned to the writings of others to see if they could throw any light on my questions about Betty's therapeutic work. I read that each type of art medium has a unique ability to bridge the expanse between the literal reality of here and now and the world of the imagination— a place "where life stories are written in mythic form and life experiences are held in symbols" (Greer Essex, 2005). Seen from such a viewpoint, the cockerel mask perhaps served as a bridge between Betty's adult life in the therapy room with me and the world of her imagination and childhood memories.

Another particularly apt way to describe Betty's work is captured by Penny Lewis' statement that "the arts provide vehicles for the accessing and re-experiencing of historical traumatic events and relationships". Lewis further states that the arts provide a "medium within which healing and transformation can occur" (Lewis, 1993). The metaphor of the vigilant cockerel, the mask-making and wearing, and the dramatic re-enactment of Betty's family dinner table experience had all provided a medium for healing and transformation.

* * *

I looked to neurobiology to see if it could assist in my understanding of what was actually happening for Betty during her mask-making and re-enactment. It seemed that perhaps the neural pathways that had split off and been buried in the recesses of her memory were reactivated somehow by this method of working. As a result, she began to feel less disturbed by sudden, post-traumatic flashbacks. She also reported a dramatic reduction in the occurrence of disturbing dreams and nightmares that had haunted her throughout her adult years. These dreams had always been situated in the house where her childhood trauma had taken place.

Bonnie Badenoch provides a neurobiological explanation that may be useful in understanding Betty's work. She says that synapses that have fired together in response to years of continual terror can become encoded and lead to an individual feeling a strong physical/emotional response to environmental and emotional triggers. These synapses over many years can become woven into neural nets that become "isolated baskets holding terror, pain and shame" (Badenoch, 2008). By working through the original trauma in myriad ways (but always with a therapist acting as "caring observer") the neural nets can begin to be integrated and a client can become less vulnerable to triggers in their environment (ibid.).

Vermetten and Bremner explain that when an individual is exposed to long-term extreme stress, cortisol baseline responses and regulatory feedback loops are altered, and the hypothalamus-pituitary-adrenal axis' synaptic connections may be permanently changed (Vermetten & Bremner, 2002, quoted in Hass-Cohen, 2008). They suggest that post-traumatic stress can involve the fragmentation of a client's personhood—dissociative symptoms and fragmented memories. It is thus necessary to provide phased treatment to a client in order to decrease phobic responses and increase interpersonal trust, and in this way carefully evaluate the possibilities for the client's reintegration (Van der Hart, Nijenhuis, & Steele, 2005, quoted in Hass-Cohen, 2008).

For Betty, long-term therapy that included a carefully graded use of art materials helped her to build trust in a three-way relationship (between therapist, art-image, and client). Later, this enabled her to also build trust in the dyadic relationship (between therapist and client). Over a longer period of time this helped reduce her symptoms and led her to greater integration.

Poetry

As her therapy progressed, Betty worked with further forms of performance and arts media. For example, she dramatically enacted moving around the room as the Vigilant Cockerel wearing the mask she had created. Later she invented "The Dance of the Vigilant Cockerel", which she put to music (with the help of a friend). Towards the end of her therapy, Betty brought me a lovely painting of the Vigilant Cockerel keeping watch over the family group (see Figure 3.2).

She also wrote a poem about her feelings around this family trauma. I had invited her to select postcards that spoke to her in some way about her situation and suggested she might weave the imagery that resulted into a poem. This seemed to help Betty overcome her initial uncertainty

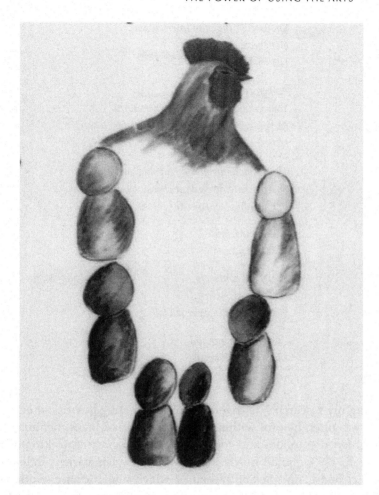

Figure 3.2. Betty's cockerel drawing.

about writing poetry. She selected postcard images of a Francis Bacon painting (of a distorted face), a broken glass, a calm sea, a stormy sea, a plant cell illustration and a ghoulish creature and then produced a poem inspired by these resonant images:

Trauma re-visited

Shards of traumatic memories
Tug at my mind
Sucking me back ...

Splintering the calm internal sea ...
Now becomes there
Here is then

As I frozenly watch
Your kindly face distorts and contorts
Merging from benevolence to sinister
Malevolence ...

The harmonious melody, in slow motion,
Shatters into discordant chaos
In a wordless whisper the message is clear

Hide your panic
Eat your fear

Every cell contracts
As the world spins ...
Hold on tight in case you fall

Clench your fear and
Make yourself small

* * *

During my research I discovered some interesting theories about why poetry is often helpful within therapy. Nicholas Mazza mentions that "heightened emotions and compressed meaning are central to poetry" (Brogan, 1993, quoted in Mazza, 2003). Poetry has variety, indeterminacy, richness, and flexibility—all of which make it an exceptionally powerful medium for "redeeming the past, assimilating the present, and projecting the future" (ibid.). Writing a poem, as opposed to speaking or producing a piece of prose, invites inclusion of the right hemisphere of the brain. Working with poetry enables a client to access deep emotions, sensory information and many other intuitive ways of *knowing* that are predominantly held within this right hemisphere. In the creative act of writing a poem, a client is also able to use imagination, image, metaphor and symbol simultaneously, making it more likely that a new "combinational leap" can be achieved (Mendelsohn, 1976).

Breakthrough moments frequently appear at the time a client writes their poem or reads it aloud in a session. A rush of emotion often follows as they hear back the hidden meaning of what they have written and recognise the deep, metaphorical truth of something they didn't know they had grasped or understood, which is precisely what happened to Betty.

Sand trays

Several weeks before her sessions around the Vigilant Cockerel theme, Betty had created a sand tray that pre-empted the work to come. Within her sand tray she had placed figures that were to represent her family sat at the table. For each of her family members she selected small figurines, but for her father she had curiously chosen a scorpion painted on stone. She told me this was because at any moment the sting in his tail could suddenly attack.

My integrative arts training favours an approach in which I let clients' images speak for themselves (with a minimum of commentary, interpretation, or analysis), so at this time I did nothing but gaze at the sand tray image she had created. After looking at it herself for an extended time, Betty reached into a basket of objects and replaced the scorpion stone (that represented her father) with a huge black spider, which she flung into the tray, knocking over the dinner table (see Figure 3.3). We both gasped in horror at the chilling scene she had created; Betty had put her hand over her mouth as if to stifle a scream. I was especially

Figure 3.3. Betty's spider sand tray.

shocked by the suddenness of Betty's action, not to mention the way she had so graphically depicted the effects of her father's erupting fury. I felt nauseous; especially when she told me her family would carry on eating despite the presence of this massive spider, "as if *nothing* had taken place". Synchronistically, the other family members in her sand tray had stayed seated on their chairs as if they were indeed carrying on with the meal.

* * *

I searched in the literature for reasons why working with a sand tray can be so compelling for clients. Bradway and McCoard suggest it is because the sand tray requires a form of active imagination in which the images being constructed are concrete and tangible (and can be viewed by both client and therapist) rather than being intangible or invisible (Bradway & McCoard, 1997). Also, there is often a "reduced consciousness" that accompanies play in the sand tray. Almost like catching a client off guard, the sand tray activity can reveal hidden thoughts and feelings for the therapist to view. This makes it particularly helpful for working with a client's unconscious processes. The images created by the objects and figures in the sand tray can become embodied with meaning for a client (Schaverien, 1999).

Bonnie Badenoch has written about the neurobiology of working with a sand tray in *Being a Brain-Wise Therapist* (2008). One of the key features, she says, is the fact that a client usually uses both their hands when working with a sand tray, which activates neural pathways in the left *and* right hemispheres simultaneously, helping a client to make meaningful connections between body, thoughts and feelings that could not otherwise be made. Badenoch describes the sensation of the sand itself sending messages to the thalamus, then the parietal lobe (which processes touch), then the occipital lobe (sight), before this sensory information reaches limbic structures where meaning is assigned. The meaning that has been attributed then integrates with the hippocampus and associated memories emerge. This sensory data converges in the middle, prefrontal cortex. The whole experience, Badenoch says, encourages vertical integration, linking body, limbic region and cortex in the right hemisphere (Badenoch, 2008; Cozolino, 2002).

I've noticed from my work with Betty and other clients that a breakthrough moment frequently follows on from the making of a sand tray. On some occasions the whole tray seems to speak to a client and become the primary means of their showing the therapist what they are feeling at a deep level. Badenoch describes this as the client and therapist sitting together and "holding" the tray between them. She suggests it allows for "interpersonal warmth and resonance to continue doing their integrative work" (Badenoch, 2008).

Trauma does not disappear in the first telling of its horror. It needs to be revisited many times (in different ways) before it can begin to be integrated more healthfully into a client's body and mind. Betty revisited her childhood memories with the sand tray and then went on to visit them again and again through her later use of the mask, drama, enactment, movement, dance and poetry. On each occasion breakthrough moments of varying size arose as she told and retold her story with new and different images and metaphors.

Ritual

For the remainder of this chapter I will present some further examples of different arts media and materials that have been used by clients who visit my practice, starting with ritual.

Grace's story

Grace was a woman in her mid forties who had come to see me to deal with perpetual feelings of emptiness. After more than a year's therapeutic work she was ready to complete a particular segment of her therapy and move on to the next. We decided to review how much Grace had changed since she first started coming to therapy.

We looked back at the many art-images she had created (by looking at photographs and original art pieces) and reminded ourselves of the most significant sessions that had taken place. We came to a decision that in our following session we would carry out a ritual that would represent Grace's development during the period we had worked together so far. Grace decided we would use the symbolism of a snake shedding its skin.

When the appointed session arrived I invited Grace to create the image of a path that she could walk along for this ritual. She chose to draw road markings along the middle of a large, rolled-out piece of paper and selected some cardboard footprints to indicate her journey. She then reached into a basket of material and draped herself in several silk scarves, each one representing a different skin. Down the sides of her "road", Grace lined up numerous soft animals, dolls and puppets. She also placed particularly significant figurines and art materials from her work at intervals along the route.

I banged a drum to mark the commencement of the ritual, and at each subsequent banging of my drum, Grace shed one of her scarves of skin and moved on to another cardboard footprint. With each step she spoke movingly of unwanted feelings she was shedding, as well as describing how the new skin being revealed underneath represented the positive attributes she had gained from her therapy. It seemed almost as though the animals and objects she had selected to flank her pathway were cheering her on along her "journey". When she reached the doorway of the practice-room I played a long single chime on a singing bowl and Grace stepped across the threshold to leave. As she did so, she discarded her final skin (scarf) to symbolise her graduation to a new phase of therapeutic work.

* * *

Ritual can serve to heighten all sorts of occasions in a therapeutic setting. For example, attention can be given to something by burning candles or playing ceremonial music. Combs and Freedman have argued that ceremonies (a form of ritual) "serve two purposes—to validate an occurrence and to promote change" (Combs & Freedman, 1990, quoted in Mazza, 2003). In carrying out rituals with a client, the neural pathways connected to an event or situation from the past can be strengthened, and aspects of the client's memories can be more fully integrated. Sometimes my clients and I create a spontaneous ritual as a celebration of something, such as their recent success with a difficult task or a happy occasion that has arisen. At other times the ritual is planned in advance, as with Grace. Grace had carried out deep work in her therapy and the ritual of "shedding her skin" served to heighten the significance of this work, as well as bestow an appropriate dignity and importance to her therapy.

Puppets

Sally's story

My client Sally, seven years old, put a large bumblebee puppet on her arm, and with her fingers operating the insect's legs began to act out a story of The Bee Who Couldn't Fly (see Figure 3.4). She narrated the tale confidently, saying this particular bee was very sad because its wings were covered in "nasty, sticky stuff" that made it impossible for him to fly. She told me the bee was going to die if somebody did not help it soon. She asked me if maybe *I* could help the bee. I told her I was certainly very willing to try and so together we began to enact a long story about our concerted efforts to help this bee. The story variously involved the bee resting on my hand as I flew it around the room, then our taking the bee to hospital to undergo an operation on its sticky wings. Finally the bee was washed in a washing machine and spun-dried until its wings were restored and it could fly once again.

During our enactment of the story I felt a number of emotions. At first I felt desperately sad for the bee then strangely powerless to help it and finally genuinely triumphant when we were able to help it fly

Figure 3.4. Sally's bee puppet.

again. I wondered if any of these were feelings Sally was having to deal with in her life. We remained inside the metaphor of Sally's bee story for a while. I wasn't exactly sure what the story represented for her but I held on to the possibility that it was helping her work through difficult feelings concerning her younger brother, who had been diagnosed on the autistic spectrum and was finding life a struggle.

I wondered if Sally felt unable to help (or heal) her brother and if perhaps she wished she had magic powers to make life easier for him. There was also the possibility that Sally was playing out her need for me to help her manage her complex feelings about her brother's inability to "fly". Perhaps the bee even represented a repressed desire to fly away from the painful situation. There were no breakthrough moments during my work with Sally, but the bee story nonetheless felt significant and reparative for her.

* * *

Puppets can be used to explore either intrapersonal or interpersonal dynamics (McLaughlin & Holliday, 2014). In other words they can be used to dramatise conflicts within a client's psyche or conflicts in their relationships with other people. They can also provide some useful distance from a client's difficult feelings and relationships whilst affording an opportunity for them to personify subpersonalities and introjects.

Drama using puppets is usually improvised and can include creating and telling stories, as with Sally. The client breathes life into the puppet and imbues it with thoughts, feelings and social interactions that are often easier to acknowledge and manage when seen as belonging to the puppet rather than the client themselves. The fact that a puppet can be taken off the hand and put down can also help a client to put some distance between the parts of themselves they may find difficult to deal with, in the sense that, "it's not really me, it's the puppet" (ibid). Cozolino tells us that storytelling and drama (both of which were involved in Sally's bee story) weave together sensations, feelings, thoughts and actions in ways that organise both internal and external worlds. He says this can enable new neural connections and pathways to be formed and thus new neural integration is achieved (Cozolino, 2002). In addition, the stories that clients tell themselves can be transformed by co-creating new personal narratives with the support of the therapist.

It was some time in our work before Sally felt confident enough to take her story out of the bee metaphor, but she was eventually able to tell me how sad and frustrated she felt about her brother's situation and how difficult it felt to live with him. She also let me know that I had helped the bee to fly.

Music

Tony's story

I frequently suggest to clients they may wish to use musical instruments in the sessions to express their feelings. Many clients feel inhibited or embarrassed to admit they have strong feelings, let alone express them in the therapy room. Tony was one such client. He was twenty-three-years-old and worked in an office. Although he had been coming to therapy for some time, it was clear that being passive-aggressive came more easily to him than expressing his angry feelings towards people and things in more constructive ways.

I found Tony would reveal his hidden feelings as sarcasm and thinly veiled caustic remarks. We had made some headway after I encouraged him to play with clay, which he slammed onto a plastic sheet spread out on the floor. He had also vigorously painted what began as a calm scene but which soon became so savage that he ended up tearing the paper, yet none of this seemed as though it was connecting to the reason Tony felt so angry.

Some time later I suggested to him that we place a series of objects in a line in front of him—each one symbolising the things and people he currently found mildly irritating (I find that very angry clients can sometimes engage more easily with a lower level of their anger or frustration). The idea seemed to mobilise him and he quickly selected a large group of irritants (from the objects and figures in my practice-room) that could form part of this line. I suggested that he speak to each of these irritating objects and characters in turn while playing a set of bongo drums; I would play a djembe (African drum). He spoke first to a little gnome-like creature, who represented his boss, and as I beat my drum softly to support him, he said (surprisingly gently) "Why are you so annoying? You really get on my nerves!"

Each of the other objects in the line was addressed in turn (some more personally than others). "Why do you always come late?" he said to a red bus that was next in the line. He was beginning to bang his drums more loudly and with more gusto, suggesting he was more than mildly irritated with the objects he had selected. We progressed down the line and arrived at a slug-like plastic creature. Tony picked up his drumsticks and smashed down on the bongos. As he did so, he shouted:

> "You are sucking the life out of me ..."
> [BANG!]
> "You are suffocating me ..."
> [BANG!]
> "... I can't breathe!"
> [BANG!]

And with this last statement his anger finally seemed to crash through to a breakthrough moment. He became calmer and seemed shocked at what he had just revealed to himself. He seemed to have reached a whole new level of understanding about something profound. At the time, I had no idea who or what the slug-like creature represented, but the important thing was that banging the drums had enabled Tony to get more fully in touch with his irritation and anger and to connect it somehow with whatever was the source of his rage.

Delia's story

In Tony's case, it was playing musical instruments that helped him to express his feelings; with my client Delia it was the act of listening to music that helped her. Delia told me she had been watching a film recently that had switched half way through from being a romantic adventure story into a full-blown horror movie. She had been so engrossed in the story that by the time the mood switched she simply could not stop watching. She told me it was the music in particular that made her realise she was watching a horror film long before the events of the story began to turn macabre. Delia had found herself haunted by this film throughout the week prior to the session. She told me about the powerful way in which the music in the film seemed to almost manipulate her feelings. I wondered if this could be symbolising something particular since it resonated so deeply for her.

"Do you think you could bring a piece of music to our next session that is similar to the horror music that upset you in this film?" I asked, "Or indeed any music that feels similar to that moment when the film seemed to switch into something more horrific?" I reassured her that we could use my own music in the practice-room if she did not feel satisfied with any pieces that she found. The following week she brought in a piece of music that she felt met the criteria. We first listened to a beautiful cantata from my own collection. It played pleasantly for a while before Delia said, "okay, now *this* is the bit where it changes ..." At that moment we put on her own choice of music and sure enough the atmosphere in the room changed dramatically. The music she had brought in was menacing and claustrophobic.

Delia looked utterly terrified listening to it even though she was familiar with the piece, having chosen it herself. I asked her what was happening in order to bring her away from what was clearly a state of deep fear. The expression of most other emotions can bring relief for a client, but entering deeply into fear is often unhelpful, as it can become magnified when it is expressed. We put the first piece of music back on the player and felt ourselves relaxing once more. Later on in Delia's therapy we would discover the link between these pieces of music and her story. But for now we can at least see the powerful effect the music had on her and on me.

* * *

Music is used in my practice-room in a number of ways. Clients may bring their own significant music or choose it from my collection. It can be used to accompany work, such as rituals and re-enactments. The drums, percussion and singing bowls can be used to express emotions such as poignancy, anger, anguish, and grief. This way of working can perhaps best be described as cathartic. A cathartic experience can release an individual from the power of their trauma and thus help them begin to heal some of their hurt. Tian Dayton has suggested that catharsis happens not only on an emotional level but also on a physical level, cleansing the body and causing a cellular release of the held memory from a client's brain and body (Dayton, 1994).

Studies on the way music is processed by the brain have generally concluded that there is no single music-processing centre. Oliver Sacks suggests there is, rather, the involvement of a dozen scattered networks (Sacks, 2007). Whether produced by voice or instrument, music has the capability to stimulate the entire brain, making it an extraordinarily powerful tool for therapy. It appears that music, whether listened to or performed, "restores our connection with our essence—the realm beyond our conscious awareness—and thus with the cosmos" (ibid.). Clients in my practice will often use music as the inspiration for their mental or visual imagery, as in Martin's case.

Martin's story (continued)

After choosing a piece of music from my sound effects collection, Martin and I sat together and listened while it played. The piece that filled the practice-room was the sound of waves crashing onto a pebbled shore, while a haunting melody soared in the background. After quietly listening to this music for a while, Martin started to draw a charcoal picture (see Figure 3.5). At first the picture seemed to depict ferocious waves descending upon a pebbled beach, but then claws could clearly be seen emerging from the crashing surf. Here they are again, I thought.

The many benefits of using drawing and painting in therapy have been investigated. Hass-Cohen speaks of "the unique contributions of art therapy to well-being and health" (Hass-Cohen, 2008). He says that in art therapy, the artwork can be thought of as a concrete representation of a client's mind-body connectivity: "mind-body approaches link nervous, endocrine and immune systems with physiological and

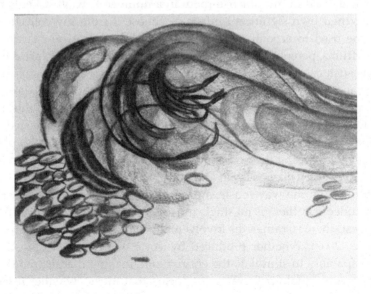

Figure 3.5. Martin's wave picture.

psychological changes", demonstrating complex, chemical bodily connections. Could the recurring claws in Martin's drawings be a physical ailment crying out for attention? Hass-Cohen also discusses the ways in which art therapy practices are informed by visual stimuli and mental imagery. Visual integration during a therapy session is influenced by intrapersonal affects, interpersonal relationships, and relational support from the therapist (ibid.). Research has shown that the processing of mental imagery and visual stimuli employs almost all the neural pathways (Kisslyn, Thompson, & Ganis, 2006, quoted in Hass-Cohen, 2008).

* * *

It is clear that using arts media within a therapy session can lead clients to experience powerful breakthrough moments they may not otherwise have achieved (whether as vividly or spontaneously, or even at all) in a more traditional, dyadic (therapist–client) form of counselling. But what is it about this special ingredient of the arts that harbours the potential for pivotal moments in the therapeutic relationship? In the next part of this book, I will begin to consider some possible answers to this question.

PART II

EXPLORING THE PRESENT MOMENT

CHAPTER FOUR

The present moment

Guy's story

My client Guy's breakthrough moment was particularly intriguing. Guy was thirty-three years old. He had come to see me to try and work out why he found it so difficult to relax and enjoy his life. On the rare occasion he *did* manage to have a good time, Guy said he would feel terribly guilty. Now he had a new girlfriend who was also beginning to complain that he never seemed to enjoy himself.

We had been going round in circles in our sessions for several weeks and Guy was growing increasingly despondent. He was always complaining that he never enjoyed himself and the less than productive therapeutic work had given him a new complaint—this time about *me*. I was not successfully helping him and thus failing in my role as his therapist.

I was beginning to feel impotent and stuck until about halfway through one session Guy pulled towards him a basket of postcards and began absentmindedly flicking through them. He rifled through the cards with almost exaggerated disinterest, as if he wanted me to know how bored and frustrated he was with the art materials and the therapy itself. After a while he pulled out one particular card and said, "Perhaps this one is significant in some way but I don't know how".

He laid it on the floor between us and we stared at it for some time. The card depicted the silhouette of a family walking along a dirt track. Up ahead of them menacingly stood the Grim Reaper, hooded and cloaked and wielding an enormous scythe (see Figure 4.1). I found myself reflecting on the malevolence of the image with its sinister depiction of a happy family unwittingly strolling towards death. I wondered what Guy was thinking, as he too was deeply absorbed in the image on the card.

It felt as though we might be on the brink of a new discovery. The atmosphere in the practice-room had changed from one of exasperation

Figure 4.1. Guy's grim reaper.

(at the repetitive cycle of fruitless work) to one suddenly charged with possibility for something new and interesting to take place. Although we had been working together for several weeks I still had no clear idea why Guy felt this image of death and the family to be especially resonant. Had he experienced a recent bereavement? Did he feel a health concern for someone?

Several minutes of silence followed, which felt far longer, when Guy finally spoke. "That's me," he said softly, "and my Mum and Dad and little brother, walking along like a happy family". He seemed shocked by his realisation and carried on staring at the image. He then began to cry softly. In a voice that was barely audible he said, "Death was *always* coming to get my Dad. We were just *pretending* to be a happy family". Guy's powerful confession hung in the room for some time. I could now see the postcard in the light of his own family tragedy and eventually said, "No wonder you can never feel relaxed or happy".

Though he continued looking at the card, I could sense that Guy felt I'd reached him for the first time. I had been witness to his moving realisation and had spoken aloud the connection that this image had enabled him to make—the link between his childhood fear of his father's mortality and his inability to enjoy his current life as an adult. He went on to explain that the entire time he was growing up he was aware that at any moment his father might die and this would make him permanently anxious. If he ever *did* feel happy for a while he would start to feel guilty about it. His father had been dead for a decade, but it was not until our session that day that Guy had been able to connect his childhood history with his present dissatisfaction.

Guy had said that he thought of himself as "a pathetic, anxious, discontented person". Now he could begin the process of replacing this attitude with compassion for the little boy whose childhood experience had been entwined so inseparably with suffering and death. I had to admit to myself that I had begun to think of him as a petulant, spoiled child in an adult's body after weeks of his complaints and less than enthusiastic work. But once his breakthrough moment had taken place it was as though we each had a new understanding of his nature, and I felt full of compassion instead of irritation.

* * *

Guy's breakthrough moment with the postcard of the Grim Reaper ended the process of going round in circles in his therapy sessions. But if I was to really understand what was happening for my clients at such times, it seemed important to ask what it is about breakthrough moments that mark them out from other moments in a therapy session. I looked to the existing literature to see if I could obtain a detailed, step-by-step exploration of what might be happening leading up to and during pivotal moments in psychotherapy. I was surprised at how few studies of this sort I could find. The most promising work I discovered was Daniel Stern's research into the Present Moment. Stern studied the different kinds of moments that can occur within the course of a therapy session. This includes moments leading up to dramatic breakthroughs as well as the dramatic moments themselves, which were the focus of my interest. It seemed like an excellent place to begin. In this chapter I will explore some of Stern's fascinating ideas about the kinds of moments that occur in therapy.

Introduction to Stern's model

Daniel Stern had always been "a reader of the nonverbal" (Stern, 1998). He studied the naturally occurring non-verbal language of infancy, which culminated in his seminal work *The Interpersonal World of the Infant*. Later he went on to collaborate with the Boston Change Process Study Group. This was a group (formed in 1995) of eminent professionals who came together to study change processes in psychotherapy.

What makes Stern's work so unique—and so relevant for my own investigation into breakthrough moments—is his interest in the small, momentary events that make up our experience. He thought that studying hours of video footage of mother–infant relationships (in the 1960s and 1970s) gave him a "sort of microscope" through which he could see interactions between two people unfold. He went on to apply his findings to the interactions between a therapist and client. The idea of taking a metaphorical microscope and examining in detail what takes place moment by moment in an arts-based therapy session appealed to me greatly. And although Stern does not directly apply his ideas to arts therapies, the non-verbal nature of the therapeutic moments he identifies make for a particularly apt comparison to arts therapies like my own.

It is necessary to gain a clear overview of Stern's model in order to assess to what extent it might be applicable to arts-based therapy. Stern developed a process called microanalysis to investigate the passage of time, moment by moment, in a psychodynamic therapy session. He developed a terminology for the different kinds of moments that make up the flow within a session. He suggested that change can be "present" (between the client and therapist) or non-conscious, and is represented by three types of moment: Moving Along, Now Moments, and Moments of Meeting. Moving Along consists of non-conscious processes as the therapy ticks along, minding its own business. But then there can be sudden dramatic moments that are conscious (and these include Now Moments and Moments of Meeting). I will attempt to clarify each of these key Sternian concepts with reference to examples from my own clients.

Moving Along

Stern suggests the therapist–client dyad of Moving Along is similar to a mother–infant relationship in which the mother and her baby play and enjoy one another for the sake of it, without any specifically stated goals within the interaction (Stern, 2004). He suggests these interactions are mainly improvised. Improvisation can be described in many ways, such as thinking on one's feet, speaking off the top of one's head, winging it, and playing it by ear—none of which are phrases one might typically associate with therapeutic interventions.

Stern suggests it is this improvisatory nature of the Moving Along process that allows implicit relational knowing (which is largely non-verbal) to surface. It allows for the arrival of the unexpected, leading to the possibility for dramatic, pivotal moments to emerge from the process. However, he is careful to make clear that implicit progressive change can occur for a client without sudden dramatic moments, during the "quieter, less charged moments" of Moving Along, but it is often subtle and needs to be revisited in order for more permanent change to take place (ibid.). So Moving Along is not just about preparing for the more charged moments; it affects significant change in the "implicit relational field" (between client and therapist), even when it does not move towards transformative moments.

Moving Along occurs in the back and forth interactions between a therapist and client. But in the specific context of arts therapies, this process more often than not includes the creation of art-images. Often these images themselves seem to precipitate more dramatic moments, but they too can sometimes provide a background to the work where "implicit progressive change" can take place in the sense of Moving Along. This is exemplified by my client Michael's story.

Michael's story

Michael had two part-time jobs in different locations. In one of his ongoing sessions with me he shared feelings of confusion as to why these two places of employment felt so different—one left him unsatisfied (although the work itself satisfied him greatly) and one he enjoyed immensely. I invited him to create two images to represent his two different experiences.

The image he created first was to represent the job that left him feeling unsatisfied. In one corner of a mat on the floor he placed an arc of colourful figures around a birdcage filled with stones, and in the opposite corner he placed two rows of seashells and a heap of wood chippings (see Figure 4.2).

Figures 4.2 Michael's first workplace image.

This image, he said, depicted an organisation where the highest level of management stayed closely closeted in their bird cage/ivory tower, removed from the next layer of management (the colourful figures). The shells were staff who felt fragile and unsupported, and the clients (of the business) were symbolised by the wood chippings that were even more fragile still.

As he made the image, Michael seemed unaware that he had placed the "middle managers" onto the mat in a manner that suggested he was irritated with them. I mirrored this back to him by placing a few figures of my own onto the floor with the same disgruntled attitude he had demonstrated. He was subsequently able to recognise for the first time where his feelings of dissatisfaction with this particular job lay: he felt unsupported by middle management.

For his second image, Michael created a sand tray in which a ring of interlinking clay people was placed around some happy, smiley figures being held by a stone hand. As he made the image, Michael became aware of how supported he (and his colleagues and clients) felt in this second job and how much he belonged there, in an environment where he was appreciated, held, and contained (see Figure 4.3).

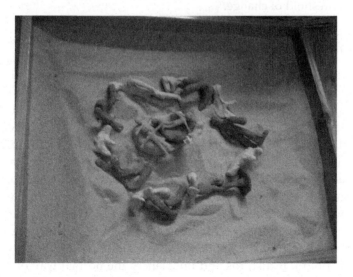

Figure 4.3. Michael's second workplace image.

* * *

The two images he created enabled Michael to gain an insight into his confusion. Later in the therapeutic work he told me that the images had supported him considerably in understanding his relationships with these two organisations. They also helped him to make decisions about his future career. In this sense, the work moved [the therapy] along (to use Stern's terminology). Or to put it another way, the implicit relational field was altered and groundwork had been laid for the possibility of dramatic moments of change in the future. What was particularly curious for me as a practitioner of arts-based therapy, however, is that it seemed as though this opportunity for future dramatic moments of change actually lay dormant within the art-images themselves.

Stern suggests there is inevitably an improvised quality, even a "sloppiness" to the process of Moving Along in therapy. I find this admission refreshingly honest and in welcome contrast to much that has been written about the need for goal-oriented therapy with the application of standard approaches. I was definitely improvising when I suggested Michael create two images to symbolise his feelings about his jobs. Michael himself was improvising when he created the resulting scenes. And these seemingly unconscious acts were able to lead us to the threshold of change.

Now moment

In addition to non-conscious moments in which the therapy is Moving Along, Stern also describes the occurrence of moments in a session where something profound takes place. He calls these Now Moments and describes them as the arrival of "moments of truth", laden with potential importance for the immediate or long-term future of the work (Stern, 2004). "Now" moments are full of possibility (or crisis) and the therapist is required to be actively present to the moment and respond authentically to achieve some sort of resolution. This goes beyond what is normally expected in the non-conscious moments of Moving Along. The Now Moment announces a "disturbance in the system that constitutes a potential transition to a new state of organisation" (ibid.). It disturbs and unbalances the normal way of a client and therapist "doing business together" and thus creates a new intersubjective context.

Stern tells us that during a Now Moment, a new state is effectively coming into being or promising to emerge for the client. There is often a mounting emotional charge and the situation requires that something *needs* to happen—a pregnancy of expectation. Such moments are also referred to as "hot present moments". This is a reference to Constantin Stanislavski's description of "a hot stage" in the world of the theatre. A hot stage is a phenomenon whereby the atmosphere on a theatre stage becomes electrified during (and after) a powerful performance (Stanislavski, 1990). Within therapy, a client and therapist seem to enter a state of heightened drama and expectation in a similar way. This shift in atmosphere means they are poised and more *available* for something dramatic to emerge, which reminds me of a most unusual session with my client Elias.

Elias' story

Elias was a young man in his early twenties who had been struggling with identity issues. He was currently working with a team of mostly women at his place of employment and was finding this difficult. I asked him to create an image to represent how he felt. Elias created the image of a plastic toy baby placed inside a rubber frog's mouth (see Figure 4.4). He then volunteered a piece of information about the image that seemed to astonish us both. He said it was intended to represent "all those women who eat babies".

Figure 4.4. Elias' frog and baby.

Immediately after he had said this Elias looked at me expectantly, as if I would automatically know what to do or say. I was tracking his non-verbal cues and noticed he had become paler and started to tremble slightly. It was clear that a Sternian Now Moment had occurred, and just as Stern describes, the question of what I did or said next was crucial to what was going to develop. I felt at a total loss. As I stared at Elias' image I felt the vulnerability of the baby and I experienced a powerful desire to snatch it from the frog's mouth (which would have gone against one of the fundamental principles of my integrative arts training—you never touch a client's image). I kept thinking about what women who devour babies would be like. It also crossed my mind that maybe he had been feeling devoured, invaded or "eaten up" by *me*. This led me to make one of my more unusual interventions, as I asked him without irony, "Can you tell me something about these women who eat babies?"

After a slight pause in which we looked at each other in surprise, spontaneous laughter erupted between us. The laughter seemed to create a strong connection, something that Stern calls a Moment of Meeting. In a Now Moment Stern says that the dyadic atmosphere becomes "highly affectively charged" (Stern, 2004). The participants (who in my example are gazing at the frog and the baby art-image) are pulled fully, even violently, centre stage and into the present moment that is now staring them both in the face. But interestingly with Elias' art-image (and in many other cases of arts-based work with clients), it seems to be the art-image *itself* that holds "centre stage" as we (the client and therapist) gaze with awe and surprise at what has been created.

Moments of meeting

A therapist's response to the dynamic created by a Now Moment has to be improvised on the spot to fit the singularity of the unexpected situation. It requires something beyond technique and theory and can lead to a peak connection being made between client and therapist; a connection that Stern calls a Moment of Meeting.

A Moment of Meeting is a "special kind of present moment" that provides one of "the key moments of change in psychotherapy" (Stern, 2004). It is always preceded by a Now Moment (although a Now Moment may also dissipate and fail to lead to a Moment of Meeting). Moments of Meeting are so powerful that the "therapeutic relationship seems to tilt on its axis" and something so vital is added that the whole session is altered and profound change takes place (ibid.).

At around the time I was immersed in reading Stern, I had sessions with my clients Amy and Ali that demonstrated the validity of all three of his categories. I will describe these sessions in turn.

Amy's story

My client Amy had been managing several significant upheavals in her life—beginning a new job, moving house, and planning a big family event. In the week prior to this particular session she had moved into her new home. She told me that curtains had been scheduled to be fitted but they had been delayed for some reason and would not be installed until the following week. Amy was surprised at how agitated she had become by her windows' lack of curtains, and how upset she felt about the idea she was being overlooked by neighbours. But as a highly intelligent and self-aware woman she also realised her reaction was rather extreme.

I suggested she choose an item from the practice-room shelves to represent her new home. She chose a plastic model of a house (with no glass in the windows) and placed it on the floor between us. She then frantically began putting up pieces of material for curtains and even went so far as to barricade the house on all sides with planks of wood (see Figure 4.5). As she carried out this work she became increasingly upset and somewhat manic in her attempts to get the curtains and planks to stay in place. "People are peering in," she was saying, "they're *staring* at us!"

Figure 4.5. Amy's houses (a)   (b)

Amy was unclear as to why she was becoming so agitated and emotional. I found myself wondering what could have caused this huge disturbance. Was her distress perhaps not actually connected to her new house at all?

As mentioned, Stern believes that all change in therapy can be divided into non-conscious moments of Moving Along and sudden dramatic moments (comprised of Now Moments and Moments of Meeting). The first stage of this session, in which Amy built barricades for her model house without either of us really knowing what she was doing or why, was an example of the Moving Along process. We were both improvising. Her actions expanded to surreal proportions when she protected the tiny model house on either side with large cushions, such that it could hardly be seen at all. And yet still this exaggerated camouflage did not seem to calm her agitation and outpouring of emotion about prying neighbours.

"Does this remind you of anything?" I found myself asking. She did not reply, which was fortunate. It was a poor intervention on my part and could have been unhelpful had she tried to answer it, as it would probably have taken her to the analytical part of her brain and away from the immediate experiential moment. Instead she continued to look for more and more objects around the practice-room to help her barricade her house. "I can't stop them looking," she was saying frantically, while the model house was being evermore enshrouded with bricks and cushions.

I watched her search for more and more barricading material with no clear idea what was happening for her or why. "Why can't you stop them looking?" I tried asking. No reply. I added, without really knowing why, "Where are the peering eyes?" At this point Amy and I could perhaps be described as "riding the crest of [a] Now moment" (Stern, 2004). She paused and began quietly sobbing. The atmosphere in the room had changed to one of charged emotion and expectancy, and neither Amy nor I knew what would happen next. But it was clear we had arrived at the threshold of a deeply significant moment in which something new and pressing was required.

"They ... they are inside the house"

Amy said in response to my question. She looked from the house to me and we locked eyes. Her emotions burst through and she began sobbing uncontrollably. Her past and present had collided.

We were each shocked by the revelation that had suddenly broken through. I was particularly surprised as I did not yet fully understand what she meant by saying "they" were *inside* the house (her neighbours?) but the statement had clearly revealed a new, disturbing aspect to her experience. Amy was perhaps shocked because she had said it out loud—and now her secret was out. She looked at me with shame and questioning in her eyes. I met her gaze with surprise and compassion and together we experienced what felt like a Sternian Moment of Meeting.

* * *

Later I would find out that the model house Amy had made was about so much more than her fears of there being no curtains at the window. It was linked to a separate event that had occurred when she was much younger. She had been unknowingly spied on for months (and possibly years) by her mother's boyfriend when she was a nubile adolescent. Unbeknownst to her or her mother at the time, the voyeur had made holes around light fittings in the attic so that he could spy on her in her bedroom and the bathroom. Once Amy had made this connection, it became something she could never not know again. And this is what Stern seems to be getting at when he says Moments of Meeting are irreversible and where real change takes place for a client.

Ali's story

My client Ali was a middle-aged woman who had suffered an extreme eating disorder when she was an adolescent. I had invited her to create an image of the part of her that had suffered from this eating disorder. The idea was that this image might reveal to us the part of Ali's younger self that still remained, long after her experience with this adolescent eating disorder had passed. She drew a picture with wax crayons of a character she called Eating Disorder Ali. It was a little white alien creature with a big head and emaciated body, surrounded by a dark shadow (see Figure 4.6).

Once the drawing was finished she placed a series of tea lights around it, which she said were "to keep her warm" because she could remember always being cold when she was in the grips of her eating disorder. At this point the therapy was Moving Along.

Figure 4.6. Eating Disorder Ali.

Sat opposite, I had an upside-down view of Eating Disorder Ali. As we both gazed at the image from our different viewpoints I became aware of the unintended simulacrum of a little gremlin or gnome-like figure hidden within the emaciated rib cage. We turned the paper around so that Ali could also see this unintended second face that had been lurking within her picture. At first she couldn't see what I meant but then suddenly she saw it too (see Figure 4.7).

We rode the crest of a Now Moment as she suddenly said in a wavering voice, "Yes! I see him! He looks like the angry voice in my head that was always telling me not to eat things ... I always had gnawing, angry hunger pangs in my stomach like a grumbling gremlin". We had achieved a profound Moment of Meeting.

At my invitation, Ali decided to create a safe place for Eating Disorder Ali in a sand tray. She cut the character out from its background and carefully placed it in the tray. Next she tried to build a canopy above the figure but it kept collapsing. I remarked that this process seemed analogous to the way she would try and build up her life when she had the eating disorder, only to find it collapse. She ignored this comment.

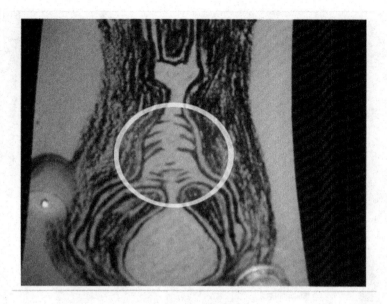

Figure 4.7. Eating Disorder Ali (with circle detail added afterwards) [not detailed as at present].

(I am always struck by the extraordinary way clients seem able to ignore what is not directly relevant for them at a particular moment). Eventually Ali created a "safe place" in the sand tray for this part of her (with feathers all around and a soft patterned scarf for the figure to lie upon) (see Figure 4.8).

At the end of the session, and with Ali attentively watching, I carefully placed Eating Disorder Ali in a special folder and ceremoniously tied up the ribbons that secured each corner. This was in order to ensure that Ali could see I was going to look after this part of her very carefully. The image was put in a safe place and we would refer to it on future occasions as her therapy progressed.

* * *

Having discovered the work of Stern, it became important to ask if my own concept of a breakthrough moment might be synonymous with either of Stern's ideas of pivotal moments: Now Moments and Moments of Meeting. A breakthrough moment is undoubtedly a highly dramatic, charged moment and in this sense has many qualities that

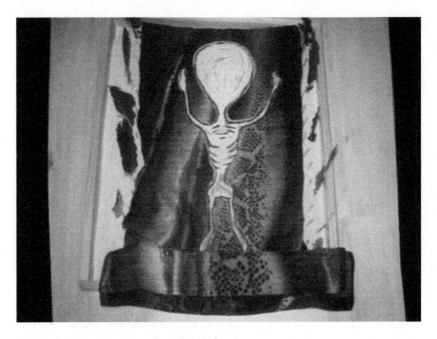

Figure 4.8. Eating Disorder Ali sand tray.

could be considered similar (or even identical) to Stern's ideas. One such similarity is that at the time of a breakthrough moment both client and therapist are dramatically pulled into the present. Something unique and authentic is frequently required of the therapist and often the client as well.

Is a breakthrough moment a now moment?

Stern suggests that a Now Moment always precedes a Moment of Meeting—that is, it alerts the client and therapist to a new crisis that must be resolved (and if pursued successfully, can lead to a Moment of Meeting). Is there a moment that precedes a breakthrough moment that does something similar? In many ways, yes. There *is* a moment of heightened atmosphere that suddenly arises and can lead on to a breakthrough moment or disappear and not come to anything. So in this sense Stern's concept of a Now Moment is extraordinarily helpful in understanding what happens at the time of a breakthrough moment.

But there is also a fundamental difference that must be noted. In the instance of arts-based psychotherapy (as opposed to traditional, dyadic therapy) a breakthrough moment is not *solely* a crisis that arises between therapist and client that demands a resolution (as with a Sternian Now Moment). This is because a breakthrough moment occurs within a therapeutic relationship that already includes art-images, and the presence of such images fundamentally alters the nature of that relationship.

Within the three-way relationship of client–art–therapist, a Now Moment can arise because of the art and not require resolution within the therapist–client dynamic at all. In this sense it stands apart from the strict concept of a Sternian Now Moment. In Ali's session, for example, the precipitating moment before her breakthrough moment was created by the reconfiguration of her art-image when the simulacra of the little gremlin figure suddenly appeared within the character she had drawn. In this instance, the art-image *itself* was providing the Now Moment, not an intervention from me (her therapist) or anything else from the dyadic nature of our relationship.

So it seems that although a Sternian Now Moment can be a deeply useful way to describe the moment just before a breakthrough moment, it cannot be considered synonymous, because in arts-based therapy it is not always predominantly a client–therapist moment. It is very often, instead, a client–art moment (albeit the therapist is still a key part of the experience). In addition to this key difference, Stern suggests that a hot present Now Moment does not last longer than ten seconds. In my own experience working with the arts, moments leading up to a break-through moment can be dramatic, charged periods that last longer than that. With both Amy and Ali, for example, there was a build up to their breakthrough moments that lasted for several minutes.

Is a breakthrough moment a moment of meeting?

I have shared with the reader many examples of powerful moments of connection with my clients that can be understood as Sternian Moments of Meeting. In each of these examples the client and I had a deep and profound connection with one another. But this is not always the case when working with arts media. In many instances with the arts, a breakthrough moment seems to be a Moment of Meeting between the client and the art-image rather than with me. I am cast more in the role of witness, although even in these instances the dyadic relationship of therapist and client does nonetheless tend to deepen and change.

In this chapter I have argued that Stern's model can usefully be applied to arts-based psychotherapy, but amendments are necessary to accommodate the uniquely triangular relationship of therapist–art–client. In the next chapter I will consider the role played by the therapeutic relationship itself in bringing about breakthrough moments.

CHAPTER FIVE

The therapeutic relationship

Lucy's story

It had been several months since Lucy first came to visit my private practice. She presented herself as a highly intelligent, middle-aged woman with a great sense of humour. But lately she had been feeling anxious and confused. She was particularly tall and her body seemed as though it was struggling to fully contain her energetic presence.

Lucy had been trying to tell me something for a while, but so far she had only been able to say it was something she found impossibly difficult to talk about. She seemed caught between desperately wanting to reveal whatever it was and needing to strongly defend against revealing it. I also felt pulled in two opposite directions. I was inclined to encourage her to talk about what was distressing her, but simultaneously found myself wanting to protect her from having to speak about it. The result was that Lucy and I had become respectively stuck. How could I help her feel safe enough to communicate what was going on?

It occurred to me that we might simply focus on trying to reach a safe place, here and now, in the therapy room and see if this encouraged anything new. In a previous session Lucy had chosen a selection of objects and figures to act as her personal defenders and protectors.

I suggested she now create a new image of a safe place. She took some black paper and put a few of the "protectors" (from her previous session) around the paper like a border (see Figure 5.1).

I noticed that Lucy became more energised at my suggestion that she create "a safe place", having seemed quite low in energy previously. She used chalk to draw a containing boundary for her image. I wasn't sure exactly what she was trying to do, so I merely reflected back that I could see she needed to make the space feel really, really safe. I also asked her if she needed to additionally protect herself against *me*. This appeared to encourage her to draw several layers of further chalk boundaries.

Finally, Lucy made a big chalk scribble in the middle of the "protected space" of her image and said she could not name this scribble. It struck me that her carefully prepared layers of containment (on the image) had enabled her to feel safe enough to incorporate a symbolic representation of what she could not tell me. This unspeakable truth (whatever it might be) was held within the scribble in the centre. The act of creating a safe, contained place to conceal her fears (without any pressure to express them in words) had apparently enabled Lucy to feel more secure. She had created layer upon layer of safety within her art-image and this appeared to allow her to give form to a nameless emotion (something that clearly involved shame, fear, or dread). The safety

Figure 5.1. Lucy's border picture.

that was symbolised by the borders around her image also appeared to indicate the fact that she was becoming more trusting of me and thus felt safer within the therapeutic relationship.

I had purposefully suggested that Lucy create a safe space in the therapy room. Schaverien talks of the "frame within the frame"—the frame of an image within the frame of the therapeutic space within the frame of the therapeutic relationship. My aim had been to ensure Lucy did not feel cajoled into telling me what she felt unable to tell me, by suggesting instead that she put her energies into making the room feel safe. This enabled her to show me how unsafe she felt in the image she created. As Schaverien says, "the depth touched by [an] image is far beyond what the client could have stated" (Schaverien, 1999).

* * *

There is something extraordinary about the bond that exists between a client and therapist. From a review of the literature (that included over 1,000 separate pieces of research) Orlinsky, Grave, and Parks (quoted in Eysenck, 2004) gleaned that it is a widely accepted fact that the therapeutic relationship is the single most important factor in client change. If I was to gain a proper understanding of breakthrough moments it was going to be necessary to better understand how this relationship provides the context in which such moments can arise. In this chapter I will use examples from Lucy's work and that of my other clients to consider the unique nature of this relationship.

An extraordinary bond

The special bond between a client and therapist grows and changes over time. As this change serves to deepen trust it can often create a context in which breakthrough moments are more likely to occur. But how could I conceptualise this near-magical quality of trust that builds in the therapeutic relationship? What could it be likened to? Stern believes the best way to grasp this quality is to liken it to the relationship between a mother and her newborn infant. There is a palpable, almost mystical bond between mother and child that is prior to language and beyond words. Stern calls this connection implicit relational knowing—it includes emotions, expectations and motivational behaviour, all of which can be communicated from infant to mother in a few seconds. It was Stern's firm belief that "the vast majority of therapeutic change is found to occur in [this] domain of implicit knowing" (Stern, 2004).

Stern believed that over time this implicit relational knowing between a client and therapist could move the relationship from state (1) to state (2). For example, my client Lucy sensed that her relationship with me had shifted from state (1) in which she protected herself against feeling pressured to tell me something, to state (2) in which, once she had shown me how unsafe she felt, she was able to trust me enough to show me what she could not tell me. Similarly, my client Ben moved from state (1) in which he experienced me as a therapist who was effectively a stranger and thus unlikely to be able to help him with his problem, to state (2) in which he experienced me as someone who had shared his deep moment of recognition. In the case of both clients, their realisation about me itself contained the potential for change. Or as Stern rather wonderfully puts it, our therapeutic relationship "tilt[ed] on its axis" (ibid.).

Martha's story

The therapeutic relationship with another of my clients, Martha, also changed or tilted on its axis. Martha and I had already developed a unique bond of trust but it deepened to a whole new level when she experienced a profound and unforgettable breakthrough moment. She was sixty-five years old and had referred herself to therapy in order to try and understand how her present relationship with her daughter had become entangled with experiences from the past. Her relationship with her (now-adult) daughter Rowena was complex and Martha found herself wondering if it could be connected to the traumatic difficulties they had experienced at Rowena's birth.

After working with Martha on this and several other related issues for about a year, we decided to re-enact the birth of her daughter. The day and time were carefully planned out in advance. What could not have been anticipated, however, was how surprisingly and dramatically things would play out. When the day in question came around, Martha was laying on her side upon cushions on the floor. She was silently writhing as she enacted giving birth (much as she had done thirty years before). As the enactment unfolded, I found myself cross-modally attuning to her by banging a drum and making noises—groans and birthing sounds—to accompany the dramatisation. We were each fully engrossed in the shared drama and I was quite caught up in moaning and banging away at my drum when something shocking happened.

After about 20 minutes of "giving birth", Martha suddenly sat up and looked straight at me. With tears streaming down her face, she spoke for the first time during the enactment. "Am I going to die?" she asked. "Is my baby going to die?" It was a powerful breakthrough moment I will never forget. It was as though we really were back there at the time she had given birth to her daughter. I could think of no correct response. My intuition told me she needed to know that I had empathically attuned to the terror of what it felt like for her back then. "You were terrified that you were both going to die," I said. I spoke in the past tense to remind her that her worst fears were from a long time ago. The session enabled Martha to revisit what had been an extremely traumatic event in her life, only this time I was there so she did not have to feel so alone. It seemed to help her ease the disturbing memory that for thirty years she had kept secret.

Martha told me later that she had made no sound during Rowena's actual birth, as it had been a home birth and she was concerned her three-year-old son might hear and become alarmed. She told me that it really helped her to hear the sounds I was making in the enactment, because back then she had suppressed all sound. Although she still felt unable to make any noise herself during our dramatisation, the sound I supplied seemed to be healing for her. Perhaps this was because at least sound was being made this time, even though it was not Martha making it. It was as though we had finally provided a soundtrack to something that was soundless in her memory. I believe this also helped to prevent the enactment from being re-traumatising. My sound effects helped to make it a very different and thus reparative experience for Martha.

Taking part in an enactment of trauma provides a client with a safe way to powerfully revisit the original event. However a strong bond needs to have been formed between therapist and client for the therapy to work. I believe it was the fact that Martha had been working with me for a year already when we planned her enactment that made it possible for her to carry out the work in such a reparative way. She had reached a deep level of trust in the therapeutic relationship and this made it possible for us to attempt this high-grade, experiential session. Due to the deep level of the work and the power of her breakthrough moment, our therapeutic relationship moved to a new level after this session.

Martha's story illustrates how crucial the therapeutic relationship can be in fostering an environment for brave, powerful work to take place. This is particularly true when the work involves the use of arts media.

Intersubjectivity

We have seen that in a therapy session I often invite clients to select a postcard image that resonates with whatever issue they are wanting to explore that day. When I am the supervisee-client in sessions, my supervisor, too, will often invite me to select images to explore my questions and concerns. In one such session, I had been discussing my work with Lucy and Martha and my supervisor asked me to select an image that depicted my feelings about how the therapeutic relationship had changed with each client. I selected an image of two trees entwined with one another in an indissoluble way. It was not possible to see where one tree started and the other ended. This was how I saw the deep bond I felt with my clients (see Figure 5.2).

Figure 5.2. Trees entwined.

Stolorow and Atwood suggest the "client and therapist together form an indissoluble psychological system" (Stolorow & Atwood, 1987). I was stirred by the way my image appeared to symbolise this intersubjectivity of the therapeutic relationship and illustrate the idea that therapist and client can become one system. I additionally imagined red apples on the tree that could symbolise the art materials, as well as one or two bright lights amidst the foliage that could represent break-through moments. The image gave me a visual depiction of the ways in which the feelings and experience of a client and therapist might meet within the therapeutic relationship.

Feeling "felt"

At times, there is a remarkable phenomenon that occurs with clients in which it can feel as though we are having the same exact thoughts. This often results in the client "feeling *felt*" as Daniel Siegel so aptly puts it (Siegel, 2010). Siegel describes the experience of this phenomenon as being "the sense that someone else feels one's feelings" (Siegel, 1999). He reminds us that in attuning to others, or being attuned to, our own internal state is "allowed to shift" and can begin to resonate with the inner world of another (Siegel, 2010). He believes this ability to "feel *felt*" emerges in close relationships, such as infant–child and therapist–client, where a fledgling sense of trust is increasingly formed that begins to bridge the seemingly "unbridgeable gulf" (ibid.).

I found the way Siegel describes this feeling to be close to my experience as a therapist (and a client). I believe Martha was already "feeling *felt*" by me when she agreed to re-enact her difficult childbirth and that after the session she felt this at an even deeper level. With my client Ben, I believe a connection was made between us with his choice of the orangutan image, my recognition of its relevance, and the act of us contemplating it deeply together. This enabled him to feel *felt*. He had only just met me but by the end of the session each of our internal states had changed and the relationship had reached a new plane.

The space between

I scoured the literature for descriptions of the intangible web of interpersonal connections that exists between a client and therapist. Schaverien, for example, speaks of there being a "dynamic field", while Stern refers to the "inter-subjective relational domain" (that includes the shared, implicit relationship between therapist and client). But I was particularly drawn to another of Stern terms. The interactions between a therapist and client take place within what Stern calls an intersubjective matrix (Stern, 2004). A matrix can be defined as "an environment in which something develops." My questions thus became centred on how and in what ways the space (or environment) between a therapist and client can develop and how this can encourage breakthrough moments and foster change processes.

Whichever way the mysterious, ever-changing relational field of client and therapist is described, it is accepted (by both psychodynamic and arts-based psychotherapy) that this includes both conscious and unconscious aspects. It also includes aspects of transference and countertransference. Nathan Schwartz-Salent believes that the unconscious dynamic between people in a relationship (including therapist and client) contributes a realm where "more than apparently harmless creatures lurk in the forest" (Schwartz-Salent, 1998). The idea of creatures lurking in the unconscious forest alongside me and my clients was an apt metaphor. Such creatures had perhaps been lurking with Lucy and it was not until she created the safe boundary around her image that she felt she could keep them from emerging. What creatures might be lurking in the forest of my relationship with other clients?

Tanya's story

My client Tanya seemed to imagine there were "more than apparently harmless creatures lurking in the forest" in the relationship with her boyfriend. Tanya was thirty-nine years old and had always found relationships difficult. In one session she was telling me about her current boyfriend and how insecure she felt with him. I invited her to create an image to show me how she wished the relationship could feel.

She first created an image that showed her feeling secure with her boyfriend (two figures lying happily beside one another). She then rapidly made a second image (in which one of the figures was placed far away) and said this was how she felt when she received no reply to her texts (see Figure 5.3). Next she made a third image (in which only one figure remained) to show how abandoned she felt when an entire day

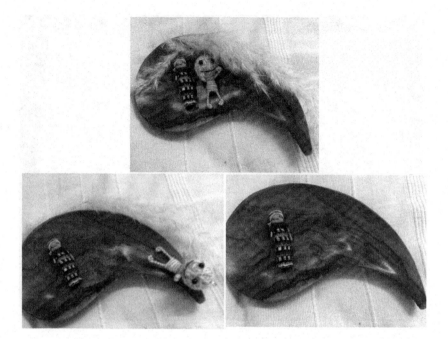

Figure 5.3. Tanya's relationship (a), (b) and (c).

went by without receiving any replies. She told me that making these images helped her to understand how disproportionately extreme her feelings were in relation to the facts. In reality, her boyfriend had simply been held up in a meeting all day and unable to receive or send messages.

Tanya drew her final image of this aspect of her work when she was invited to show me once again how she wanted her relationship with her current boyfriend to feel. She created a warm chalk drawing of a figure engulfed in the wide embrace of another (see Figure 5.4). She later told me that creating this image had helped her imagine what it might feel like to be secure in a relationship and that she had held this understanding in mind whenever she began to feel abandoned. Over time this had helped her to separate what she experienced as disrespectful behaviour from her boyfriend from her childhood fears of abandonment. With this lovely image she had provide herself with a positive talisman.

Figure 5.4. Tanya's chalk picture.

The triangular relationship

It is clear that there is an intersubjective matrix within which the therapist–client relationship takes place. But what happens when this matrix is extended to include the use of arts media, such as with Lucy, Martha, and Tanya. Tessa Dalley et al. describe the resulting relationship as triangular (image–client–therapist), a concept that has become common in art therapy theory (Dalley et al., 1993). My colleague and I devised a diagram to represent this triangular relationship (see Figure 5.5).

The diagram offers a simplistic overview of something that is in fact far more complicated. The therapist, art and client are each represented by a smaller triangle in each of the three corners of a larger triangle. Within the middle of this triangle is a small circle that represents a breakthrough moment.

I chose to place the client at the apex of the triangle and to use the term "art" rather than Dalley's term "image" so as to remind the reader that a whole variety of art forms and arts media are implied.

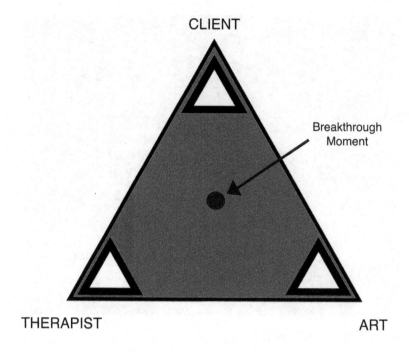

Figure 5.5. The triangular relationship.

It is important to remember that although each corner of the triangle contributes to the context in which a breakthrough moment may occur, together they create an intersubjective matrix that cannot be separated out.

Susannah's story

In response to how she was feeling one afternoon having just visited her parents, my client Susannah drew a lone bird on the ground, surrounded by a flock of other birds flying around. Having finished the image she sat back and stared at what she had drawn for a considerable time. Suddenly she drew a cage around the lone bird then looked up at me with surprise and said, "I never knew I felt like a caged bird when I go back to visit my parents. I always felt like that as a child and I never realised that before" (see Figure 5.6).

Figure 5.6. Susannah's bird in cage.

Susannah and I already had a dyadic therapist–client relationship but the bond was extended or triangulated by the addition of art—in this case, her drawing of the bird in the cage.

Phil Jones, a drama therapist, says that one way of looking at the triangular relationship is to see therapist, art and client as co-creating the "drama-therapy space" together (Jones, 2010). The art-image takes a central place as a means of "expressing, exploring and resolving material over the use of words alone" (ibid.) within the therapy process.

A shifting perspective

Schaverien warns us that the triadic relationship of client–art–therapist should not be viewed over-simplistically. She says that the primacy of the client–image relationship and client–therapist relationship is in continual flux, with one or the other asserting themselves more prominently at alternate times (Schaverien, quoted in Gilroy, 2000). For example, when Ben first arrived and reported his problem of clinginess, the relationship between us was predominantly one of therapist–client. But when his focus was on the orangutan image, the key relationship became our connection with the art. Both of us were drawn to the image, almost to the exclusion of an awareness of the other. In this sense, it felt more accurately like two parallel relationships—client–image and therapist–image—than it did a therapist–client interaction. But following Ben's breakthrough moment, when we looked at each other and experienced a deep connection (a Sternian Moment of Meeting), the client–therapist connection became central again and the role of the art receded. This idea that the figure-ground of the triangular relationship can shift its primary focus from client–art to client–therapist (and back again) can be illustrated by a story involving my brave client June.

June's story

June worked as a hospice counsellor supporting adults who were suffering from terminal illness. In her ten years of work at the hospice, she was required to practically and psychologically support terminally ill patients (and their families). She would aim to provide them with "the best possible death". She would even attend funerals, providing further support to her clients' friends and families on these occasions.

June kept referring to a recurring dream she was having that disturbed her greatly and which she had never described to anyone. She said that it had the quality of a nightmare and that she would wake up trembling and filled with terror, which made her afraid of the fact that she was alone in her house. In particular, her anxiety centred on the fear that someone was lurking in the cupboard under her stairs. She mentioned this dream to me frequently but said she was not yet ready to speak about it any further.

Several months went by and June worked through many different concerns in our largely successful therapy sessions. One day when she was telling me that things in her life had greatly improved, I found myself asking, "What about death?" I was aware of her job at the hospice and how inevitably she was surrounded by death and I also remembered the recurring nightmare that she hadn't felt able to tell me about. This led June, for the first time, to tell me the details of her nightmare. I knew how difficult it was for her to speak about it, so I did not suggest she recall it in the present tense (something I frequently do with clients to make the dream recall more intense). But interestingly, on her own accord, she chose to tell it in the present tense anyway:

I am standing in a graveyard and behind me there is a church.
I can see through [the] open doors that stacked up everywhere in
this church are coffins, as far as the eye can see—coffins stacked to
the ceiling, coffins covering the floor space, coffins on pews, coffins piled high *everywhere*. The church is practically *full* of coffins …
I dare not turn around because I know they are there. I can *feel* them
and see them in my mind's eye. Now I sense that more and more of
these coffins are stacking up and they are spilling out of the church …
It feels as though they are coming after me. I am terrified and try to
run away but I cannot move … I am completely paralysed.

June looked petrified at this point in her recollection. I suggested that
perhaps she might *draw* the dream for me. My thinking was that such
an exercise could provide her with some containment (by having the
dream exist on paper). The image she drew depicted coffins stacked
within the arch of the church. Crosses depicted tombstones in the
graveyard and she represented herself as a stick person alone in the
cemetery (see Figure 5.7). She explained that the pathway between
the trees to the right of the picture was where she wanted to run away
to, but her legs would not allow her to move.

Figure 5.7. June's graveyard.

One week after describing her dream, June told me that she had experienced a dark night of the soul. Ever since our session she said she had been haunted by the art-image she had made and that it somehow presented her nightmare back to her in a completely new, vivid way. She had spent a whole evening on her own, crying about her fears of death. During this night she visited a series of imaginary scenes that all began in the graveyard of her drawing: in one of these it was her own young son lying in a coffin; in another it was her in the coffin and she mourned her son and husband that were left behind. She told me that she cried and cried.

* * *

It seems that telling me about her dream and then creating an image of it had unlocked the fears June had around death. The outpouring of tears (and years of grief) seemed to have loosened the grip of terror that had been trapped in the recurring dream. Most interestingly, however, for our current purposes, is that June's breakthrough moment took place while she was on her own and *not* as a result of any direct connection to me as her therapist. It was as if her creation of the art-image based upon the dream had enabled her to "meet" and face her own unprocessed fear. This seemed to support her to bring about significant changes in her internal world. She told me in a subsequent session that if she was back in the dream now she would no longer feel immobilised; in fact, she would be halfway down the path, looking back at the church and coffins (although she did acknowledge she would still feel frightened). Interestingly, she has not had the recurring dream since.

Perhaps June's dream had enabled her to "meet" her deepest fears about death. Her job at the hospice and having to face the deaths of individuals she cared about on an almost daily basis meant she had perhaps needed to repress and deny this fear. The fact that June's breakthrough moment seemed to take place while she was alone offers us a further illustration that the pivotal relationship in arts-based therapy can take place almost entirely between a client and the image they have created—the therapist does not have to be involved (or even present).

But the dyadic (therapist–client) relationship between me and June took centre stage once again when she returned to tell me about her powerful breakthrough. It was also instrumental in giving her the confidence to work further with arts media. The therapist–client bond was critical to the context in which her work took place. But her breakthrough moment itself did not take place within the intersubjective matrix of therapist and client. This illustrates Schaverian's idea that the primacy of the relationship can shift in arts-based psychotherapies.

* * *

In this chapter I have argued that there is something about the triangular relationship (of client–art–therapist) that has a chameleon-like ability to shift relational fields—to tilt on many axes. I began to wonder if this could be the very quality that makes arts-based psychotherapy more conducive to the arrival of breakthrough moments. In the next part I will go hunting for clues in each of the three corners of this mysterious triangle.

PART III

THERAPIST–CLIENT–ART RELATIONSHIP

CHAPTER SIX

The role of the therapist

Melissa's story

"I've been to see lots of therapists in the past and none of them have helped me."

This was the opening statement of my client Melissa, a successful accountant in her late forties who came to see me one afternoon. We decided we would talk about her reasons for seeking therapy in a one-off assessment to see if we wished to work together any further.

"What is it that you need help with?" I asked her.

"I can't speak about it," she said, "I've never told anyone before and it's just too terrible to speak about".

"That must be very hard," I said, "to be holding on to something that feels so dreadful you can't speak about it, but which bothers you so much that you must seek help. Perhaps something in this room could help you find a way to show me what it is you need to tell me without having to use words?"

"That feels a bit scary," said Melissa, and she glanced nervously at the crowded shelves of my practice-room (see Figure 6.1).

Figure 6.1. Practice-room.

"I expect it does," I said, "but it can be fun and even insightful to use something other than words to try and understand things in your life. Especially when it's something you don't feel able to talk about".

After a little more gentle persuasion I suggested that we try something there and then. I chose a few items that I felt were not too threatening (some scarves and bits of material) and put them on the floor in front of her.

"Now, how about you choose a few objects from the shelf?" I said. "Pick anything that you feel represents what it is you can't tell me. You can cover the objects up with one of these scarves and maybe that way you will be able to show me what you don't feel ready to tell me about yet".

Melissa took a long time deciding and she carefully selected a snake, a furry spider, a large wooden cheetah, and several painted stones. She placed these on the floor between us. Next she selected, just as carefully, a black silk scarf and covered her chosen objects with it completely.

When she had finished we sat together staring at the scarf, now bulked up by the objects beneath. It felt as if the issue Melissa could not talk about was right there with us in the room, concealed by the metaphor of the objects she had chosen (I did not yet know what they signified) and literally covered up by the scarf. Melissa had grown pale and alert. She seemed to be strongly defensive when I asked what it was she found too terrible to speak about. I don't usually ask such a starkly penetrating question of any client at an assessment session and felt that if Melissa did choose to return for therapy I would wait until she was ready to reveal what was troubling her.

I asked her towards the end of our session to think about whether she wanted to try out six therapy sessions as a starting point, after which we could review whether she wanted to work with me further.

"I already know I want to work with you," she said immediately, "can we put the six sessions in the diary now please? I feel comfortable with you!"

* * *

What is it that I (the therapist) contribute to the relationship that determines whether or not a new client such as Melissa wishes to return for therapy with me? And how might this contribution influence the possibility that they go on to experience breakthrough moments? In this chapter I will focus in detail on the therapist's corner of the triangular relationship (of client–art–therapist) and consider specifically what it is that I bring to the therapy that might increase the possibility for my clients to achieve breakthrough moments and change.

Clients come to see me for the first time via many different routes and for many different reasons: I may have been recommended to them, I may have been randomly selected from a list of therapists in their area, or the client may simply have chosen me because I work with arts media. But no matter what reason they have for coming (and whatever the client's ultimate goal for their therapy), I am always placed in the unique position of being about to meet a brand new client for the first time. I may speak to them briefly on the phone before they arrive (to pick the date and time or give directions to my practice) but often that is all.

Having been a client myself I know firsthand the apprehension and curiosity one feels prior to meeting a new therapist. As a therapist I am always intrigued to meet a new client and excited to see if I can help them reduce whatever suffering they might be experiencing. What takes place in a first meeting is in some ways the sort of conversation that might take place between two strangers meeting for the first time. However, it is also the beginning of an entirely unique relationship. The client will not find out facts about my own life, but will rather respond to me as someone who they feel may or may not be able to help them with their particular issues. Clearly there are a vast number of different traits and characteristics a therapist might possess that can impact upon their client and the therapeutic relationship. These include, but are not limited to, gender, age, background, demeanour, voice, sense of humour, energy levels, physical appearance, and ways of relating.

The Mindful therapist

Researchers and theorists have suggested a number of important qualities that are necessary to be an effective therapist. Dan Hughes (2006) suggests that psychotherapy is at its core a special relationship. It "provides the safety and supportive presence of another [person] that helps clients to explore themselves and the events of their lives that trouble them the most" (Siegel & Solomon, 2013). The way that a therapist imparts this sense of safety and supportive presence, he says, is through a process of mindful intersubjectivity. Here Hughes is referring to Daniel Siegel's seminal work *The Mindful Therapist* in which Siegel uses research to demonstrate that a therapist's presence and the way they bring themselves fully into connection with their clients' selves are some of the most crucial factors in helping the client respond positively to the therapy. He believes therapists can cultivate this quality of presence (Siegel, 2010).

According to Siegel, the mindful therapist possesses qualities such as being creative and open to possibility. They have an awareness of the present moment without grasping onto judgements or expectations, which enables them to be flexible, receptive and have presence (ibid.). When a therapist feels confident enough to be mindful in such ways, Siegel believes their clients can begin to flourish (ibid.). Readers should note that this is the case for a therapist in any therapeutic approach, but in the case of arts-based therapy it applies in a slightly different way, as the therapist must also be mindful of the art-image as well as their client.

As well as being an integrative arts-based therapist, I am also a supervisor of other (qualified and trainee) arts-based therapists. One of these trainee therapists, Craig, was fraught with uncertainty in our session one day. He revealed that he had been finding it hard to be fully present and open to spontaneity with his client Joe. Every time Craig made an intervention, instead of feeling free and in the moment, he wondered whether the intervention would be approved of by his training institution and by me (his supervisor). It transpired he was using these interventions to make analytic and interpretive demands of his client's use of arts media instead of allowing the work to proceed more organically. To use Siegel's term, these qualities could be seen as inhibiting Craig's ability to be a mindful therapist. In his supervision sessions with me we explored the possibility of Craig finding a way to be more open to the metaphor of what his client Joe was presenting, without feeling pressure to get Joe to explain it.

Joe's story

Craig was a trainee therapist working with children using arts media and play. Joe was nine-years-old and had become so quiet and withdrawn (at home and school) that his parents had requested he come to see Craig for therapy. In keeping with his silent tendencies, Joe hardly said a word to Craig when he first came in and made little eye contact. But he quietly discovered the sand tray and week after week began creating new variations around the same theme.

Joe would place different figures in the sand tray each week and play imaginative games in which these characters would be busy minding their own business when, all of a sudden, a cataclysmic disaster would take place. One week it would be a huge bird descending upon the group and attacking them; another week it was a train crash, and at other times it would be a tsunami of poured water or an earthquake (for which the sand tray was shaken violently).

Craig was bewildered as to what these disasters might signify in Joe's life. Joe's parents had not mentioned any traumatic events or calamities in their son's short life and Joe offered no explanation himself for why these disasters were such a natural part of his sand tray scenes. Craig told me that he kept making interventions to ask Joe what his sand trays were about and what they meant, but each time Joe would simply ignore him and continue playing.

In our supervision sessions, Craig and I discussed how fascinating it is that clients (particularly child clients) will ignore an intervention when it's not something they wish to respond to. We also considered how Craig might find a way to let go of the inner critic that kept judging his therapeutic prowess and find a way instead to be more mindful with Joe. He said he would try this and eventually it paid off.

In their next session together Joe's sand tray again depicted a crowded scene of figures: this time a bus was driving along and a puppy suddenly ran into the street. The disaster enacted on this occasion involved the puppy being run over by the bus. All the sand tray "passers-by" (other objects and figures) stopped and the scene became still, as though everything and everyone had been turned into statues. This time, instead of asking Joe what the event signified, Craig remained mindful and fully present and thus did not ask any questions or make any interpretations. In fact, he didn't comment on the accident at all; instead a silence ensued that Craig said "seemed to magnify the intensity of the moment". With Craig's new mindful and accepting presence, it seems Joe slowly felt able to reveal some of the hidden meaning in his play. For the first time in a session he looked up from the sand tray and met the eyes of his therapist. In a hushed tone, he said simply, "everything can change in a moment".

Staying with his new-found mindfulness, Craig repeated back, "Yes—sometimes everything can change in a moment". And this simple act of Craig mirroring back his words seemed to lead Joe to a breakthrough moment. He rubbed fiercely at his eyes then gently placed all the figures to one side of the sand tray to frame this frozen scene of the dead puppy and the bus. Craig never did find out exactly what had precipitated Joe's deep fear that "everything can change in a moment". Joe had never owned or lost a dog, but maybe he had witnessed an accident at some point, or seen one in a film or maybe it was a metaphor for an underlying fear of change. Whatever the cause, it seems that Joe eventually received from Craig exactly what he needed—an open, accepting presence that validated his play.

In subsequent sessions, Joe's creations moved on. He now used Lego bricks, painted pictures, built models, and even created music. There were no further catastrophes. It seemed something had been resolved for him through this repetitive sand tray play that culminated in a breakthrough moment.

A relationship of trust

In the case of Craig's work with Joe, it seems reasonable to assume that Craig's own mindfulness—which included his new-found ability to adopt a non-questioning, non-judgemental stance—had influenced the success of their work to a powerful degree. In addition to the importance of presence, Siegel suggests that attunement and resonance are also key to creating clinical conditions of trust and enabling a client to change (Siegel, 2010).

Presence, attunement and resonance form a sequence. Presence describes how a therapist is able to be open, accepting and curious about their client and the unfolding of possibilities within a session. Attunement is how the therapist focuses their attention on the client's internal state (not just their outward behaviour) and attempts to empathically attune to their non-verbal patterns. Resonance—which describes two elements in sympathetic vibration (such as musical tones) that synchronise into a new harmony—describes how the therapist allows their own internal state to be informed and shaped by what they sense and perceive about their client's state. This is not an act of mirroring; it is an act of resonating. As the client begins to feel his or her therapist's resonance (from presence and attunement), he or she can begin to develop trust. When this sort of resonance is enacted with positive regard, Siegel says that a deep feeling of coherence emerges, containing the subjective sensation of harmony (ibid.). It results in the joining of the therapist and client into a functional whole whereby each is attuned to the other and both are changed as a result.

He suggests that this sequence of presence-attunement-resonance sets the stage for trust to grow in the therapeutic relationship and that this trusting state can itself create the conditions for change. We are hardwired to connect with others from the very beginning of our lives, he says. Our brains seek positive forms of contingent communication in which we send a signal that "is hopefully received, made sense of, and responded to in a timely and effective manner" (Siegel, 2010). This rings true with what I have observed when supervising qualified and trainee therapists, namely that those who display qualities of presence, attunement and resonance tend to be the most able to engender trust in their clients. Once this trust begins to grow, pivotal moments can arise and clients are able to make progress in the therapy. The more mindful and present the therapist, the greater the opportunity for breakthrough moments and change.

Rowan and Jacobs (2003) have suggested that the non-verbal, reactive response of a therapist, such as being moved to tears, can provide an "I–Thou" type of emotional connection with a client. This response is one way that a therapist can self-disclose, albeit not in a way that is verbal or consciously presented. A therapist's self-disclosure might be in response to their client's story, but in arts-based therapy it can also be in response to a client's art-image, as in the case of my client Henry.

Henry's story

One afternoon, Henry, a care worker in his mid thirties, created an image of a figure stood alone in a vast desert to represent how he felt (see Figure 6.2). I found myself looking beyond the image and imagining Henry himself as a little boy, all on his own in a desert with nobody to turn to for help. I was suddenly moved to tears. I knew a number of details about Henry at this time; he had an emotionally unavailable

Figure 6.2. Henry's toy in the desert.

mother and an abusive father so that throughout his childhood the very people he looked to for help had been the ones who were hurting him.

Henry's image in itself may not have had the power to touch me so deeply, but alongside my increasing comprehension of what had happened to Henry as a child, I felt that I was now expressing his own unexpressed tears. When he saw, however, that I was so moved it appeared to unlock his own feelings and he began to cry in earnest.

By creating the image of a lonely figure in a desert landscape, it seems that Henry had created a metaphor for how he felt without showing any actual emotion. My own tears of self-disclosure precipitated a breakthrough moment for Henry in which he was able to access his own previously hidden feelings.

* * *

Mark Welch identifies the most important attributes a therapist can possess that may foster the arrival of pivotal moments in the therapeutic relationship: understanding and empathy, seeing the client as unique, being genuine, and demonstrating respect (Welch, 2005). It seems almost self-evident that a therapist should need to be able to demonstrate understanding and empathy and be seen by their clients as supportive. In his book *The Gift of Therapy*, Irvin Yalom says that when his clients are looking back on their therapeutic work, they frequently recall "positive supportive statements [from] their therapist" (Yalom, 2001). But on the other hand, he says, "beware of empty compliments". Positive support should be informed by specifics—real details the therapist has learned about her client's life and particular experiences. For example, one of my own clients said that she appreciated how positive I was about her tendency to present many ideas simultaneously. She said that others had been critical of this habit whereas I delighted in it. I still tried to find a way to weave her often conflicting ideas together into a coherent narrative, but told her I appreciated them all.

Welch also asserts the importance of the "here-and-now" (or the immediate events within a therapy session) as being vital for effective therapy and a "major source of therapeutic power" (ibid.). I notice with my supervisees that it is the times they are able to be authentic and real in their therapeutic relationships that they report having had the best connections with their clients. Laughter and play are also key ways in which a therapist can demonstrate their authenticity and find a way to meet their clients. Many clients remark that they did not know therapy would be such fun or that we would laugh so much. Humour is one of the ways I try to bring authenticity to my own practice. It is hard not to be genuine when laughter is involved because laughing comes from a place that bypasses pretence. It is a real response that erupts spontaneously and thus communicates authenticity and warmth. Laughing with a client creates a connection to the therapist, bringing both parties abruptly into the present moment. In this sense, much like tears (and emotion), shared humour can lead a client to a breakthrough moment.

Shadows and the therapist

The Code of Ethics and Practice Guidance for Professional Conduct suggests that well-being practitioners should possess and promote many positive qualities and values, including honesty and dependability, clarity in thought and communication, integrity and wisdom. It also warns practitioners that the shadow or "polar opposite" of these qualities "may also be encountered". This serves as an opportune reminder that however much we therapists seek to demonstrate certain ideal qualities, we frequently fall short of our lofty aspirations. This is one of the reasons why the professional framework of supervision is so vital for a practising therapist, so as to analyse, critique, digest and understand these "shadow" aspects and prevent them from surfacing (or influencing the therapy) in a way that could be harmful to his or her clients or themselves.

We have identified a number of critical attributes a therapist should possess (and cultivate) to best support clients—mindfulness, presence, empathy, understanding, honesty, authenticity, clarity of thought, resonance, staying in the here and now, being creative, and being open to possibilities. But what about those times when a therapist is not able to be fully mindful or present? If I am honest, in my own experience there are more of these occasions than I might wish! On such occasions I might be inadvertently presenting shadow qualities. I might, for example, be distracted by events in my personal life, thinking about another client, or even thinking about what I'm going to have for lunch. But however distracted I might become, one of the most fascinating things about being a therapist is that my clients will frequently say (or do) something that pulls me sharply back to the present. In arts-based therapy, the image *itself* has the ability on occasion to make me more fully present. For example, one day in a session with my client Susan I was feeling rather tired and listless and my mind was wandering, when Susan jolted me dramatically back into the present.

Susan's story (continued)

On this particular afternoon I was tired and not ready to be an effective therapist at all. My mind was running over the many things I had to do that week. But in the instant Susan arrived for her session, I was shaken out of my distracted, less-than-present state. In fact, no amount of experience or training could have prepared me for what happened that day.

Susan had been coming to therapy for about six months, and as she arrived she was attempting to conceal something behind her back. "*This is that other part of me I was hinting at last session,*" she announced in a matter-of-fact way and revealed a large sculpture. I was no longer distracted by my thoughts. I was drawn completely to the present moment—shocked, amazed and filled with awe at this gawky yet elegant object she had made. It was even taller and thinner than Susan and it seemed to be imbued with an almost lifelike (but also deathlike) quality.

Despite the tumult of conflicting emotions that swept through me, I managed to say to Susan (in what I hoped was a relatively ordinary voice): "She is very welcome here. Would she like to sit on your client seat so I could meet her properly?" Susan agreed and sat her sculpture down on the seat (see Figure 6.3). I felt a surge of excitement at the unexpectedness of the situation, along with a frisson of intrigue as to what was going to come next. I had a compellingly strong desire to find out more about this new character in my therapy room. I was fully present and all distracted thoughts had been banished.

What in fact transpired in the session was an extraordinary three-way discussion between Susan, myself, and the new sculpture, which she had named Thin Susan. It started to feel almost like couples therapy with Susan and Thin Susan. They were beginning to find a way to get to know each other while I acted simply as their facilitator and mediator. It turned out that Thin Susan represented the anorexic part of Susan—a part that urged her to stop eating when she was thirteen. It seemed to have disappeared by the time she was seventeen and she had kept it hidden ever since.

Figure 6.3. Thin Susan sculpture.

Later in her therapy, Susan brought in a disturbing picture she had seen at a friend's house. She told me this picture was another way to show me what it felt like to be her at the time of her eating disorder. The image was of a beautiful ballerina dancing on pointe with a macabre skeleton (see Figure 6.4). She said the picture made her think of Thin Susan (represented by the skeleton) dancing with one of the other Susans (represented by the ballerina).

Figure 6.4. Susan's dancing with death.

Susan explained that it had felt as though she was dancing with death at the time of her eating disorder. She had been hospitalised for several months as a child following the death of her mother. During this period she had been literally starving herself to death as a way of trying to cope with the grief. Susan's mother herself had been dieting prior to her death and began to lose a lot of weight. Once Susan's mother became ill, Susan made a pact with God that if she lost weight, too, somehow her mother would be saved. By the time her mother finally died, Susan was well on her way to becoming anorexic.

Susan was thirty years older now and this was the first time since then that the Thin Susan part of her had been acknowledged, let alone conversed with somebody. I felt as though we were literally witnessing a reintegration of her cut-off self in action. These events with Susan demonstrate that what a client brings to their therapy has the ability to dramatically affect my own ability to be mindful as their therapist and to be fully present in the here and now. I can (and do) try to cultivate my abilities at being an effective therapist, but at the end of the day I am a human being and inevitably fail sometimes to be fully present to my clients. Luckily my clients themselves bring so much of interest to the relationship that this frequently has the power to arrest my attention and bring me back entirely to the here and now. Through their use of arts media in particular, there is the opportunity for endless unexpected events—all of which have the ability to keep me fully present to the wondrous process of the work.

The Therapist's worldview

We have considered some of the essential qualities an effective therapist should possess (or aspire to possess) in order to fully support their clients and enable the therapy to be maximally effective. It is equally necessary to consider how a therapist's training and methodology can be significant to these ends. It is widely accepted in the literature that a therapist's view of many aspects of life—their worldview—is largely influenced by their training. The particular therapist that I am, for example, has been directly informed by my specialised training as both a gestalt and integrative arts psychotherapist.

The importance of the therapist's worldview is strongly endorsed by expressive arts therapists Knill et al., who suggest that every therapist's approach implies, either explicitly or implicitly, "a philosophical framework within which its particular activity can be understood" (Knill, E. Levine, & S. Levine, 2005). This framework may or may not be directly explained to a client but it cannot help but be influential. If I could make explicit my own therapist's worldview, perhaps this would help me understand how I might influence my clients' experiences and, in particular, the context in which they are able to achieve breakthrough moments.

When asked to describe my own particular style of therapy I typically state with confidence that it lies within the existential-humanistic paradigm. But what does this mean? There is a useful description in Dave Hiles' paper "Defining the paradigm of existential-humanistic psychology" (2000). Hiles argues that what sets this paradigm apart from others is the themes it is interested in. These themes, he believes, are informed by the answers a therapist would give to five fundamental questions: What is a human being? What is the nature of a subjective, lived experience? What is our potential? How can we best promote growth and change? And what are we a part of? Hiles reminds us that each of these questions reflect a phenomenological theme.

Phenomenology is central to my approach as a gestalt and integrative arts psychotherapist (and also as a heuristic researcher). This philosophical method originated with Edmund Husserl in the early years of the twentieth century and was an attempt to describe conscious experience purely as it appears to the subject who experiences it. A phenomenological approach to therapy places emphasis on a client's own perception and understanding of their life situation, rather than a therapist's analyses and interpretations.

As a therapist I am interested in my client's subjective, firsthand, uniquely personal experience rather than in any conscious interpretation. For example, my client Ben embodied the images of the orangutans with his own meaning. Whatever I might have believed this image symbolised for him was not relevant. I used Ben's own report of his phenomenological, subjective experience to make my interventions. I mirrored back to him his own term of feeling clingy by saying that the orangutan baby looked like it was "clinging" to his mother. I then asked him about his relationship with his own mother when he was young. Ben was able to arrive at a breakthrough moment when he himself put together these different elements of his life story for the first time and saw that they were connected. The only thing that mattered was the significance he gave to the image, not any interpretation of my own.

The humanistic-existential paradigm is the bedrock of my theoretical and practical approach as a therapist and it inevitably influences the context within which my clients' breakthrough moments arise. In this sense, it is an approach that forms the background to most of the ideas in this book. The humanistic approach places critical emphasis on the potential of human beings and their ability to utilise their own resources to develop and change. It was my firm belief, for example, when Susan first came to see me that she possessed the resources within her to improve her life experience. This is a key difference between the humanistic paradigm and other approaches. Although Susan was a successful professional, she showed me that she felt more like separate, fragmented *Susans* than a single integrated person when she tipped the basket of stones on the floor. Her unstated goal for her therapy was to feel more like an integrated whole person or "one Susan". I strongly believed she contained the potential to grow and change, particularly with respect to her experience of feeling like separate selves. And I believed this despite the fact that some of her selves were not available to either of us consciously. I also believed that revisiting difficult events in her past, such as her mother's death, could help her begin to rediscover and comprehend the less successfully integrated aspects of herself. These beliefs were implicitly present within the therapy room at all times (and on occasion were also explicitly stated).

The way that each client subjectively experiences their life is of paramount importance to me as both a gestalt and integrative arts psychotherapist. Fritz Perls suggests that the gestalt therapist should observe and describe present behaviour and attempt to bracket off their own assumptions about the client's way of being. In this sense the therapist's role is to encourage in each client increased awareness of themselves.

The Researcher's worldview

We have seen how much a therapist's worldview influences what they bring to the therapeutic relationship. And we have seen how much this worldview is informed by the therapist's personal values and their specific training. A word or two should also be said about the worldview of the researcher.

When I first began researching this book it was necessary to select a methodological approach that would be in line with my therapist's worldview. The heuristic method is perfectly suited to this end. It allowed me to emphasise the phenomenological, subjective experiences of my clients and also include my own phenomenological experience as their therapist. It is not possible to be an objective observer of clients' breakthrough moments. As a therapist I am an integral and inseparable part of the context that brings these moments into being. The heuristic approach allows me to accommodate this fact because it is autobiographical. Despite this fact, however, virtually every question that matters to the heuristic researcher involves a matter of social, even universal, significance. In the next chapter, I will consider what contributions the clients themselves make to the triangular relationship (of client–art–therapist).

CHAPTER SEVEN

The role of the client

Gillian's story

The first thing that struck me about my client Gillian was her hair. It virtually covered her face. It was as though she was trying to hide behind a wavy black curtain. This made it difficult to see her eyes, and the resulting lack of eye contact made it difficult to engage with her directly. Gillian was in her early twenties but appeared much younger. When we spoke about her life—her family, boyfriend, and housemates—she remained flat and disinterested. I almost felt like I was intruding on her and this didn't seem to fit with the fact that she had referred herself to therapy. In our initial assessment session she told me that her parents and boyfriend didn't know she'd come to see me.

An image popped into my head as I tried to navigate Gillian's lack of enthusiasm. I felt as though I held a fishing rod with bait and was trying to entice her to come up to the surface of a lake. This mental image reminded me that I needed to stop "fishing" for answers. Instead we sat in silence for a fairly long time. Eventually I asked her if she could tell me why she had come for therapy. Suddenly her demeanour changed and she seemed to come alive.

Meeting my gaze for the first time she said, "I want things to be different". I immediately warmed to this determined, open desire she had expressed. But what did this young woman want to change? Was it her life circumstances? Her feelings and beliefs? And were these realistic changes or did she in fact wish to be someone else entirely? In a short space of time Gillian had shown me that she felt the need to stay hidden and as a mindful therapist I had to respect that need. She had been hard to reach until the moment when she spoke about her desire to change. As soon as she made this statement she became available and we connected. We had a shared goal that we would work tirelessly to address: Gillian's desire for things to be different.

* * *

In this chapter I will focus on the client's contribution to the triangular relationship (of client–image–therapist) and consider how clients themselves influence opportunities to experience breakthrough moments and achieve change.

Why can't I change?

Much like therapists, clients bring an almost infinite variety of traits and characteristics to the therapy room. They might vary in age, gender, intelligence, sense of humour, ways of relating, energy levels, and creativity. They may also differ in terms of how the past has affected them, how they perceive the meaningfulness of their lives, and whether they have positive or depressive tendencies. In short, clients are individuals and each client's therapy is unique.

Therapy is, more than anything else, a relationship such that a client and therapist's contributions combine to form an alchemical mix deeply significant to the success of the work. This makes it difficult to speak in isolation about qualities a client brings to the therapy. But one thing that virtually all clients have in common is that they choose to attend therapy because they desire some aspect (or aspects) of their lives to be different. They long to learn more about themselves or a particular life circumstance and in the process change, develop, and grow.

The changes that can be achieved by a client vary in magnitude, rate, and consistency. They might be intense or subtle; they can be temporary, lasting, planned, or serendipitous. They can spiral into constructive actions or indeed lead to a downward spiral (Kottler,

2014). In short, when we therapists (and others attempting to quantify client progress) refer to client change we are signifying a vast range of differences in a client. And we must acknowledge that sometimes we won't be able to detect these differences, let alone be able to articulate or measure them (particularly when they are not discernible in behavioural terms).

"I just want things to change" is a frequent opening plea from my clients when they first arrive for therapy. It is often accompanied by, "whatever I do I seem to end up back in the same place". All too often clients seem to know exactly what they want to change but nonetheless get caught in not changing. The change they desire might be in one main area of their inner or outer lives (involving emotions or life circumstances) or it may involve many aspects simultaneously. Gillian, for example, wanted to stop feeling permanently anxious; Ben wanted to change his clinginess in relationships; Amy wanted to understand why she would suddenly be overwhelmed by fear (despite being a highly successful professional); Susan wanted to gain an overall sense of being one Susan and not multiple, fragmented Susans.

The changes clients seek for themselves might be vague or unclear. Indeed, one of the primary tasks of therapy is to help a client ascertain precisely what they would like to change about their lives. But what is change? And how does it happen for a client? Jeffrey Kottler suggests that even after centuries of systematic study, "we still don't really know what's going on" in human change processes (Kottler, 2014). The myriad phenomena that constitute change are just too complex and multilayered to present any clear definition or single set of variables. Change occurs for all kinds of reasons, depending on the individual and their context, issues, problems, and desired goals. These variables are "woven into the threads of each story of change" (ibid.).

A conflicting pull

Michael Mahoney reminds us that we are all seeking (and achieving) some form of change at every moment of our lives. We are shifting and adjusting to the ever-changing demands of each "micro moment that changes with the flux of our worlds" and making "never ending adjustments to our own adjustments" (Mahoney, 1991). Many of these changes take place at a bodily level and are partially (or totally) outside our awareness.

Even though some change is completely inevitable, other aspects of our lives that we seek to change will nonetheless stubbornly stay the same. In such cases it is almost as though we fiercely defend against having to make the very changes we seek. For example, some clients arrive for therapy desperately wanting to change addictions to eating, spending money, alcohol or drugs, sex or gambling. Sometimes in such cases the best that can be accomplished is for the client to become aware of how they are caught between two conflicting pulls—one towards the addictive activity or substance and one towards the desire to cease the behaviour. The case of my client Caroline provides a good illustration of this conflicting pull.

Caroline's story

Caroline arrived for her first therapy session exhibiting shame, guilt, and desperation. "Please help me," she begged, "I can't stop buying things on TV shopping channels". As her story tumbled out, it transpired that this addictive behaviour had caused all manner of problems, such as getting her into debt and angering her family, and had even contributed to the breakdown of her marriage. Shortly after pouring out her story and shedding plenty of tears, Caroline spied a puppet whose head was poking out of a basket of dolls in the corner of my practice-room. "That's it!" she said, pointing at the spindly skeleton-puppet. "That's what the voice looks like ... the one that tells me to buy things!" (See Figure 7.1).

"Oh, that's it?" I replied casually, my own gaze now fixed on the ghoulish puppet. "And what is its name?"

"Persuasive Pete," she said without hesitation.

"Ah yes," I said. "Persuasive Pete. Would you be able to speak for a moment as if *you* were Persuasive Pete?"

Caroline paused for a second, apparently considering how best to respond to my request, and then suddenly spoke in a voice that could perhaps best be described as a wheedling falsetto:

> *"Go on, Caroline,"*

she said as wheedling Pete:

> *"Buy it! Buy it!!! I'm so fed up with your life*
> *Caroline—you deserve more money than*

you earn. You are worth more. You deserve to have nice
things—why don't you buy something to cheer yourself
up and cheer your kids up? Go on, why not—just do it!"

Caroline told me she found it so hard to resist this persistent voice. And the more difficult her life situation became, the more the voice would urge her to treat herself to just *one more thing.* I asked if she could see any other character (or object) in the room that might help her resist the taunts of Persuasive Pete. Her glance fell on a floppy lion puppet perched on top of a guitar in the corner (see Figure 7.2).

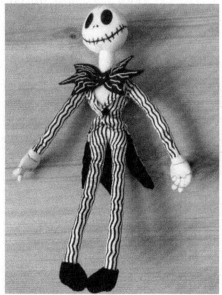 

Figure 7.1 Caroline's skeleton   Figure 7.2 Caroline's lion.

"Him?" she said, although at first her voice did not indicate much hope that he (or anyone) could help her. She told me this lion pup-pet was called "Helpful Henry". She placed her arm inside the pup-pet and found a voice to suit the lion's character. For many weeks of therapy we carried out dialogues between Persuasive Pete and Helpful Henry (with interventions along the way from Caroline and myself). These puppet interactions provided Caroline with a new approach to add to the many previous attempts she had made to curb her shopping addiction. It would be nice to report that this led to the end of her addictive behaviour, but in truth she would get to a point where the habit somewhat improved before she would slide back down again. This went on for many cycles of her therapeutic work.

Caroline was looking for a reasonably straightforward change in her behaviour—she just needed to stop shopping. However, it seems that the impetus for her to stop (as characterised by Helpful Henry) was frequently countered by an often stronger part of her that could not help but continue (characterised by Persuasive Pete). This created a conflicting pull between two opposing forces within her and resulted in a spell of positive action (to rectify her habit) that would then be followed by a downward spiral. This seems to echo Kottler's idea that change will often consist of cycles of constructive action followed by downward slides.

Complexities of change

Whenever we say things like, "I want things to be different," or as my client Sally said, "I just want to be different," we speak as though we are clear on what desirable human change would look (or feel) like. In truth, however, the nature of such change is highly complex. I have created an octagonal diagram that identifies eight key areas of experience a client might expressly desire to change (see Figure 7.3)

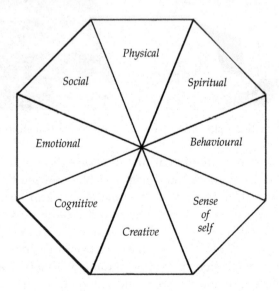

Figure 7.3. Areas of experience that could be changed.

The change that takes place for a client is not always a linear process but can present itself more as part of a dynamical system. This can be illustrated with reference to my client Susan.

Susan's story (continued)

When Susan tipped the basket of stones onto the floor and arrived at her breakthrough moment she seemed to be expressing conscious (and unconscious) feelings of being many Susans. She communicated this in a way that was entirely contained within the metaphor of the stones. This paved the way for most of our future work together.

Over the course of the following year of her therapy, Susan presented many aspects of herself through the use of different arts media. She explored and reframed her thoughts and emotions, discovered and reintegrated lost parts of herself, modified her relationships with people and, most importantly, reconfigured her own view of herself. To put it another way, she strengthened her sense of self.

It seems that Susan had had to deal with the feelings surrounding the traumatic childhood experience of her mother's death on her own. This led her to split herself off from these feelings, which in turn led to a breakdown in the cohesion of her sense of self. In addition to this split (and perhaps because of it) she developed a severe eating disorder as a pathological strategy to attempt to manage her emotions.

Even twenty years after these traumatic events she still felt like many different Susans and had little sense of an overall unity of who she was. Being able to paint, model in clay, act and express herself with puppets all enabled Susan to gain insight into these different parts of herself and the various roles they played. The parts of her that had been denied were given a voice and she was able to express some of the grief, rage and fear she felt over the death of her mother in the safe environment of the therapy room. Later she would explain that although she still had the sense of feeling like a group of Susans she now felt as though the separate parts had been linked (albeit loosely) together. And this may well have given rise to temporary or permanent changes in the neural pathways of her brain (Kottler, 2014).

Later in her therapy Susan increased her ability to trust me even further by drawing a big red pause button to remind herself that she could stop the therapy at any time if it ever felt too overwhelming. This led her to begin to be able to speak about her mother's illness and death for the first time, which brought changes in the way she understood these events. Whenever she felt too much emotion in a session she would press the red button image. Later still she brought her sculpture of Thin Susan to see me and this too brought new aspects of her hidden selves to light. It seems more accurate to view Susan's changes as having taken place as part of a non-linear dynamical system, as with my client Ben.

Ben's story (continued)

Ben's breakthrough moment with the orangutan postcard seemed to deeply affect his emotions and self-awareness. Before leaving the room at the end of our one-off counselling session, he picked out two toy gorillas and placed the infant close to its mother for protection (see Figure 7.4).

Figure 7.4. Ben's gorillas.

It was as if he left the session having indicated (metaphorically) that at least a part of *him* still needed a mother to care about him. Ben appeared to have replaced the orangutan postcard with this new image. Now the baby was not clinging to its mother; now it seemed the mother was standing close by and offering less cloying protection and support.

It would be wrong of course to suggest that Ben was making a declaration of "now I am fine" with this second image. Rather, it was a way for him to symbolise what he *hoped* to feel in the future. There was no inevitability that things would improve, or any guarantee that they would improve in a linear, upward trajectory. But Ben now had an awareness at least of a new way to understand the aspects of himself he wished to change.

It would be unwise and indeed arrogant to assume that the ways in which clients desire to change are always the same. Sidney Bloch reminds us that when a client seeks therapy it is usually because they have some overwhelming need (Bloch, 1982). A client may desire an internal, subjective change, such as Gillian's desire to feel calmer and less anxious. Or the client may wish to make external changes, such as quit a job, assert themselves in a relationship, or break an unhealthy habit. Positive change for a client can involve improvements in reducing suffering and distress, discovering new strategies to cope more effectively with life's demands, identifying psychological blind spots, gaining new awareness and insight, strengthening a sense of self, living more creatively, improving relationships, increasing the ability to regulate overwhelming emotions, reducing self-harming activities, and much more.

There are some particularly illuminating discussions of client change in gestalt theory. One useful idea is that of contact. Through contact (between client and therapist), Erving and Miriam Polster assert, "one does not have to try to change; change simply occurs" (Polster & Polster, 1974). Similarly, Fritz Perls (1973) suggests that "full contact is implicitly incompatible with remaining the same". William J. Coburn (2014) argues that in considering therapeutic action it is important to distinguish between that which a therapist can do with the *intention* of bringing about change and that which the therapist can actually change. The latter, he says, critically includes the management of unconscious and conscious material.

Kottler reminds us that the most impactful thing that can bring about client change is often not something the therapist has said or done but rather, "a cascade of events that occurred indirectly or tangentially from that experience" (Kottler, 2014).

I won't change

Coburn reminds us that sometimes a client seems unable to change. He says that however painful a client's emotional themes might be, if they were suddenly stripped of these, he or she may be plunged into an unmanageable abyss or "structureless chaos" (Stolorow, Attwood, & Orange, 2010, quoted in Coburn, 2014). This can leave the client with no firm ground left on which to stand. Sometimes they may feel it is better to be oriented to the world through repetitive suffering rather than free themselves and risk losing the essential ground on which they have stood. As Erik Erikson has said, for some clients "a negative identity is better than no identity" (Stolorow, 1992). We can be drawn to the familiar even when the familiar is undesirable. This can be exemplified by my client Diane's story.

Diane's story

Diane was clear that she wanted things in her life to change. But every time she started to create the kind of change she yearned for she would relax and begin to feel dissatisfied all over again. This included her desire to earn more money, find a nicer place to live, enter a new relationship, and take on a healthier lifestyle. Within a few months of adopting more satisfying behaviours, she said that "things would start to slip away" from her again. She would end the relationships or they would become less satisfying; she would spend too much money and incur debts again. She would then feel depressed at the new turn of events and start to live in an increasingly unhealthy way.

In our therapy Diane identified a part of herself (perhaps a subpersonality) that she realised would sabotage any new-found successes. She chose a plastic figure with massive hands to represent this internal saboteur and placed it in the sand tray. She then added a doll to represent herself and placed one of the saboteur's large hands tightly around her hair (see Figure 7.5). Diane said it was as if this saboteur-personality grabbed hold of her each time (with its giant hands) and reversed any aspect of her life she was finally managing to turn around.

Figure 7.5. Diane's saboteur.

This image helped her to recognise the repeating pattern. Having gained the new awareness, we were hopeful she would find a way to elicit permanent change without always reverting back to how things were before. After six months of therapy with me she moved away from the area. Sadly, when she last contacted me she still seemed caught in the grip of the same pattern.

Art and change

We have looked at some of the aspects a client might wish to change about themselves and some of the attributes that may assist them in making those changes. But given the uniquely triangular nature of the arts-based therapeutic relationship (client–art–therapist), it is necessary also to consider how a client relates to the use of the arts.

Some clients are immediately able to embrace working with arts media in the therapy room whilst others feel lost and intimidated. Some clients, with little support or preparation, are able to imbue the images they create with rich metaphor and meaning, whilst others just stare at them blankly. For the clients who *are* able to embrace this way of working, the arts media frequently become the most important aspect of their therapeutic work. They will regularly be surprised by the power of their own images to reveal something they did not know they knew. The clients' stories presented in this book provide many such examples.

But what of the clients who find working with the arts more difficult? These might be reluctant clients in general or clients who are particularly overawed by the idea of using art materials. Some clients would simply rather talk and not use the arts. Others (especially children) would rather use art than talk. However, even the clients who are the most reluctant to work with art materials are often intrigued by the presence of them in the practice-room. This means that with a little bit of encouragement from me they will tentatively begin to use them. It might be something simple to begin with, like choosing a postcard to encapsulate a feeling or dilemma (as with Ben), or using a sand tray to show me their predicament.

Sometimes a client will talk about the objects they have chosen (or images they have created) and stay firmly with a literal understanding of what they signify. At some point during the course of their therapy, however, even these clients will usually be surprised by a breakthrough moment in which some new and previously unmade connection is revealed. Their therapy will often be irrevocably changed from this point onwards, which is what happened to my client Dave.

Dave's story

Dave was an eighteen year old who was plagued by indecision. He found it almost impossible to decide what he wanted to do when he left school, where he wanted to live, whether he wanted to stay with his current girlfriend; in fact, what he wanted to do about *anything*. He was in the fortunate position of having doting parents who provided for him financially and supported him in whatever decisions he made. But he was unable to make any decisions.

When we began to work together, Dave's indecision transferred itself to his use of the art materials. He could never decide which objects to choose and became immobilised in the therapy room, much like he felt immobilised in his life. I rolled out a long piece of paper across the length of the practice-room floor and told him it was to represent his future stretching out before him. I then asked him to choose any three items he felt symbolised the things that might arise in his future and to place them somewhere along the trail. I told him not to worry if he did not yet know what these items represented.

After much encouragement (and many suggestions) from me, he eventually chose a rubber snake, a plastic scorpion and a large piece of rope and placed these onto the paper. I wondered if he might be able to respond better to his chosen objects if they took on different "personalities", so I began to speak as if I were each of the objects in turn.

"I am a snake," I said first. "I am curled up here in Dave's future."
Silence.

"I am a scorpion," I said next, "and I am sitting here ready to sting anyone who comes along!"
Still silence.

At this point Dave was gazing deeply at the objects that lined his pathway to the future. The atmosphere in the room had changed and I suspected he had entered some trance-like form of altered consciousness.

Finally I began to say, "I am a rope and I ..."

But before I could finish my sentence, Dave became deathly pale. With his attention fixed on the rope (as if it truly had just been addressing him), he said:

> *"You just want to get round my neck and squeeze all*
> *the life out of me until I'm dead!"*

This was shocking and so unlike anything he'd said so far that I'm not sure which of us was the more surprised. Recovering myself quickly I asked him:

"Why do you want to strangle Dave?".

Dave, who by now seemed to be deeply immersed in speaking as though the rope itself was speaking, replied immediately,

> *"Because whatever Dave decides to do, I am lying in*
> *wait to trip him up and spoil things".*

This was new.

No wonder he couldn't make decisions about his future if he was beset by such fears. Following Dave's breakthrough moment we had a new handle on the reasons for his indecision and we could finally begin to untangle them. We had much work to do, but in time Dave was able to obtain a deeper understanding of the different parts of him that prevented him from making decisions.

Clients arrive at my practice with differing levels of confidence in their ability to use arts materials, but they tend to grow more comfortable with them throughout the course of their therapy. Dave's original inability to embrace the use of arts materials changed in a breakthrough moment. Following this pivotal moment—and despite his own reservations—Dave was able to embrace the arts in future sessions and this helped him to mobilise his life and thus achieve change.

* * *

In this chapter I have looked at some of the many different ways a client can contribute to the therapeutic relationship. I have argued that a client's desire for change is one of the most critical things they can bring to the therapy and that their increasing preparedness to use arts media will often directly influence their ability to achieve breakthrough moments and change. In the next chapter I will focus on the role played by the arts themselves in this triangular relationship (of client–art–therapist).

CHAPTER EIGHT

Art-images and the art-experience

Barbara's story

Barbara was trapped in a controlling relationship. She had become completely obsessed with a song she had heard playing on the radio. She bought the song on CD and told me that she kept playing it on repeat. I suggested she bring this CD and a copy of the song's lyrics to our next session. We sat together and listened through the song twice, each of us following a copy of the words as Barbara entered what appeared to be a trance-like state.

The lyrics were about a person feeling caught in the web of an addictive love triangle. As we listened I felt unaccountably sick. There was no connection to the song from my own life that could account for this sudden onset of nausea. I imagined it had to have something to do with Barbara's own feelings and her obsession with the song. At the end of our second listen, and while she was still in her trance-like state, I invited Barbara to select or draw an image of what she was feeling and to do this without thinking about it too much. My desire was for her to act without breaking the spell that seemed to have woven itself around her and also to give myself some time to recover from feeling nauseous.

Without appearing to awaken from her trance, Barbara first selected a picture of the earth (from a pile of images in my practice-room) and then placed a huge plastic spider on top of it. Next she selected a small plastic fly, almost too small to be detected, and carefully placed this at the very edge of the earth (see Figure 8.1).

I invited Barbara to pretend that *she* was this spider and to describe what was happening in her web. She was comfortable and familiar enough with this way of working to accept the invitation readily. Still seemingly in a trance she said,

> *"I have made this web and that little fly over there is going to get tangled up in it! And my web stretches over the whole world, so she will never be able to get away, wherever she goes to try and escape!"*

Figure 8.1. Barbara's spider on earth.

The sudden rush of new emotion and insight that arose for Barbara as she spoke these words had all the hallmarks of a breakthrough moment. A stunned silence followed that felt deeply significant for us both.

At some level it seems Barbara had a clear perception of the fact she was in a relationship with a man who was intent on ensnaring her. And yet she expressed no desire at this point to disentangle herself. Following her statement that the "spider" was never going to let her go, I started to make sense of the sick feeling that had come over me. I sincerely hoped that whatever came next in her therapy would help Barbara extract herself from what was clearly a destructive relationship.

When eventually she did appear to come out of her trance, we discussed what had happened and how she was feeling. Barbara told me she had been identifying herself with the fly and that by speaking as the spider and referring to the web (the relationship she was caught up in) she had experienced the song from a new perspective. What had previously seemed to be a song about a love triangle between her, her boyfriend and another woman, she now recognised as being a song about the triangle between her, her boyfriend, and his web of control. She said it made her feel sick that she had got so caught up with this man, which in turn made further sense of my own sick feelings.

* * *

It took many sessions to disentangle Barbara from her spider's web, but by working therapeutically with the metaphor she created in this session, she began to understand what her destructive relationship was doing to her. In future sessions she often referred to what *the spider* had said, which seemed to further demonstrate the importance it held for her. But how was this dramatic shift able to occur for Barbara, seemingly just from the act of listening to a song, creating a spider image, and speaking as the spider? What was it about these arts-based activities that enabled my client to arrive at a powerful new realisation—one that had previously eluded her? In this chapter, I will focus on what happens to the therapeutic relationship when arts media are introduced and consider some of the many ways they can help lead a client to breakthrough moments and change.

Part I: the art-experience

Gestalt and integrative arts psychotherapists each use various techniques to enable clients to gain a deeper experience within their therapy. A client will often experience this during (or following) an act of creation (or enactment), because it seems to enable them to move from left-brain explaining into more right-brain experiencing (that is often trance-like) and provides them with a different type of insight. It is also frequently accompanied by a heightened charge in the therapy room. This charge may occur while the client is making the art-image or just afterwards—when they experience the often startling work they have created. As we have seen, this can frequently bring about a breakthrough moment. But what can be said about the nature of the heightened charge that occurs at these times? And what might a client actually be experiencing when their experience is tied to an art-image?

A heightened charge

It is never quite possible to know how a client is experiencing something in the therapy room. One of the few theorists who have speculated about the nature of client experience is Daniel Stern. Was there a moment prior to Barbara's breakthrough moment that could be understood as a Sternian Now Moment? Barbara was involved in an extended period of heightened charge while she was in her trance-like state. And this continued for most of her session (while she was listening to the song, creating the image, and speaking as the spider). This certainly had many of the qualities of a Sternian Now Moment in that it was full of potential and dramatic resonance, but it extended to almost fifteen minutes—far longer than the ten seconds Stern dictates as the maximum length for a now moment.

It seems Barbara was having some sort of extended art-experience. It was not a single instance of heightened charge. Perhaps the moment immediately prior to her breakthrough moment could be described as a Sternian Now Moment, but the fifteen-minute period that came before this could not sensibly be considered one. Barbara's state of altered consciousness extended far beyond a single now moment—as did Amy's when she created her model house and Ali's when she created a safe place for Eating Disorder Ali. In each of these cases an extended period of time had acted as a precipitator for the clients' breakthrough moments—more like a series of Sternian Now Moments woven together (not that Stern allows for such a thing). It seemed that Stern's model could not sufficiently accommodate these instances of a client's extended *experiencing* and I needed to search elsewhere in the literature.

I looked to other theoretical models to see if any of these could satisfactorily describe Barbara's extended period of heightened experience involving her use of the arts. The experiential part of her session involved direct contact with the spider image. It also involved unconscious aspects of her awareness. A client's relationship with the image they have created (or chosen) seems, in part at least, to involve deeply unconscious processes. I wondered if depth psychology could provide an explanation for these periods of heightened charge, seeing as it is an approach that specifically explores the relationship between the conscious and the unconscious. Could depth psychology explain Barbara's trance-like state while she listened to the song, created her image, and spoke as the spider? All of these actions had seemingly enabled her to bring unconscious aspects into consciousness.

Depth psychology is a field of theories and therapies concerned with exploring the hidden or deeper parts of human experience. It involves deep inquiry into the symbolic meaning of images that might influence a client, whether they are aware of them or not (Ellenberger, 1970). Barbara certainly seemed to be involved in deep inquiry into the symbolic meaning of her spider image (ibid.), so this seemed like a promising lead. According to Carl Jung, depth psychology seeks to take notice of that which is "silenced, marginalised or hidden at the edges of what we believe to be normal in our culture and our world" (ibid.). It generates further questions rather than settling on fixed answers. The best art, of course, does this too. Art in general is a profound vessel for marginalised or unspoken truths, because it is a language with few universally agreed norms. It seems clear that this is at least one of the reasons it can enable a client to discover new and multiple symbolic meanings within an art-image.

Throughout the fifteen minutes of her extended period of deep experiencing, Barbara appeared to be using her imagination. I looked to Jung's method of the active imagination to see if this could explain what might have been going on for her during this time. Active imagination is a technique Carl Jung developed to help uncover the hidden meanings of his own dreams and fantasy images (Jung, 1997). The technique can be carried out in a number of ways, which include painting, dance, music, automatic writing, visualisation, and play. The ultimate aim is to bring aspects of the unconscious into consciousness for a participant and Jung believed that active imagination provides a bridge between these two domains. The key to the technique is to exert as little influence as possible on the mental images (provided from a dream or imagined scene) as they unfold (ibid.). Jung believed this process would involve not only the individual's personal unconscious but also the "collective unconscious"—including shared myths and archetypes (Jung, 1948).

There are similarities between Jung's technique of active imagination and the way I had worked with Barbara. But active imagination is a *technique*—a way of working with the self or with clients. I had not wittingly used this technique and it could not therefore fully be applied to an understanding of Barbara's experience.

The "as if" falls away

Perhaps a theory from the arts therapies could help me under-stand more about Barbara's experience of heightened charge. Cathy Malchiodi speaks of therapeutic work as being deepened by the use of arts approaches. She says working with the arts often includes a cathartic element and can be transformative because it taps the senses as "source[s] of stories and memories" (Malchiodi, 2005). This is a lovely way of describing *how* the experience of therapy can be deepened by the image, but it does not account for what the experience *feels* like for a client at such times.

Looking elsewhere, Tian Dayton suggests that when a client takes part in a psychodrama (or enactment) based on a past traumatic event they may enter a psychodramatic trance somewhat akin to a dream-like state. In such cases, she says, the "as if" seems to fall away, leaving both client and therapist in a new and unfamiliar landscape. This cer-tainly appeared to fit with Barbara's experience: the "as if" certainly appeared to have fallen away for a short while when Barbara spoke as the spider in her trance-like state. And it was from this altered state of consciousness that she spoke about her relationship (the web) from the new vantage point.

Dayton's suggestion that a client can experience altered states of con-sciousness in a session certainly fits with what appeared to happen to Barbara. It is also helpful in showing how the use of dramatisation by a client can be beneficial in accessing past memories of their trauma. Dayton suggests that when we experience a traumatic event we have a tendency to freeze and our brains do not function normally. We are not fully able to process the experience and are thus not able to fully integrate it. This means that when the memory is triggered at a later point, a fully integrated memory is not available and what comes back is the unresolved state of frozen fragments of the event (Dayton, 1994). This was a fascinating way to think of Barbara's period of extended deep experiencing—memories of how controlling and hurtful her boyfriend had been towards her over many years seemed to have been frozen, and she was just beginning to become aware of the fact that he had been controlling her. These memories were slowly being pieced together like a jigsaw so she could begin to see the full picture of his web of control over her.

The enactment or dramatisation of an issue can often enable a client to re-access the original event in a powerful way (always assuming the therapist takes great care to prevent any possibility of the client being re-traumatised). I have undertaken some psychodrama training in my career and experienced firsthand the power of this approach. It provides participants with a powerful opportunity to deepen their therapeutic work because of its full engagement of body, memory, and experience. Barbara's session had a quality not dissimilar to my experiences in these psychodrama workshops. And in this sense it seemed like the most promising avenue so far—it was at least phenomenological (the client's actual *experience* was involved in the description). But although Barbara's enactment had some similar features to a psychodrama, it was *not* a psychodrama. So this aspect of Dayton's model could not be said to literally apply.

Barbara's trance-like state extended across several of her actions, including creating the spider image and listening intently to the song. Dayton's model could perhaps account for when she spoke as the spider but it is not able to explain why she felt mesmerised during these other non-drama based creative activities. I was looking for an explanation that would allow for all the diverse aspects of Barbara's deep experiencing with the arts.

Extended deep experiencing

I wondered if the world of experiential psychotherapy could offer any explanation for the extended period of Barbara's heightened, emotionally charged experience while she engaged with different aspects of the arts. Experiential psychotherapies believe that *experiencing* is the basis for a client's change rather than other more commonly identified mechanisms of change—such as the bond with the therapist or the therapist's particular interventions (Mahrer, 1986). My own way of working with clients could be described amongst other things as being an experiential approach (as both a gestalt and integrative arts therapist).

Alvin Mahrer suggests that therapeutic experiencing "provides the key to [the] process of change in therapy" (Mahrer, 1986). Therapeutic experiencing can make an event visited during the therapy session appear so real that the therapist and client feel as though they are actually existing in that situation in the present. He says it can feel like "being in a dream or a hypnotic state". It provides the client with an experience that is "alive and vivid" and thus creates an opportunity for the expression of profound emotion. This seemed a fitting way to describe Barbara's experience. She became very emotional whist in her state of altered consciousness. But it would be wrong to say that she was back in the situation with her controlling boyfriend, because the situation she appeared to be immersed in (at least to begin with) was her sand tray image of the spider and fly. Could it be that using arts media in the therapeutic relationship somehow enabled her to vividly exist in the present of her own metaphor?

Mahrer's term "therapeutic experiencing" refers to his own single method of experiential psychotherapy with expressly directed steps for the therapist to follow (Mahrer, 1986). One of these steps is described as the client "entering into an experiential state". For my own purposes (although there were some clear resemblances) I was not going to be able to adopt Mahrer's terminology. Therapeutic experiencing described Mahrer's own particular method and I was not following its directed steps. It was becoming clear that I needed to create my own term.

I decided to describe this aspect of my clients' work as extended deep experiencing. I felt this term was ideal for a number of reasons. First, it captured the phenomenological quality of the experience for Barbara when she was creating and interacting with all different aspects of the arts media. Second, it allowed me to denote that her mesmeric state had extended over a long period of time. And third, it allowed me to incorporate two phrases I had found most helpful in my research—"entering into an experiential state" and "*deeper* in-session experience". In addition to all this, it was a term that implied the deepening of the work and thus also made reference to depth psychology.

Now I had a specific term to describe the extended, deep, mesmeric states that my clients would often enter into when working with arts media. And I could state with confidence that extended deep experiencing was one of the crucial ways in which arts-based therapy can support clients to arrive at a breakthrough moment.

Part II: the art-image

We have seen that a client's extended deep experiencing with an image has the ability to increase the chances of achieving a breakthrough moment. But what is it about the use of arts media that so frequently supports the deepening of a client's experience? In this section I will consider the role played by the art-image itself. It is important to remind readers that although I am using the term art-image, I am also including clients' creations with sand trays, music, drawing, painting, re-enactments, ritual, clay modelling, puppetry, and more. Indeed, a client may move between these various arts media within the one session (as was the case with Barbara).

How does an image deepen the therapeutic work, precipitate break-through moments, and bring about change for a client? In an attempt to answer this question, I looked to Joy Schaverien's work. I had found Schaverien's writing on arts therapies insightful in the past—in par-ticular, the distinction she draws between two different types of aes-thetic effect: the diagrammatic image and the embodied image. The diagrammatic image is equivalent to a map or diagram, usually accom-panied by a spoken description from the client. Therapy involving the diagrammatic image is similar to that of psychodynamic talking therapy, but the image is used as a sort of diagram. I was looking to explain ways that therapeutic work can be deepened, so this was not a category I found particularly helpful to my quest. Schaverien's concept of the embodied image, however, seemed much more relevant for my purposes.

The embodied image "conveys a feeling state for which no other mode of expression can be substituted" (Schaverien, 1999). It is as if the client imbues the image with a "magical investment"—one that can contain unconscious and unwanted feelings (ibid.). In this way, she says, the image itself has powerful potential to bring about change. This seemed highly relevant for my research.

One morning a new client arrived to see me whose work seemed to provide a wonderful illustration of Schaverien's concept of the embodied image.

Sarah's story

Sarah was an attractive research assistant in her mid twenties. When she presented for therapy she was dressed in a smart, careful way and spoke in a rather unexpressive voice—as though she were tightly holding in her emotions (in case something spilled out that she didn't wish to acknowledge). She had been telling me for several weeks how wonderful her father was and how he had loved and protected her throughout her childhood. But something about her demeanour led me to suspect there was more to this relationship than she was letting on. I discussed the suspicion later with my supervisor when I said something like, "I can't help wondering if this is only *part* of Sarah's story … No doubt she will show or tell me when the time is right".

A few weeks later, Sarah was busy painting some stones. On one of these she painted a face that loosely followed the contours and cracks of the stone (see Figure 8.2). This was in direct contrast to other art-images she had produced to date—all of which had been very neat and aesthetically pleasing. There was something more organic and instinctive about the way she created this piece.

Figure 8.2. Sarah's stone face.

Sarah was quiet as she worked. When she had finished, she pushed the stone away with a look of surprise that suddenly turned to dismay. The silence between us seemed to grow heavy with the anticipation of something ... I waited. Slowly, for the first time in her therapy, she began to quietly sob. After a long time she whispered in a voice noticeably younger than her usual voice, "That reminds me of my Daddy—he wasn't always kind to me. Sometimes he got very mean and I became frightened".

I was taken by surprise at the sudden arrival of these feelings. The emotion had come first, before her admission (to me and herself) that her father had this other side to his character. The room felt charged with emotion and it was clearly a breakthrough moment for Sarah. I was in awe that this stone face had somehow enabled Sarah to finally be able to tell me about her father. It was as if events and feelings she had not been able to reveal (even to herself) had been lying dormant within the stone. Making the image had somehow embodied her unwanted and unprocessed feelings about her father, and when Sarah saw them given form in this way she was able to viscerally recognise a truth she had previously denied.

* * *

Schaverien suggests that when an image is "embodied" in this way, a client's feelings arise in relation to the image itself and that "change is possible" (Schaverien, 1999). It seems the image can embody unconscious forces for a client and in this sense become a talisman, or lucky mascot for change—although it can equally become a "scapegoat" or vessel to hold and evacuate unwanted feelings (ibid.). Sarah's painted stone face seemed to embody her unspoken and unexpressed feelings about her father and yet she had created it by following marks that were randomly embedded in the stone. The grotesque, contorted face that appeared was an inadvertent simulacrum. This seemed to embody her feelings and provide a "scapegoat" for what she could not allow herself to acknowledge. Up until this point she had only said that her father had been kind and supportive of her. Sarah's stone face confronted her with a reminder of her father's angry face when it became contorted, and her memories and feelings were triggered accordingly.

The reader may recall that my client Ben was also mesmerised by his chosen image of the two orangutans. I made a comment to him about the infant ape appearing "clingy" and this allowed him to make a connection with his own situation when he was a child. From here he was able to reconfigure his experience. Once again, it would seem as if the image had somehow embodied the client's dilemma and presented it back in a way that could be perceived more directly.

The idea of the embodied image is a useful way to explain how an art-image is able to deepen a client's therapy work. It is frequently this embodiment of meaning that appears to support the client in reaching a breakthrough moment. The embodied image holds the client's unwanted and often unrecognised unspoken feelings and presents them back so that they can be seen—sometimes for the first time and this can provide the tipping point for powerful breakthroughs.

The image as catalyst

Tessa Dalley et al. (1993) argue that the centrality of an image and its ability to communicate visually provides a "powerful catalyst for change" in the therapeutic process. In science, a catalyst is defined as a substance that increases the rate of chemical reaction whilst remaining unchanged itself. It can be useful to think of the image in a similar way—as a catalyst that can trigger client change whilst it remains unchanged itself. For example, an image might trigger a client to express, explore or reveal something not previously realised, or symbolise something from their unconscious. This idea of the image as catalyst certainly fits with my clients' experiences. But it sometimes happens too that an image keeps recurring in a client's therapy *without* becoming a catalyst for change, or at least not until much later—as in Martin's case and his pictures of claws. It struck me that an additional term was thus needed to account for those instances when an image holds the potential for *future* change. I chose to call them latent catalysts.

The way that images work as catalysts and latent catalysts provides us with another reason as to why arts-based therapies increase the opportunity for client breakthrough moments—namely, because there are *two* potential catalysts at play in the triangular relationship (of client–art–therapist): the arts media *and* the therapeutic relationship, both potentially providing their own catalyst for healing to occur.

Stephen's story

The story of my client Stephen provides a clear example of the image as latent catalyst. Similar to Martin with his endless images of inexplicable claws, Stephen too had an obsession in his artwork. Using black charcoal over several sessions, he sketched a series of images of birds and bird parts emerging from the clouds. These sketches were multi-dimensional and seemed to contain all sorts of literal and hidden messages we could not at first fully understand (see Figure 8.3). For a long time in Stephen's therapy it felt as if the embodied meaning held within these images would provide us with the key to Stephen's secret (or hidden) story if we could only uncover it.

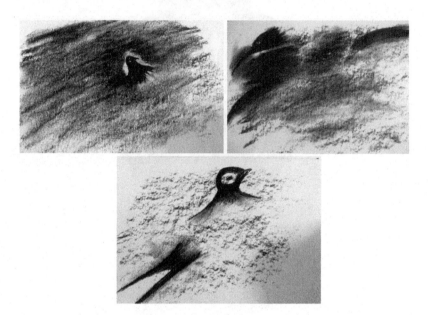

Figure 8.3. Stephen's birds.

Stephen told me he was not aware what his images were about—only that he felt compelled to create them. And that in the act of creating them it was almost as if he were attempting to hunt down their meaning and crack the code hidden within. After several weeks of producing these illustrations, Stephen found a postcard at a market that finally seemed to unlock the meaning embodied in his bird drawings. The postcard depicted a man with a rook's head (see Figure 8.4).

Stephen brought the rook-man postcard to his next therapy session and we explored its significance for him. Some aspect of our discussion allowed him to make a new realisation. In a powerful moment he told me that he suddenly saw what these birds meant. They were

Figure 8.4. Stephen's rook-man.

inextricably linked to something that had happened to him in his child-hood. When Stephen was a little boy he would regularly have to watch on, horrified and helpless, as his father took drugs and fell into an intoxicated stupor. At such times, Stephen now understood it was as if his father morphed from a loved and trusted man into a wild bird that flayed and flew around blindly. He realised that the bird images were a metaphor for this shocking transformation that used to take place in his father.

To make matters worse, no one in Stephen's family had ever spoken about his father's addictive behaviour and the young Stephen had thus imagined he was the only one who saw it; that he or his father must somehow be insane. At some point earlier in his life he had embedded the story of what happened with his father into images of birds. His own sketches of birds and bird parts emerging from the clouds seemed to mirror (or illustrate) the slow unfolding of his unconscious need to re-address this trauma. Discovering the postcard of the rook-man was a catalyst for his conscious awareness of something that had been relegated to the depths of his unconscious. Our further work together revealed another layer of metaphor embedded within Stephen's image. When trapped at home with his drug-addled father, Stephen had felt his heart thumping in his chest: "It was as if a bird were imprisoned in my ribcage, flapping around, unable to escape".

Stephen was finally able to uncover his "story that should never be told" of the father who would transform into a terrifying bird every night (after taking drugs) and awake as his dad once more the next morning. His untellable story was embedded within his sketches—like a code or riddle set up by his unconscious for his conscious to crack.

Illuminating the transference

Donald Winnicott has argued that in regular dyadic therapy (i.e., client–therapist), a therapist can "hold" their client's difficult feelings and feed them back in small and manageable chunks so that the client can process them (Winnicott, 2013). In triadic therapy (client–art–therapist), Schaverien speaks of the image as "holding" unconscious unwanted feelings in a similar way.

During the course of my research, I found some equally resonant suggestions of ways that an art-image "holds" feelings for a client:

- By acting as a vessel in which transformation can take place (Schaverien, 1999).
- By containing: ambivalence and conflict (Case & Dalley, 1992), pre-verbal or non-verbal feelings (Malchiodi, 2005), conscious or unconscious feelings too difficult to speak about (Schaverien, 1999) or "unspeakable" anxieties (of total isolation and falling forever) (Winnicott, 1965).

- By giving form, expression and "a voice" to existential fears (Sunderland, 2000).
- By revealing something that was not previously known to the client or therapist (Case & Dalley, 1992).
- By providing a bridge between the client's inner and outer world (Case & Dalley, 1992).

Schaverien, Waller and others have argued that the art-image can "hold" a client's projections and that these may include positive and/or negative transference of feelings towards their therapist (Waller, 2000). Images frequently "illuminate the transference"—that is, they reveal a client's feelings towards the therapist and the work in overt and covert ways (Schaverien, 1999). This can be illuminating for subsequent therapy sessions and can bring deeper feelings to the surface that may have been hidden. My client Brenda's art-image provides an example of this idea of illuminating the transference.

Brenda's story

Brenda, my nine-year-old client, was making a sand tray in her session one day that depicted a war going on between two sides of her family. She placed the lone figure of a Dalmatian amongst a series of more macabre-looking plastic toys (including a gun) (see Figure 8.5). Feeling

Figure 8.5. Brenda's family at war.

for my client (and for the poor puppy surrounded by these grotesque objects/creatures), I invited Brenda to add one more character to the sand tray who might help her in this situation. She chose a superhero figurine, which she placed beside the lone Dalmatian to protect him. She told me that this superheroine represented me.

Here Brenda was using her art-image to demonstrate positive transference towards me, her therapist. I was struck nonetheless by the fact that the gun was pointing *directly* at the character who represented me. I found myself wondering whether a negative transference might emerge. And this was indeed the case a few weeks later when Brenda lined up a row of figures and said they were "guarding her" against me (see Figure 8.6). She said they would turn me to stone if I "came any closer". In this sense, the art objects starkly held both negative and positive transference for Brenda. The way that other clients' images symbolise their transference is usually more subtle than this.

Figure 8.6. Brenda's protectors.

Rehearsal of the possible

The image has a powerful ability to provide a client with a vision of their desired outcome. During my integrative arts training this was known as a "rehearsal of the possible" (Sunderland, 2000). The use of arts media enables a client to rehearse new ways of experiencing a situation (such as a relationship) by creating images that can then lead them towards the outcomes they desire.

Working with images can help a client focus on their goals for the therapeutic work. The images made in sessions are also extremely helpful for reviewing what has taken place so far. The image is concrete and permanent and can thus act as a physical document of the therapeutic process that cannot be denied, erased, or forgotten. It also offers possibilities for reflection and further understanding in the future (Dalley et al., 1993).

Evoking the transpersonal

Another powerful way that the art-image can support a client involves its evocation of the transpersonal. Schaverien says "we are humbled and elevated by the images the client (and occasionally the therapist) creates and [we are] brought together by their presence", which, she says also, "enables the transpersonal, the mystery, the use of something greater than us to be felt" (Schaverien, 1999). Frequently the image reveals another layer of existence because of its multidimensional form. This is what happened with my client Christine when the ray of sunlight appeared to emerge from her image of the hand holding the crystal ball. It also happened for Ali with the grumbling gremlin.

Ali's story (continued)

Unexpected events will often occur when a client is using arts media and this element of surprise can itself deepen the experience. The simulacrum of the grumbling gremlin that appeared in Ali's image of Eating Disorder Ali arose quite separately to anything she had consciously created. And yet the appearance of this unexpected, imp-like figure that had been hiding in her work helped Ali to make substantial progress in her therapy. A further surprise took place in a subsequent session.

Ali was describing a dream to me. In the dream she was chasing her brother (who in reality had died in a motorcycle accident some five years before). Following this chase, the environment of her dream switched to her family sitting around the dinner table. I invited Ali to re-enact the dream in a sand tray. She created with figurines the family sitting round the table. Although she had the option of using a doll's house dinner table, Ali chose to use a small trunk. Some time later I wondered aloud why she had chosen the trunk. At first she seemed thrown by my question but then she stopped in horror. We each seemed to realise simultaneously that the trunk she had chosen looked like a coffin (although it was Ali who voiced this first) and that without realising she had placed it right at the heart of her family's dinner table in the sand tray. Ali experienced another emotional break-through moment at this point. She realised that she had poignantly and unconsciously shown how her brother's death (as symbolised by the coffin) remained at the centre of her family life many years after he had died.

Synchronicity

Sometimes within an arts-based psychotherapy session something synchronistic happens and this too can precipitate a breakthrough moment and become the catalyst for client change (much like the element of surprise in Ali's therapy). For example, before we began Martha's re-enactment of her daughter's traumatic birth, a whole jar of stones got knocked over and created a loud clattering noise that set the scene for the enactment that followed. Martha's silent screams (which the reader may remember I attuned to with vocalisation and drums) were framed from the start by what felt like more than a coincidental occurrence of a sudden noise. It felt like an accidental gift. When Martha recounted later that she'd had to give birth silently and how this had added to her trauma, we both realised the sudden clattering of stones had been synchronistically important in lead-ing the way for her extended deep experiencing and breakthrough moment.

Carl Jung tells the story of a young female patient he was treating. She had had a dream in which she was given a golden scarab beetle. At the exact same moment she was recounting this dream to him, Jung heard a noise behind him like a gentle tapping. When he turned around he saw a flying insect knocking against the windowpane from outside. He opened the window and caught the creature as it flew in. It was a scarabaeid beetle (the nearest type of beetle to the golden scarab that could be found in the area) (Jung, 1948). Whatever the reason for a syn-chronistic event, such as the clattering stones in Martha's enactment or the scarabaeid beetle in Jung's practice-room, the transformative effect on the client is the same. They are able to feel there is something pro-foundly greater influencing the moment and this frequently leads to a deepening of the work.

* * *

In this chapter I have focused on some of the ways arts media have the ability to deepen a client's experience and increase the opportunity for breakthrough moments. In the next chapter, I will turn to the sciences and ask what might literally be going on in a client's head at such times.

PART IV

TURNING TO THE SCIENCES

CHAPTER NINE

Inside the brain

Julie's story

My fifteen-year-old client Julie had a secure and loving attachment to her mother. The strength of this relationship had enabled her to develop a number of ways to regulate and calm her feelings when faced with difficult circumstances. But Julie's father had an alcohol problem and it seems that her otherwise-nurturing mother had never quite known how to explain or acknowledge this to Julie. Julie had not understood at first that her father's erratic behaviour was caused by alcohol and thus now whenever she found herself in a situation where someone was acting strangely or exhibiting detached emotions, she would become overwhelmed by anxiety. She would feel inexplicably fearful and could never understand why. Julie had come to see me in order to try and help her understand and manage these difficult feelings.

Julie's mother had privately made me aware of her husband's alcoholism and I observed almost immediately that Julie herself would show great anxiety (often appearing to become frozen) whenever she was trying to say anything connected to her father. She also seemed anxious about the idea of using arts materials, so I suggested that she and I might make art-images *together*. I sensed intuitively that this was easier for Julie than being asked to create something on her own. She readily agreed.

From then on, frequently in our sessions, we would draw or paint side by side and sometimes create an art-image together involving objects and figures. During one such session we began to create a sand tray. Julie placed some beautiful bird feathers in the sand and took a wooden tortoise shell from my basket of objects and placed it alongside these feathers. We each added further items to the image. At one point Julie buried a twig in the sand close to the tortoise shell and the image suddenly appeared to depict a trapped bird, half submerged in the sand (see Figure 9.1). We worked silently for some time creating a safe place for the sand-drowned bird to rest. I found myself feeling deeply moved and inexplicably choked with sadness. I wondered if these feelings were a countertransference of Julie's own unexpressed sadness or if they were my response to the fact that Julie was looking after the bird so tenderly.

Julie and I were each trying to make the bird more comfortable with the addition of extra objects to the sand tray. It was as if we each

Figure 9.1. Julie's wounded bird.

understood it would be a long time before the poor creature recovered. I felt almost *desperate* in my desire to give this bird a warm and comfortable resting place. I wondered if this feeling, too, was influenced somehow by Julie's own unexpressed feelings.

When I asked her if she had a title for the sand tray image we were making, she said without hesitation "the wounded bird". The naming of this image seemed to bring her to a breakthrough moment because she then suddenly found the words to tell me (through tears), "my father is ill and he needs help".

It was unclear if the bird in the image symbolised her father or herself, or maybe both of them. Perhaps it unleashed feelings of compassion, sadness or helplessness in her. But what is certain is that making and naming this art-image had somehow enabled Julie to acknowledge for the first time that she felt anxiety around her father. From this session onwards she seemed better able to find ways to calm herself whenever she became stressed or upset by her father's behaviour. From our weekly therapy sessions, which took place over a period of eighteen months, she seemed to gain a secure attachment to me (as her therapist). This gave her the experience of a reparative relationship that further helped her access the trauma. It seemed that at first Julie had not developed the necessary mechanisms to calm herself with regards to this particular aspect of her life. Our therapy appeared to help her develop the necessary neural pathways.

Over the course of the next eighteen months, Julie used many different forms of arts media, such as drama, music, story, enactment, ritual, sand trays, drawing, and painting—some of which prompted further breakthrough moments in her therapy. I hypothesised that these arts-based activities were assisting her in acquiring new neural connections that would help in the process of integrating previously cut-off feelings connected to her father. They would also enable her to establish a new narrative about what had been happening throughout her childhood. This helped her begin to be able to manage experiences that would previously have triggered strong and disconcerting responses.

* * *

In this chapter I will consider what might be taking place in a client's brain at the time they experience a breakthrough moment and in particular how the use of arts media might be contributing to this neural activity. It should be noted that I am not a neurobiologist and the following discussion is no more than a perfunctory consideration of some basic neurobiological ideas and how they might apply to arts-based psychotherapy.

The brain as regulator

All organs and tissues of the body are composed of cells. But unlike other cells in the body, brain cells (or neurones) communicate and exchange information directly with one another. Each individual brain (and thus each individual person) has a unique combination of neurones that provides them with their distinctive qualities and characteristics (LeDoux, 2002). The brain is a series of neurones and nerve cells organised into systems that are mostly interconnected by synapses. A synapse is a term derived from the Greek word *synapsis*—meaning to clasp, connect, or join. But what is a synapse exactly? A synapse has been defined as a small gap at the end of a neurone across which information must pass in order to connect to another neurone. Synapses are thus found in the brain wherever nerve cells connect with other nerve cells.

There are three parts to the synapse: 1) the presynaptic nerve ending, which contains neurotransmitters; 2) the synaptic gap (or cleft) between the two nerve cells; and 3) the postsynaptic ending, which contains receptor sites. Electrical impulses travel down the axon of a neurone and trigger the release of neurotransmitters (Pert, 1997). These neurotransmitters—effectively chemical messages—allow the transmission of signals from one neurone to the next, across the synapse or gap. A group of connected neurones can form a more or less durable electrical pathway, which may last briefly (as in a short-term memory) or more permanently (as in the case of longer-term memories). In some cases these neurones may stay connected for the whole of an individual's lifetime.

Young children often cannot moderate intense emotion as they do not yet have sufficiently matured neural pathways in their brains. This is often the case for older children too, as well as for some adults who have not been "wired" to calm themselves or self-regulate their emotions. Sometimes this will present as an individual's *overall* inability to regulate difficult emotion or it might be specifically related to one or more particular experiences in their past (as was the case for Julie).

My client Amy, for example, was an intelligent, self-aware and high-functioning student who later became a fully qualified professional. But she would occasionally nonetheless find herself in situations in which she would feel overwhelmed by her frightening and confusing responses (such as when she discovered there were no curtains at the windows in her new home). From a neurobiological perspective it seems that Amy's past trauma had in all probability fired her amygdala (the primitive response for learned danger in the brain), and that this had prepared her body for a fight or flight response (or perhaps to freeze). She would have stress hormones, such as cortisol and adrenaline, coursing through her bloodstream. And crucially, she would have insufficient neural pathways to moderate her extreme emotion with no way of understanding why she was feeling so overwhelmed. Through the experience of therapy Amy was slowly able to understand her difficult feelings in the *present* and then connect them with what had happened in her past. From here she could begin to reintegrate denied, repressed and cut-off experiences. This meant that over time—much like Julie—she was able to form new neural pathways that helped her begin to manage her emotions whenever she encountered experiences that had historically triggered a fearful response.

I became fascinated by this notion that the brain is not hardwired in childhood; that it leaves the door open for further neural changes to occur throughout life, given the right circumstances and conditions. Research has suggested that an infant acquires emotional regulatory abilities through a secure attachment with a caregiver. This important interaction allows the child's brain to develop neural connections with a balanced capacity to regulate emotion. This suggested that an infant acquires emotional regulatory abilities through a secure attachment with a caregiver. Later in life, a new caregiver for the child (or a new partner/new therapist for the adult) can become an "interactive regulator" and provide the means for an individual's brain to be rewired for self-regulation of emotions (Sunderland, 2000).

Louis Cozolino suggests that a therapist "attempts to restructure neural architecture" by helping their client "self-soothe" or "self-regulate" (Cozolino, 2002). It would seem that Julie, Susan, Ben and Amy (and many of my other clients) were able to create new neural pathways from their experiences within the therapy work. The relationship with a therapist can lead to the rewiring of a client's brain for self-soothing, which can then provide support outside the therapy. As we have seen in Chapter Five, this relationship with the therapist can be strengthened and deepened following a breakthrough moment.

The brain circuits responsible for interpersonal communication are surprisingly the same as (or at least closely linked to) the circuits that regulate modulation of emotion. This is significant for clients who have not experienced a secure attachment to a caregiver, as it almost always means they will have great difficulty in regulating their emotions (Bowlby, 2006). Julie had a secure attachment to her mother, but she had not developed neural pathways to regulate her emotions concerning her father's alcohol addiction. This was partly due to her mother's inability to acknowledge it or comfort Julie about it.

The slow, gradual development of an individual's brain allows for the possibility of its being influenced by environmental factors. This means the brain can be flexible and adapt in appropriate ways for survival in a particular environment. However, if these environmental factors are less than favourable, the brain may be "sculpted in ways that can become maladaptive" (Cozolino, 2002). When an individual is aroused by disturbing, strong or overwhelming feelings (hyper-arousal) this can threaten to disrupt their equilibrium and they may become "dis-regulated" (Sunderland, 2000). If they have no other means to successfully calm themselves, this can lead the individual to neurotic auto-regulation in an attempt to soothe him- or herself—for example, the continual rocking or head banging of an infant, or the use of alcohol or drugs by an adult. Alternatively, it might also lead to dissociation—a process whereby overwhelming feelings are denied, partially shut down, or entirely split off.

The ability of an individual to regulate their emotion is vital for psychological health. Noah Hass-Cohen states that "at the core of mood disorders, such as depression and anxiety, are problems with the regulation of affect" (Hass-Cohen, 2008). He asserts that arts therapies provide a unique opportunity for practising this regulation. For example, following her mother's death, my client Susan created her pause button in order to be able to explore emotions that threatened to become unmanageable within our sessions. If ever she felt overwhelmed by her emotions Susan would press this "button" and we would stop the therapy until she felt able to continue. In this way she was able to face traumatic feelings along with her fear of becoming out control within our sessions. The image of the pause button gave her the opportunity to practise the "regulation of affect".

The associations of memory

In studying neurobiology in my research for this book, many new ideas formed and a number of my previous thoughts reorganised themselves.

One might say I was able to create new neural pathways regarding my understanding of clients and breakthrough moments. One such idea came via the idea of the plastic brain. Joseph LeDoux and other writers speak about the brain as having plasticity. By this they mean that it is "changeable, malleable [and] modifiable" (LeDoux, 2002). The term plastic brain can be applied to an adult brain as well as a child's, since it is no longer believed (as it once was) that the brain is hardwired after the developmental phase of childhood has passed. LeDoux suggests the brain is a far more open system than we ever imagined and that nature has gone to extensive measures to help us perceive and take in the world around us in ever-developing ways. Nature has in fact given us a brain that "survives in a changing world by changing itself" (Doidge, 2007). Change is thus central to all brain activity even though from a phenomenological standpoint as adults we may experience ourselves as changing very little.

LeDoux believes that almost all brain systems have the "ability to be modified by experience". This means that all experiences—including those in a therapy session—have the potential to modify an individual's brain. I found this to be a particularly exciting discovery, as it tacitly acknowledged the potential for therapy to bring about neurobiological changes in clients. That is, if the plasticity of the brain continues into adulthood, my clients' brains are malleable and modifiable and thus open to change in their therapy sessions.

At around the time I discovered this idea of the plastic brain, I came across Siegel and Bryson's book *The Whole-Brain Child* (2012), which they wrote for parents to explain brain processes to their children. Siegel and Bryson explain that memory is not stored in the brain in categories such as years, people, events, and relationships, as many people typically believe, but rather that memory "is all about associations" (ibid.). The brain processes an idea, a feeling, a sensation or an image in the present and then links it with similar experiences from the past. This is because when we undergo an experience, neurones fire electrical signals. These neurones link with other neurones that are firing simultaneously. In this way they become associated with each other and a memory is formed (Hebb, 1949). This process is neatly encapsulated in the famous axiom: "cells that fire together, wire together".

This idea seems particularly helpful in understanding what might be happening for a client at the time of a breakthrough moment and how the art-image may contribute. For example, the depressed expression of the adult orangutan depicted on Ben's postcard may have connected with a memory he had of his own mother's depressed expression when he was a child. It may have been this memory association that enabled his breakthrough moment to arise. Vague associations he had previously made about clinginess with his girlfriends then suddenly came together and led to his new realisation. When I spoke to Ben later he informed me that now whenever he felt clingy around his girlfriend (after our single session together) he would associate this with the orangutan image. He said this helped him remember that the clingy feelings he was experiencing were associated with past experiences, which in turn helped to put the clingy feelings about his girlfriend into a new perspective. In this sense, the image of the orangutan had helped him make new associations, which significantly helped his understanding of the problem.

Siegel and Bryson acknowledge that memory associations like this can set up expectations for the future. If Ben's mother was unavailable and kept "disappearing" into her depression, it was perhaps not surprising that by association Ben developed the expectation that his girlfriend too might disappear somehow, or become unavailable. This would activate a separation anxiety in his current relationship that really belonged to his historic experience as a child towards his mother.

Bryony's story

At around this time a moving session with my client Bryony presented me with an example of the power of memory association. It also provided an illustration of how working with the arts can present a client with an opportunity to access hidden feelings. Bryony felt she had to "get things right" all the time in life and had come to therapy to address her suffocating feelings of perfectionism. She drew a large red tick (check mark) in the centre of a white piece of paper, surrounded by further little black ticks that she said were to represent the many things she had to get right. Next she added several blue teardrops, which she said were her tears. She then coloured inside the tick with a thick red marker, some of which bled outside the lines into the tears. This felt deeply important, although I had no idea what its significance might be.

I chose, somewhat unusually, to comment on her art-making process by saying, "I notice the red tick has bled out into your tears". From this, Bryony had a sudden and powerful breakthrough moment. She began to sob deeply and spoke for the first time about her "lost babies". It transpired she had experienced several miscarriages earlier in her life and although she now had four healthy children the pain of this loss clearly remained deeply buried inside her. The memory-association that had arisen seemingly randomly from the red ink bleeding into the tears in her image (and my observation of this) had provided a key to unlock her hidden pain.

Left and right brain

On delving deeper into the literature, I discovered that the brain is, broadly speaking, organised into left and right hemispheres. It has been recognised that if one hemisphere of the brain is damaged, the other hemisphere can take over some of its functions. However each hemisphere predominantly provides a different main focus (Sunderland, 2000).

The left hemisphere is usually focusing on the external world, details, words, logic, and milder feelings. It is less good at regulating stress. The right hemisphere is involved in context, overall meanings, intense feeling, sensory information, and empathy. This includes detecting and processing the mood of another person (including their tone of voice, body language, eye contact) as well as emotional regulation. The right hemisphere is also involved in bodily sensations and the processing of images (ibid.).

Iain McGilchrist in his book *The Master and His Emissary* (2009) describes how an ability to view the world from a detailed perspective whilst simultaneously being able to see the greater context is important for the survival of all animals. He gives the example of a bird peering at the ground with one eye to find grains of food while keeping the other eye out for predators and other potential dangers. In the case of humans, the brain is divided into two hemispheres to keep these separate ways of viewing the world distinct, but they are integrated across the two hemispheres. McGilchrist suggests that the left brain frequently hijacks the right brain and develops a story or narrative for why something is the way it is. An individual will then frequently wrongly believe this version of events to be the truth. In Western culture in particular, the left brain tends to play a dominant part, as if this were the most important way to view the world. In reality, however, both ways of viewing the world are required. For the most healthy and emotionally adjusted individuals, these two separate perspectives or ways of viewing the world are accessible and integrated across the two hemispheres (McGilchrist, 2009).

One of the main tasks of therapy, according to Cozolino, is to help foster this integration between the right and left hemispheres. I was arrested by an image that shows visually how I imagine the two sides of the brain to be organised (see Figure 9.2). A few days after finding this image, my client Chloe came to see me.

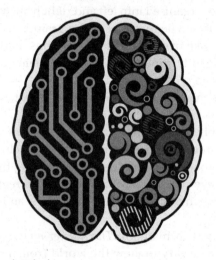

Figure 9.2. Left and right brain.

Chloe's story

Chloe was attending therapy with me as part of a recommended requirement for her training as a play therapist. She needed to make a decision as to whether or not to leave her current part-time job as an aromatherapist and focus entirely on the new training. We went over and over the practical aspects of her decision, such as whether she should reduce her hours as an aromatherapist and when exactly she might go if she did decide to leave. We discussed many logical reasons for why she might carry on working and many logical reasons for why she might leave. However this pulled her simultaneously in two separate directions and no decision could be made. I too was pulled simultaneously in both directions. We each felt stuck at an impasse.

Part way through one session when we were addressing this impasse, I suggested that Chloe might try to act out her dilemma with puppets. She chose a pig puppet to depict the "aromatherapist" part of herself and a penguin puppet to symbolise the "play therapist" part. I chose a lion puppet, which would represent a narrator character. The enactment began with the pig telling the lion-narrator how much she always used to love being an aromatherapist but that now her heart wasn't really in it. The lion rephrased this statement and said back to her, "So you are doing aromatherapy without a heart?" At this point Chloe was overcome by a sudden rush of emotion and began to cry—a breakthrough moment. It was intensified when I reached for a red ceramic heart and placed it on the floor between the pig and the penguin. It was a profound moment but we were unclear as to what exactly Chloe's strong feelings were connected to, so we continued the enactment.

The penguin said next that she felt that her heart was involved in being a play therapist and Chloe balanced the ceramic heart between the penguin's feet. Chloe then animated a new puppet character, Snappy Dragon, who seemed very practical and adamantly and persuasively said that she must continue working as an aromatherapist. From our dialogue between these four puppets it became clear that money was not the main factor in Chloe's decision.

The outcome of the session was that although Chloe had not yet made up her mind, we were now at least aware that there were multiple layers to her decision—including layers she had not previously known about until this emotional breakthrough. Following this session, Chloe was able to view her decision in a different way and also became more aware of (and more curious about) her own decision-making process. It seems that by using these puppets, Chloe had engaged the right hemisphere of her brain in considering her dilemma and had been able to access intuition, deep feelings, and unconscious aspects. She had revealed to herself via a period of experiential, extended deep experiencing that her heart was not involved in being an aromatherapist. This realisation had taken her to a breakthrough moment. The next time she came to therapy, Chloe announced that she had made a decision with her *heart*—and she was leaving the aromatherapy position.

* * *

In Chloe's case, working therapeutically with puppets assisted her ability to access right hemisphere brain processes. It seems reasonable to believe, therefore, that the inclusion of arts media into the therapeutic relationship can enable a client to gain new (and often profound) access to the right hemisphere of the brain. I was beginning to understand that with Chloe, Bryony, Julie, Ben and Amy, the introduction of art materials seemed to enable them to access and integrate right hemisphere ways of "knowing the world". Seeing as the right hemisphere is predominately involved in intense feelings and images, it would seem that working with the arts may enable clients to move away from *talking* (which predominantly involves the left hemisphere) and encourage them to access deeper, hidden feelings (from the right hemisphere) and lead them to breakthrough moments.

It is speculative but it seems reasonable to assume that the use of arts media might also assist in the quietening of a client's chattering, left-brain *voice*—enabling deeper forms of knowing to emerge. I notice that clients frequently say something like: "I didn't know I knew that" after they have experienced a breakthrough moment. It is as if they knew something with one part of their brain but had never consciously thought about it with the other. Chloe left her session with the puppets saying, "I've been struggling with this decision for so long—but today I actually *felt* it and can now see it in a very different way".

The brain at a breakthrough moment

Interesting though these discoveries were, I still did not have a tangible understanding of what was happening in a client's brain at the time of a breakthrough moment. I was unclear where to turn next when yet again I found myself drawn to an image. I came across another digital representation of several neurones firing together in the brain and I felt as though the answer to my question lay within the image (see Figure 9.3).

I wondered if this sort of image of electrochemical activity at the site of a synapse could be a helpful way of visualising what was happening in the brain at the time of a breakthrough moment: several synapses firing at once—or perhaps even *millions* of them all connecting thoughts, experiences, feelings and physical sensations in a new way for the first time.

The cerebral cortex, the outer mantle of the human brain, contains about 100 billion neurones and one million, billion synaptic connections (Edelman, 1987). Given the huge number of ways in which circuits or loops can be excited, this would mean that there are hyper-astronomical numbers of possible synaptic connections (a ten followed by at least a million zeros). Perhaps it would not be unreasonable to imagine that

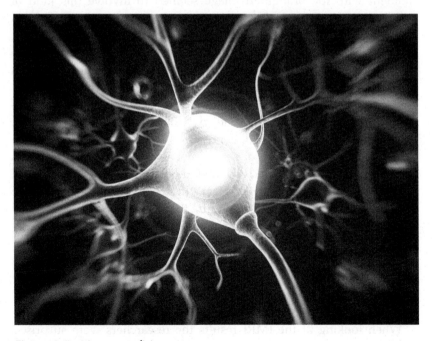

Figure 9.3. Neurones firing.

a breakthrough moment involves the simultaneous firing of many of these synapses across a range of different parts of the brain. We have seen that a breakthrough moment involves the coming together of several ideas, feelings, thoughts and possibilities into a new combination and usually in one sudden *rush*. Could the experience of such a moment be successfully captured by this sort of digital representation of several neurones firing together?

Gerald Mendelsohn has written at length about the creative process. He suggests that when an artist or creator moves from the preparation stage of their work, through the incubation stage, to the ultimate "a-ha moment of insight", this frequently involves a leap of inspiration or new understanding. He describes the creative act as a sudden insight where two or three images or ideas previously thought to be unrelated are held in focus simultaneously. This he says brings together the conditions for a new "combinational leap" to occur (Mendelsohn, 1976). This combinational leap in turn creates a new connection from which an original idea can be born. For example, Ben's breakthrough moment with the orangutan image seemed to involve this kind of sudden insight. Two or three ideas came together and were held in focus simultaneously, which led to a "new combinational leap" for him. Joseph Zinker also speaks of such leaps occurring within the creative (and therapeutic) process (Zinker, 1977). Breakthrough moments with my clients Julie, Susan, Amy and Ben certainly felt like creative leaps.

Researchers at the Weizmann Institute of Science in New York conducted research into what they called "a-ha" moments (Nauert, 2015). These moments were defined as points at which a participant experienced the sudden grasping of a new concept or insight. The scientists wished to discover what exactly was happening in the brain at such moments of revelatory discovery. fMRI (functional magnetic resonance imaging) is a neuro-imaging procedure that measures brain activity by detecting changes associated with blood flow. In the experiment, photographs were chosen of everyday things like dogs and hot-air balloons. The images were systematically altered until they resembled inkblots that the volunteers could not identify. When these inkblot images were switched for a split second with the original unaltered pictures, the subjects experienced an "a-ha moment" of recognition.

When looking at the fMRI results the researchers were surprised to observe that the amygdala was among the areas of the brain that lit up at the time of the a-ha moment, demonstrating that blood flow had increased to that region. The amygdala is mostly thought of as activating the body's learned response to emotions—particularly fear. The study concluded that it may play another important role in the creation of long-term memories. This was an exciting revelation to me. Perhaps the amygdala may have registered that at the time of a breakthrough moment, the shift in perception was significant and worthy of preservation. As it suggested the intriguing possibility that in the event of my clients' breakthrough moments (during which there is a sudden reorganisation of information and a shift in perception), the amygdala may be triggered.

In the 1970s Candace Pert demonstrated the importance of neurotransmitters in the brain. A chemical neurotransmitter is a "messenger of neurological information that is transported from one cell to other cells". This message is only able to be received if it has a receptor that is compatible with the neurotransmitter. Pert explains that for information to enter cells there needs to be an available chemical that binds selectively to its own specific receptor on the surface of the cell (Pert, 1997). This serves to unlock the receptors and enable information to cross the gap or synapse between neurones (see Figure 9.4).

Deepak Chopra puts this another way when he says that internal chemicals are the biological underpinnings of our awareness—

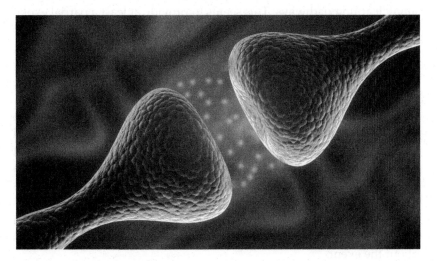

Figure 9.4. Crossing the synapse.

manifesting themselves as emotions, beliefs, and expectations. They profoundly influence how we experience and respond to our world. He goes on to say that these neurotransmitters or biochemical messengers act with "intelligence" by communicating information and orchestrating a vast complex of conscious and unconscious activities at any given moment (Chopra, 2003).

It now appears to be undisputed that neurotransmitters affect and are affected by an individual's emotions. For example, chemicals such as endorphins can be produced by: laughter, enjoying one-self, making love, exercising, or just generally feeling happy. On the other hand, steroid hormones (such as cortisol) secreted by the adrenal glands in times of stress can block the receptors and prevent them from being unlocked (especially if this stress carries on for a period of time). This can prevent information from entering the cell and stop the body from being able to function smoothly. The result is an individual who is unhealthy or emotionally unstable (Pert, 1997).

So perhaps breakthrough moments (and even smaller events that occur in the therapeutic process) affect the chemicals and neurotransmitters in a client's brain. Pert explains that endorphins serve as the body's internal reward system, providing us with a rush of pleasure whenever we learn something that is conducive to our survival as a species. Endorphins, our natural opiates, are a filtering mechanism to the brain. Moments of insight are rewarded with floods of endorphins along learning pathways. This seems to provide at least a partial explanation for why the experience of a breakthrough moment can feel so stimulating and significant for a client.

Joshua's story

Joshua was a twenty-year-old medical student who had requested to come and see me during a mid-semester break from university. He had a vague feeling that something bad had happened when he was out with his father one day at the park when he was very young. What in fact had happened is that a three-year-old Joshua had been out with his father when a gunman randomly opened fire on the crowd. Joshua's father had pulled his son to the ground and lain down on top of him until the danger passed. Joshua seemingly remembered no details about the event.

He was dealing with issues of feeling hyper-vigilant about things when he came to see me. It was starting to interfere with his ability to relax. We worked on this together for some time until one day we decided he would carefully re-enact the scene of being at the park that day with his father. During the enactment Joshua found himself lying on the floor of the practice-room, frozen in silent terror. I was able to reassure him that his feelings belonged to something that had happened a long time ago and remind him he was safe with me. After some time he went back to his seat and for the first time was able to recall new details of the previously forgotten event.

Before his next session he had a new discussion with his father and was able to acquire an even fuller narrative of what had happened that day in the park. This provided Joshua with new neural pathways linking his extreme hyper-vigilance to this event he had not been able to access. In turn this helped him regulate his emotions and make new neural connections between the past trauma and his new under-standing. It seems the integration of these previously cut-off thoughts and feelings was pivotal to Joshua's increased sense of harmony and well-being.

* * *

Bessel Van Der Kolk carried out groundbreaking research when he observed the neural activity of subjects who listened back to a tape recording for which they had described significant personal traumas from their past (Van Der Kolk, 2015). Even though they had recorded themselves telling their own traumatic stories, when it was played back to them, all the participants showed signs of being re-traumatised. There was strong evidence that their amygdala was activated in each case. But more surprisingly, when listening to the tapes there was a sig-nificant decrease of activity in their Broca's area—one of the language centres of the brain. In circumstances when the Broca's area is not fully functioning it is not possible for a person to put their "thoughts and feelings into words". And this explains why even years after a trauma has occurred, a person often still has great difficulty telling other people what happened to them (ibid.).

It seems that a person's brain when experiencing terror, rage and helplessness is often cut-off from language. The details of a traumatic story and its associated feelings cannot be recounted because they haven't been laid down in memory with words. The person thus has no access to language with which to describe their trauma and may find it returns to them via horrifying flashbacks and nightmares. Research shows that this can still be the case many years after an original traumatic event. This would certainly explain Julie's inability to speak to me at first about her own trauma and why Bryony had never spoken to me about her miscarriages. It also provides at least a partial explanation for why working with arts media—rich as it is in symbolism and visual metaphor—can enable a client to process a trauma that they were not otherwise able to acknowledge or express. The image *itself* is able to create new and significant neural connections that can bypass the need for words.

CHAPTER TEN

Chaos and complexity

Ben's story (continued)

I had often found myself wondering if Ben's breakthrough moment with the orangutan image had precipitated any changes in his life, and, if so, whether these had been lasting changes. After his single counselling session with me, Ben moved to London and I resigned myself to the fact that I would never know what had happened following his experience. To my surprise, however, several years later, he returned to see me. He revealed that after his session with the orangutan image, a cascade of new changes had taken place in his life. He had felt his behaviour, thoughts and feelings all change for the better—especially in the area of his relationships. He had moved to London as planned but soon after had broken up with his girlfriend. A few months later he began a new relationship, which felt more suitable.

One major change, which he attributed to our session, was that he now had more of a handle on his feelings of clinginess. He still frequently felt clingy with his new girlfriend but he now had a different approach for how to deal with it. Thanks to our counselling session, he told me that he now had a clear understanding that these feelings belonged to events in his past. As a result, he felt able to speak to his new girlfriend about the feelings and felt greater insight around them in general. This gave him increased confidence because it raised his self-esteem, which in turn helped him secure a new job (and later led to his being offered a post at the educational establishment where I first met him).

When asked about the lasting effect of his therapy session, Ben described the experience as having started "a chain reaction of changes". Naturally, a host of different variables were involved in this chain reaction and some of the changes may have taken place anyway, but he said that the orangutan image had stayed firmly in his head as a reminder of his tendency towards clinginess in relationships. Whenever such feelings resurfaced in his current relationship he would remember the orangutan mother and baby and this would serve to remind him that his clingy feelings were connected to the past (the little boy clinging to his depressed, unavailable mother) and not to his present relationship with his girlfriend. He could tell himself that he was an adult now, which also helped him manage the clingy feelings in a new way.

He summed up his single counselling session with me as having been a turning point that had the knock-on effect of precipitating many further changes in his life. But how exactly might we understand the changes that followed from Ben's session and his breakthrough moment with the orangutan image? It is tempting to describe the changes as the result of simple cause and effect—Ben's therapy session caused the multiple changes he went on to experience. But as Ben himself acknowledged, there were in fact myriad elements—many of them unrelated to the session—that also came into play.

* * *

In this chapter I will look at one of the most curious questions of all—how does a breakthrough moment actually bring about change for a client? And is such change always lasting? Before we begin it should be noted that change for a client does not necessarily mean desirable change. There are clearly events in therapy (as in everyday life) that do have the power to directly bring about change. But how might such change be measured? It is difficult to gauge how one event—such as Ben's breakthrough moment with the orangutan image—can be seen to affect the overall system. This is because a system is vast and unpredictable; it is impossible to quantify the many different factors that might be influencing it at any given time. The impact on a particular individual's life (of all the many things that have happened to them at different stages) constitutes a highly "complex tapestry" (Baugh, 2010).

Dynamic systems

According to Daniel Stern and his contemporaries at the Boston Change Process Study Group, the key to understanding how change takes place for a client lies in gaining an appreciation of how dynamic systems change in general. In 1963 the meteorologist Edward Lorenz was working on a computer program that simulated a complex weather system. The story goes that a slight variation in some data he re-entered created a vast and unexpected difference to the system (Lorenz, 1963). Lorenz concluded from this that within some dynamic systems there are (in some respects) sensitivities to tiny differences in the input of variables that have the power to dramatically alter the course of the later development of the whole system. This is known as sensitive dependence on initial conditions, or in more popular terminology, The Butterfly Effect, which refers to the idea that air turbulence created by a butterfly's wings can theoretically influence the weather on the other side of the world, through a vast series of compounding knock-on effects.

On the basis of Lorenz's discovery it seems reasonable to extrapolate that one particular event—such as a breakthrough moment in a therapy session—might be able to affect any number of further changes for a client. These changes could be to the client's thoughts, feelings, behaviour, and/or relationships, and each of these changes might in themselves trigger additional change. For example, one seemingly small change within Ben at the time of his breakthrough moment—namely, his making a connection between his feelings of clinginess and the orangutan image—led to changes in his future relationships, which then led to further change, such as his increased self-confidence. In this sense, Ben's breakthrough moment created a knock-on effect of further changes and a compound interest effect was achieved. It is important to remember, however, that other aspects of Ben were also shifting and thus affecting these changes at the same time. This will have caused greater unpredictability and variability in the outcome. It will never be possible to trace or predict such ongoing changes in a linear or precise way. This is because change that takes place within a dynamic system tends to involve a non-linear dynamic.

But what exactly is a system and how might these curious ideas about systems be seen to apply to the change that follows a breakthrough moment? A system is basically a group of dynamic relationships. The members of this group—which might be cells in a human system, players in an orchestra, or bees in a colony—act as a whole through a process of feedback signals (or loops) that enable a "higher level of order to emerge" (Meadows, 1993).

Could my clients themselves be considered dynamic systems? Consider Susan, for example. Is it sensible to think of the different Susans as being subsystems who were failing to act together as a coherent whole? Perhaps there were no interconnected processes or feedback signals between the different Susans and this was preventing a higher level of order emerging—one which would have enabled her to feel like a single, coherent Susan. Perhaps my job was to help enable her to gain greater awareness of all the Susan subsystems and to lead her towards new organisation by strengthening the connections between them.

With Ben it seems there was a lasting subsystem from his childhood that was sabotaging his current relationships—namely, his habit of clinginess, stemming from the experience of having an unavailable mother when he was a child. Until our session it seems that this had not yet been in his awareness and was thus not giving him any feedback signals, but becoming aware of the effects of this past experience in his present enabled considerable change to take place for Ben. It might be possible to conceptualise this change as involving the creation of new feedback loops in his brain that were able to remind him that any "clingy" feelings in the present had their origins in his historic relationship with his mother. This enabled him to recognise that his feelings should not all be attributed to his present relationship.

Some systems are closed and some systems are open to their surrounding environments. Bill Harris reminds us that human beings are made up of systems (and subsystems) that are both open *and* closed (Harris, 2007). We are constantly in flux—changing, growing, healing and learning in adjustment to our environment. It is this flexibility that enables us to be so adaptable to our surroundings. There is a constant interchange between the individual and their environment that is physical, cognitive, emotional, behavioural, social (and I would add spiritual) (Lapworth, Sills, & Fish, 2001). In our everyday thinking we are accustomed to viewing people as self-contained systems, somehow separate from their environment and from one another. But in reality, human systems are constantly exchanging information and energy with their environment and with others.

Although Ben described many changes he felt had taken place, these were not linear, causal changes but rather seemed to spread out like a fan from his breakthrough moment. One ostensibly small change for Susan—seeing herself as a multitude of Susans—also fanned out to include a series of changes in her life, including changing her therapeutic relationship with me (which offered new potential for the therapy). In daring to reveal to me the presence of her hidden Susans, she was no longer locked in a secret world that nobody knew about. Together we explored the other Susans and hoped that each new revelation would enable her to feel more like one person and less like several people.

The client in chaos

The second law of thermodynamics states that a closed system reaches equilibrium by arriving at a state of maximum disorder. Ilya Prigogine discovered that open systems become increasingly ordered by dissipating (or dispersing) their disorder to the environment (Prigogine, 1984). Could it be that clients who frequently express feelings of discomfort, confusion and disorder at the start of their therapeutic work, do so similarly because they are on their way towards new levels of order, harmony, and organisation? This perspective certainly provides an attractive way to view the change processes that took place for Ben and Susan.

In addition to highlighting the idea that order emerges after a system has tipped into disorder or chaos, Prigogine showed that the resulting order does not appear to emerge in spite of the chaos, but rather because of it. Evolution and growth are the inevitable products of open systems slipping into temporary chaos and then reorganising themselves to emerge at a higher level of complexity and functioning (ibid.). This resonates with my frequent experience of new clients, who present themselves for therapy in a disordered and chaotic state of mind, often saying things like, "I am not myself", "I feel lost," or "I don't know where I'm going any more". Ben presented himself as feeling confused and "pathetic" with regard to his intimate relationships because he felt so "clingy" and could not work out why.

It seems that in order to reach a new level of organisation, a person might need to experience a new level of dissatisfaction with their current circumstances, or indeed feel chaotically overwhelmed to such a degree that this pushes them to make changes and thus precipitates the new organisation to emerge. Ben was feeling hopeless about how every relationship resulted in him becoming "clingy". Susan was feeling desperate because she thought she would not live beyond forty (the age her mother had died). She also believed she was doomed to remain disconnected from other parts of herself, unless she made a concerted effort to understand how the death of her mother had affected her.

This fascinating idea of order arising out of a chaotic system provided me with a new way to think about client change. It also gave me a new respect for what is perhaps the *need* for discomfort or "chaos" in a client when they first begin therapy—a kind of prerequisite feeling of disorder before new levels of order can be achieved. Perhaps Ben and Susan were feeling themselves slip into chaos and disarray, no longer feeling they knew who they were—uncoupling from their old patterns along the route to experiencing new ways of being. This could equally be conceived as the systems of Ben and Susan reaching a higher level of functioning and complexity and being able to integrate to a greater extent the different subsystems.

We have seen that following a breakthrough moment a client will often slip into uncertainty or confusion—sometimes in spite of the fact they have achieved positive new clarity or made significant new neural connections. It seems fair to imagine that this could be part of the necessary disorder or chaos required for a higher level of organisation to emerge. Even a simple, single-celled organism like slime mould can entirely reorganise itself due to the signals received from neighbouring cells (Johnson, 2001). Is it fair to imagine therefore that Susan, Ben and my other clients could arrive at a place where they might feel, from a phenomenological perspective, that they had reorganised themselves to reach a higher level of order. To speculate even further, could it be that in periods of extended deep experiencing when a client is mesmerised by an art-image, various subsystems are shifting and slowly reorganising themselves. Could this at least partially explain the trance-like experience of my clients at such times?

Bill Harris speaks of raising the threshold of what a client can manage as a key form of reorganisation. This would ensure that a client is no longer "derailed by thoughts, experiences, feelings and the past" and this can beneficially mean that symptoms evaporate or have a less pressing effect (Harris, 2007). Considering my conversation with Ben when he came back to see me, this seemed to be true of a number of issues. In particular, his new way of understanding why he felt "clingy" with his girlfriend, as well as his raised confidence and self-esteem. My client Amy also no longer appeared to be so overwhelmed by her experiences (such as having no curtains in her windows). Perhaps it is not too far-fetched to think of my clients' thoughts, feelings, relationships and behaviour as being plunged into chaos, reorganising themselves and then emerging with a higher level of order.

In psychology and psychotherapy there seem to be both direct and oblique references to the emergence of a higher level order. Peter Philippson, for example, speaks about the self as an emergent process. He asserts that the emergent self can be thought of as a description of an individual moving towards a "higher level of personhood" (Philippson, 2009). Abraham Maslow suggests that all human beings have a hierarchy of needs and the highest level culminates in self-actualisation (1971). Carl Rogers' concept of "becoming a person" also seems to embrace this idea of a disparate individual aiming for (and perhaps achieving) higher levels of integration (Rogers, 1961).

The emergence of self

A few writers have made connections between the notion of change in open systems and what might be happening for a human being in distress. I found such ideas useful in helping me to reflect upon my clients' experiences. Joanne Wieland-Burston writes that, "change [in systems] takes place at certain critical points" (Wieland-Burston, 1992). She suggests "the same may well be true for individuals". For example, when water is cooling, nothing much may appear to be happening until the critical point of freezing when it starts to produce ice crystals. Similarly, when pressing needs create stress that becomes so great, change becomes an unavoidable necessity.

In the case of ice, nothing much may appear to be happening until the critical point or crisis arrives. In a parallel sense, Wieland-Burston says that sometimes an individual is less sensitive to pressing signals and ignores the physical or emotional warning signs until they reach some sort of crisis point. In such a case, rather than finding ways to change and reduce the stress, "chaos may erupt and force/enable the individual to begin the search for a new order" (ibid.).

This application of systems theory to the subject of client change gave me a new way to think about my clients. They arrive in distress and frequently need to sit in uncomfortable feelings for a time before (hopefully) gaining a greater sense of well-being and enjoyment of their lives. This certainly seemed to be the case for Susan in her continuing therapy.

Susan's story (continued)

As demonstrated by her first session, Susan was looking to find a way to feel more like one person and less like a group of Susans (including some hidden selves) frequently in conflict with each other. She did not have a multiple personality or dissociative identity disorder (as it is now categorised) but she did feel strongly that she was not a fully integrated person. I wondered if the integration she was seeking could be thought of as her desire for the emergence of a higher level of order. The death of her mother at forty had triggered a fear in Susan that she too would not live beyond that age—she had reached forty herself when she first came to see me. This fear had instigated a pressing desire to understand more clearly what the effect had been on her as an adolescent when her mother had become so thin from her illness that she had literally wasted away.

After her fourth therapy session with me—when she described her inner world as feeling like there were a plethora of Susans (symbolised by the stones she had tipped on the floor)—a tacit agreement was made: together we would explore these various Susans. Susan did not experience herself as predominantly one person (an integrated, interconnected series of complex parts or networks) but rather as a series of different characters, each with a differing motivation, some of whom were vying for control over her. Could Susan arrive at a more integrated way of experiencing herself—a higher level of order?

Susan first came to therapy saying that she believed her mother dying suddenly had deeply impacted her as a teenager. She wished to understand the many complex ways it seemed to have affected her. After she tipped the stones (Susans) onto the floor, I hypothesised that there were aspects of her that were cut off and had not yet been fully integrated. There was also perhaps a degree of dissociation—whereby some of these parts of her had become almost completely split off from her awareness and remained buried in her unconscious. This gave me a broad idea of how to proceed with her therapy.

Working with arts media meant that there were always multiple ways for Susan to meet and become familiar with the other Susans, although I did note that several of these Susans seemed to be less accessible and were perhaps even pre- or non-verbal. I felt a quiet confidence that the art materials would help us reach them. There was always the possibility at any time during this work that Susan might have slipped deeper into confusion and disordered feelings, but I kept an awareness of Prigogine's theory that this disorder itself could be a necessary precursor to the emergence of a higher level of order.

Susan and I discovered that several of the Susans with whom we tried to get acquainted were not able to speak. We thus needed to find creative ways to communicate with these non-verbal aspects of her. The expression of these particular Susans (or aspects of Susan) had been denied and repressed following the death of her mother. They had never had the chance to *speak*. As the work progressed, together we found many creative ways to allow these Susans to find their "voice". For example, one of the Susans posted me a letter. It contained the following sentence:

> "She—the Susan who goes to therapy every week—will
> pretend I don't exist and blab on and on, week after week,
> about all sorts of unimportant things and never tell you
> about ME!"

In a series of further extraordinary letters this same part of her told me how she felt banished from Susan's life and had been left powerless and overruled.

On another memorable occasion, she drew a spiked stick figure with a veil over its face on a white piece of paper. She then built a wall of stones and clay around it. While she was doing this I had the peculiar experience of feeling like she was receding further and further away from me, until I felt I could no longer reach her—almost as if she were drifting away in a boat from the island of the practice-room where I remained. Trying to imagine what to say was difficult. There seemed to be no right intervention and I felt immobilised. I was worried that if I said the wrong thing I could lose her altogether. Eventually I found myself remarking, somewhat inadequately, "It feels as though you are a very long way away". There was no reply. She didn't even acknowledge that I had said anything. After a long pause, she spelt out with bits of clay:

H-E-L-P   M–E

I found myself feeling helpless and cut off from my client. I realised that this was probably how Susan herself was feeling and it was imperative that I shake off my own feelings in order to reach her somehow. I realised also that I was being provided with a startling opportunity to communicate with one of the Susans who could not speak and was buried deep inside her psyche. How could I reach this terrified part of her? How could I build a bridge between us when she was so scared and far away? After a long pause it occurred to me that I might create an *actual* bridge (made of stones) that stretched from where I sat in the therapy room, all the way up to Susan, on the other side of the clay wall she had built. Her eyes were closed as I told her: "I am making a bridge of stones that reaches out to you from me".

After several minutes of silence that felt far longer she opened her eyes and sat staring at the "bridge" I had made. Somehow, and only after this considerable period of extended deep experiencing, a door seemed to open suddenly for the part of her that had been deeply buried beyond tears or speech. I could sense she was beginning to feel more connected to me. She didn't *say* anything but there was a distinct change in the atmosphere—I sensed strongly that I had reached out to her and she had let herself be reached. We were nearing the end of the session and the intensity was palpable, so I reminded Susan of how to rescue herself (by pressing the red pause button she had painted previously). This seemed to help bring her back into the room.

As the session came to an end, we spoke at length about what had just happened, and after a while she felt able to describe how this particular voiceless part of her must have become buried when her mother died and had not surfaced until now. It felt like the beginning of a profound change for her. Over the following weeks, she started to provide me with vivid memories of her childhood family home—including occasions when her mother had been desperately ill. She described how her mother had been on a diet to lose weight before being diagnosed with a terminal illness. When she had become really sick, Susan made a pact with the universe that she would match her mother's weight loss as a trade-off for her mother's recuperation. When the pact failed and her mother died, Susan continued to lose weight—perhaps because by then it had become the only thing she felt she had any control over.

It was, in this sense, a strategy to try and manage feelings that were ultimately unmanageable when tragically there was no one available anymore to help her with them.

* * *

But how might we understand Susan's story with regard to chaos and complexity theory? We have seen that Prigogine states that order emerges not in spite of chaos but because of it and that evolution and growth are the inevitable product of open systems slipping into temporary chaos and then reorganising themselves to emerge at a higher level of functioning and complexity. From this I speculate that when Susan was experiencing herself as disintegrating, lost and "falling apart", she was perhaps paving the way for a higher level of order to emerge. In addition, perhaps Susan's separate subpersonalities (the different Susans) were all separate subsystems and not linked together. The Susan (subsystem) that spelt out "h-e-l-p m-e" seemed to have been the part of Susan that had been split off at the time of her mother's death. Perhaps it was the part of her that had needed to scream or cry but seeing as there was nobody around to help her manage these overwhelming emotions at the time, they had become silenced.

In enabling this non-verbal Susan to surface during the session, we were possibly creating the beginnings of its reintegration with the other Susan subsystems. If indeed this analysis is correct, it provided me with a new respect for the need for discomfort or "chaos" in a client. Susan needed to explore and reach out to the other Susan and this caused her much distress during and between therapy sessions. But ultimately this exploration enabled Susan by the end of her therapy to feel she had reached a new level of order and self-coherence.

Patterns and attractors

Even in a non-linear, unpredictable system there is still some sort of order to be found (Baugh, 2010). This order may show itself in the form of patterns. David Ruelle coined the term "strange attractors" to denote the patterns of order within a dynamic open system. These patterns never exactly repeat themselves but they nonetheless display a quality of orderliness (Ruelle, 1993).

I learned that a non-linear dynamical system can have three basic states: stability, bifurcation, and chaos. Prigogine states that systems far from equilibrium (i.e., in chaos) give birth to new structures (Prigogine, 1984). Chaos emerges when the trajectory of a system reaches a threshold of change (bifurcation). The system at this point of change may break down and follow an earlier pattern imprinted into its structure, or alternatively, as a result of its sensitivity to fluctuations in the environment, may break through to a pattern of higher order. I found myself thinking of my clients and how these three basic system-states might be seen to apply to them at different times in their therapeutic work. In looking at breakthrough moments it seems clear I was addressing the threshold of change or the bifurcation state. And yet a client who has been stable but has grown increasingly distressed might slip towards the edge of chaos. This seems to suggest the possibility that such a client might fall back again into an earlier pattern (repetition compulsion) or experience a higher level of organisation.

I created a freehand drawing of a computer simulation to show the pattern created when a system is pulled between two attractors (see Figure 10.1). The system is pulled to each attractor in turn, never following precisely the same route but always staying within the broad parameters of the overall pattern.

This might be seen as a powerful metaphor for how a client can be pulled between different ways of being (or between different

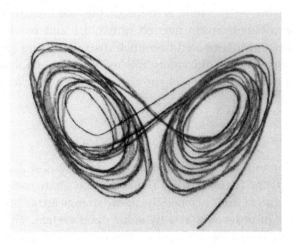

Figure 10.1 Pulled between two attractors.

subpersonalities). For example, the client might be pulled between an unhealthy agenda (such as an addiction to something destructive) and a healthy agenda (the desire to overcome that addiction), which reminds me of my client Stephano.

Stephano's story

Stephano, fifty years old, was a client who was struggling to overcome his addiction to gambling. We did some gestalt "two-chair" work in which he explored his subpersonalities by sitting in various different spots in my practice-room and speaking as the various characters. This revealed that there were two primary subpersonalities in conflict whose contradictory natures were preventing him from overcoming his addiction. Gary Gambler was the name he gave to the part of him that wanted to make lots of money fast (and who believed that gambling was a quick route to this). Sensible Simon was the part that was always telling him to stop gambling and to be more cautious with his money. I imagined Stephano being pulled between these two subpersonalities (or attractors) and the routes taken being not unlike the picture I had drawn.

Later, as Stephano was switching seats between Gary Gambler and Sensible Simon (acting out vehement arguments between the two), he unexpectedly revealed a new character (for whom he sat in a new seat). This character, he said, was Arnold Arbitrator. My own drawing shows the increased complexity that can be created by the introduction of a third attractor (see Figure 10.2). I realise this is

Figure 10.2. Pulled between three attractors.

an over-simplistic way of thinking of Stephano's pull between his subpersonalities but nonetheless it seems a useful way to visually represent the idea. It was interesting to think of Stephano (theoretically at least) as a *system* being pulled in three ways, attempting to achieve a degree of balance whilst also containing much conflict and complexity.

* * *

The Chinese word for crisis (a word that might describe the point at which most clients arrive at therapy, feeling that something about themselves or their lives is falling apart) has two concurrent meanings—crisis and opportunity (Butz, 1997). This is a useful way of looking at the crossroads at which clients frequently find themselves. A breakthrough moment is often experienced as a crisis of intense feeling, but, as we have seen, it can equally provide an opportunity for new insight and, eventually, the arrival of a higher order.

Erik Erikson's theory of human development seems to echo this dichotomy. He presents eight stages of human development where a crisis occurs that needs resolution. Four of these stages are listed as examples: autonomy versus shame/doubt (2–4 years), identity versus role confusion (13–19 years), generativity versus stagnation (40–65) and ego integrity versus despair (65–death). According to Erikson these stages of development are critical, as inherent in all these crisis points is an opportunity for change (Erikson, 1994).

Whether the individual will be able to negotiate this change in a healthy or unhealthy way is dependent on choices, such as Stephano's choice between Gary Gambler and Sensible Stephen. While the crisis is being faced, there is frequently a feeling of chaos and disorganisation and out of this the client may revert to a previous state (regression) or pattern (repetition compulsion). In the most positive case scenarios there is a spontaneous emergence of a new order within the (human) system.

Fractals

The psychologist Terry Marks-Tarlow has suggested that fractals can provide us with a useful metaphor for shedding light on deep mysteries, such as "how we maintain a feeling of continuity and identity despite the myriad changes going on within us" (Marks-Tarlow, 2008). She maintains that different aspects of an individual's self can emerge at different times and across different situations in a similar way to fractals, which are multidimensional and display self-similar detail on multiple levels. To put this another way, she believes the fractal metaphor can be used to illustrate the repetitive dynamics of an individual. For example, a client may show similar elements of their belief system, personality or characteristics at different levels.

Benoit Mandelbrot has been coined the "father of fractal geometry" (Butz, 1997). Mandelbrot used powerful computers to provide a "visual tool for understanding the dimensional consequences" of chaos and complexity theory and self-similarity (Mandelbrot, 1997). A fractal is a mathematical set that typically displays detailed self-similar patterns (which may be exactly the same or nearly the same) at multiple levels. For example, a digital representation of swirls clearly shows the self-similar, repeating patterns described in the definitions of a fractal (see Figure 10.3). It seems that nature is diffused with such patterns. They can be seen, for example, in the branching of a tree, a floret of cauliflower, the pattern of a snowflake, or the bifurcations in a human lung.

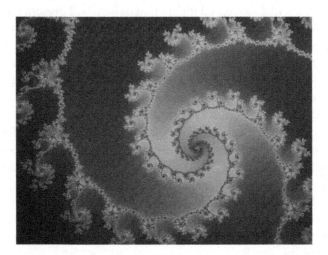

Figure 10.3. Mandelbrot's spirals.

I started to wonder if breakthrough moments could be similar to bifurcations in a non-linear dynamic system and if self-similarity might be displayed in a clients' therapeutic work. To illustrate this possibility, we can consider Gordon.

Gordon's story

Not unlike the self-similarity of a fractal, my client Gordon seemed to present a similarity of response to his life at various different levels. He appeared to have a basic feeling of entitlement and this revealed itself across several aspects of his life. He believed that he was entitled to be supported emotionally and financially by his parents, because he had concluded that many of his difficulties stemmed from the way they had raised him. He also felt he was entitled to be supported by the State, because it was his parents' fault he could not hold down a job. He felt he was entitled to be tolerated and understood by his housemates because his problems were not of his own making. He even felt he was entitled to have more than the usual six sessions of therapy typically allocated by the charitable organisation he was accessing to see me. He depicted himself as the black sheep of his family and took no responsibility whatsoever for why he was seen this way, believing it to be purely a result of their victimisation of him.

There is a widely accepted theory that a client will present the essence of their difficulties right at the beginning of their therapy. Gordon came into my room for the first time angrily proclaiming that he was entitled to be seen promptly by the receptionist at the educational establishment where I was working and infuriated that he had been left waiting while she was on the telephone to someone else. I did not comment on this at the time but held it in mind for future reference. As time went by and Gordon demonstrated his deeply held belief that he was entitled to special or preferential treatment in multiple contexts, I recalled his opening comment about the receptionist. He had demonstrated the same pattern basically at numerous different levels of his life—with the receptionist, with his housemates, with his parents, with the State, and now with me as his therapist. This might be seen as illustrating Marks-Tarlow's idea about the connection between fractals and clients' repetitive patterns across multiple levels.

CHAPTER ELEVEN

The quantum world

Christopher's story

"I think I'm having a nervous breakdown!" These were the first words uttered by Christopher—a smartly dressed student in his early twenties who came to see me for therapy one morning. He volunteered the nub of his difficulty without any prompting: "I'm stuck," he said. "I can't write my college paper and it's *so* important that I do well." Whenever he tried to start writing the essay, he said he would feel sick, panicky, and compelled to stop. He had not had any difficulty completing assignments before. He was so desperate for help that he had now referred himself for therapy.

I felt instinctively that Christopher was an intelligent, conscientious student who had *become* anxious rather than someone who was by nature an anxious individual. I noticed he kept fidgeting in his seat.

"What is the subject of this college essay you have to write?" I asked.

"Quantum physics," he said, tapping the floor nervously with his foot. "What can and cannot be understood about the quantum world."

In addition to working as an integrative arts psychotherapist, I offer an unusual form of intervention whereby a client who is a student can also sign up to receive academic support, which includes psychological assistance. This enables me and the client to work therapeutically on any academic blocks that involve an existential or emotional element. As well as supporting trainee psychotherapists with their dissertations, my work as an academic supervisor has involved supporting students in a wide range of subjects. Sat in this session with Christopher, however, it was the first time I had been required to help a student where I had no knowledge whatsoever of the discipline being studied.

Seeing as I had no entrance-way to even *begin* discussing the lofty subject of quantum physics with him, I suggested to Christopher that he make an art-image of the essay he was having trouble with. This is a suggestion I frequently make to clients who are students. I explained to him that it sometimes helps to approach a subject from a completely new and unexpected angle. Christopher stood up and considered the vast array of objects and materials on the shelves of my practice-room for what seemed like an inordinately long time. Eventually I asked him if there was anything in particular he was looking for. He shook his head and silently continued to study the display, picking up objects and putting them down again. He finally selected a series of baubles, string balls and bits of ribbon, and placed them on the floor between us. I invited him to introduce me to the image he had made (see Figure 11.1).

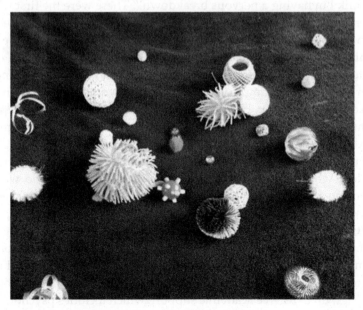

Figure 11.1. Christopher's quantum image.

"This is the world of sub-atomic particles," he said. "Nothing is ever certain in this world."

I felt a jolt of excitement at the image and Christopher's unexpected words.

"You never know what might happen when you get to the tiny quantum world," he continued, "things jump around for no particular reason. *It's completely random.* There is no certainty anymore!"

He began to pick up some of the objects he had assembled and started throwing them up and down in a random manner. I was transfixed. I imagined this quantum world he invoked—far, far smaller even than the world of neurobiology I had been researching. I felt another jolt of excitement at the idea that uncertainty ultimately lies at the heart of this world. Suddenly, I realised I had been so drawn to the image of my client juggling baubles and string balls (and the quantum ideas he was illustrating) that I was not fully attending to him. I was pulled up sharply when he stifled what I thought was a cough but was in fact a *sob*. He continued to throw a few of the objects from hand to hand whilst quietly weeping.

I wondered what was going on for him. Clearly Christopher had had some kind of emotional breakthrough moment but as yet it was not a moment of insight—he was in a state of chaos with no new level of order having yet emerged. Seeing as neither he nor I yet understood what had happened, I felt unsure what to do next. When a therapist is uncertain how to help their client it is often best merely to summarise, clarify or even present back the same words the client has uttered. This way the words can be heard as stated by somebody else, which often enables the client to understand or receive them differently. So I said, "Everything is uncertain and that seems to carry strong emotion for you?"

"That's it!" he said. "Everything is *uncertain!* Heisenberg's Uncertainty Principle. That's it! That's the problem!"

He suddenly seemed like a little boy filled with anxiety, and now I had my first real clue. He was perhaps connecting to an experience from his past—an event that appeared to be linked to uncertainty.

"Were you frightened of feeling uncertain when you were a little boy?" I asked him gently.

A dam had broken now. New tears rolled down his cheeks and he told me in a narrative, punctuated by pauses and sobs, that when he was a little boy he had felt panicked by the idea that he could not be sure about anything.

Christopher's grandfather had died when he was about five. He told me that he vividly remembered he had gone downstairs one night when he couldn't sleep and sat on the bottom step. His mother had sat down beside him and asked what the matter was. He recalled asking her, "if grandad has died, how can I be certain *you* won't die?"

"Well, I'm not ill and I'm not old," his mother had said, "so it's very unlikely I will die for a long time yet. But every living thing does die some day and we can never be quite certain when that will be. Nothing is ever completely certain in this world".

Christopher remembered these words had hit him like a punch in the stomach. He felt claustrophobic and panicky and recalled finding it very difficult to breathe. His brain, he said, just couldn't comprehend. Of course he couldn't comprehend—he was only five years old! It was his first real awareness of his own and others' mortality and he was realising that it was completely uncertain when the inevitable time would come. It seems the shocking realisation of uncertainties in the quantum world had resurrected the childhood part of Christopher that had been so shocked and terrified about the uncertainty of when death might come. At the time he had no way of managing these vast and terrifying existential questions, or the feelings of angst they inspired.

Christopher explained that as a young adult he had turned to what he felt would be the rigorous certainties of science in an attempt to help him manage his overwhelming feelings of uncertainty. If he could try to understand fixed and stable facts about the world, it might reduce the apprehension he felt around death and other mysteries. But now that his scientific education began to focus on the seemingly random, chaotic world of quantum physics, he was discovering that at the very heart of science there was no certainty at all! The very discipline he had turned to in order to calm himself was now stirring up that same panic from his past. Except now it had become the cause of his fears rather than the antidote it had been previously. And this seemed to have tipped him into chaos.

What could I say to this anxious young man that could help him feel able to write his essay? How might I help Christopher recognise that his study of the quantum world had reactivated memories of his five-year-old self? I noticed at this point that it was coming to the end of our session. Christopher was calmer but in some ways none the wiser as to what had just happened. I said to him, somewhat inadequately, "It seems that your research into the strange world of quantum theory has become associated with your childhood feelings about uncertainties in the world. Some of that panic from the past has now transferred itself to the writing of your thesis. We have to finish our session for today but we can pick this up again from this point next week at our next appointment."

In the week leading up to his second session I began avidly reading about the quantum world of Christopher's thesis. Many weeks of sessions followed during which I supported him in an attempt to understand why he had become so upset and stuck in his work. At the same time, my attempt to understand quantum theory enabled me to help him to organise and structure his research ideas around the subject. I wanted to ensure that the little boy part of him that was being re-traumatised by the uncertainty of the quantum world was also being supported and calmed by my presence this time around. I hoped he might be able to develop a new way to think about the subject without becoming frozen with uncertainty. In this way, over several months, Christopher became able to write his thesis and I was introduced to the bizarre world of quantum physics.

* * *

In this chapter I show how my work with Christopher led me to discover the fascinating and puzzling ideas of quantum physics. I will consider how these ideas might be seen to apply to aspects of the arts-based therapeutic relationship, the creative process, and clients' breakthrough moments.

The quantum realm

Reading about quantum physics, I could understand why the shock of these ideas had resurrected Christopher's childhood terror of uncertainty. The findings of quantum physics are shocking for anyone. The Nobel Prize winning Danish physicist Niels Bohr notoriously said "if quantum mechanics hasn't profoundly shocked you, you haven't understood it yet" (Bohr, 1958). As I began to investigate, I quickly experienced unsettling and shocking feelings of my own. Were these feelings a reactive countertransference from Christopher's own feelings or were they pro-active countertransferential feelings of my own?

As I read further I uncovered a new motive for wanting to find out about these ideas. Quite apart from enabling me to help Christopher with his own study, my research into quantum physics suddenly seemed (at least potentially) to be relevant to my own study for this book. The arrival of breakthrough moments seems to be full of weirdness and randomness—much like the events of the quantum realm. Might quantum ideas therefore be able to help me understand what is happening at the time of a breakthrough moment? Could they also perhaps help me understand the role of creativity and the success of using arts media in psychotherapy?

Quantum science emerged at the start of the twentieth century when developing technology enabled physicists for the first time to measure the behaviour of subatomic particles (such as electrons and protons). The physicists were deeply shocked to find that the particles did "not follow the classical laws of physics at all" (Van Lommell, 2010). I had to read and reread this puzzling statement several times.

Richard Dewitt describes three different aspects of quantum theory. First, there are empirical facts resulting from the outcome of experiments with subatomic particles—facts that are "mind bogglingly" surprising but cannot be disputed. Second, there is the mathematical core of quantum theory, which is reliable (and not at all controversial) and describes the motion of submicroscopic objects. And third, there are issues related to the interpretation of quantum theory and what it might mean for our everyday macro-reality—this is an area that is (and has historically always been) fraught with disagreement and controversy (DeWitt, 2010).

Putting the (to me) unfathomable mathematics to one side, I set out to explore some of the empirical facts and interpretations of quantum theory. The arrival of breakthrough moments seemed to be full of randomness, weirdness and uncertainty—much like the events of the quantum world. The lack of determinism perhaps means that human beings can truly make their own free choices and shape their lives.

Up until now I had believed that things moved from one point to another based on cause-and-effect relations—according to Newtonian mechanical laws of motion. But this is not at all how things move in the quantum world. At the quantum level it seems that everything is one dynamic—an interconnected pattern of probability that can include consciousness. This is in contrast to the view of dominant classical physics where everything has a local cause. I was beginning to feel my world was turning upside down. The more I read the more surprised and shocked I felt. It was a radical shift analogous to believing the world was flat and finding out that it was in fact round.

Quantum physicists have shown that the discontinuous movement of subatomic particles is entirely different to movement in the everyday world. In the quantum world things can move in a disjointed way. I began to speculate if there might be a link between this strange quantum behaviour (that does not involve strict determinism) and the suddenness of a breakthrough moment. Breakthrough moments also appear to move in a disjointed way; they appear to jump out of the triangular relationship (client–art–therapist) in a discontinuous way and seem to come suddenly, without having followed a logical step-by-step process. Similarly it is uncertain if some quantum events will happen at all and uncertain when and how they will arise if they do.

Quantum creativity

In the subatomic world, electrons can move in a disjointed or discontinuous way. The excited electron "jumps" (or disappears) from one orbit and reappears in another. There is an uncertainty as to when and where it might jump next. This means that the results of a quantum leap are uncertain. Quantum physicists have discovered that when an electron jumps orbits it does not travel through the intervening space between; rather, the electron is first in one orbit and then in the other. The movement happens in a discontinuous way.

Amit Gotswami suggests a comparison to the human creative process. He argues that the indeterminacy and discontinuity of the electron is akin to the discontinuity of a sudden creative insight—an old pattern of thought dies as a new thought pattern replaces it. Or to put it another way, a window of opportunity is opened for something truly *new* to arrive in a creative moment (Gotswami, 1993). I was excited to read Gotswasmi's idea and felt this could provide me with a way to imagine what might be happening for my clients. The creative act is similarly discontinuous and it feels very much as though a client "jumps" to a new creative insight. It struck me that such a creative insight could perhaps be a breakthrough moment. Ben's breakthrough moment arrived and a new explanation seemingly appeared in his mind's arena. Having previously felt stuck and bewildered by his habitual relationship patterns, Ben suddenly recognised and understood the link between his image of the orangutans and his feelings of clinginess. Could the arrival of this moment of insight be akin to a quantum leap?

The observer effect

In experiments carried out within the subatomic realm, an observer inherently interacts with the system and influences what is observed. Or to put this another way, the very experiments designed by scientists to observe nature at the atomic level partially "created and determined what was seen" (Wolf, 1989). This conclusion was based on the now famous double-slit experiment where a stream of light particles was directed towards a screen. It was irrefutably proven that a single photon of light would go through one of two open slits in the screen in both a particle-like state and a wave-like state simultaneously, and that the state the observer saw depended on what kind of observation was being carried out (Zohar, 1990). The outcome of this experiment showed that a quantum particle at this tiny level is in fact neither a classical particle nor a classical wave but follows its own laws that have similarities to both. Which aspect is detected depends on the kind of question the scientist asks of the system. This has led physicists to assert that there can be no such thing as an objective experiment. We have to see ourselves as part of what we are measuring. As observers, we are aspects of a participatory universe (Wheeler & Zurek, 1983).

It would appear that consciousness affects (and interacts with) all aspects of the subatomic world. Consequently, the classical scientist's desire to be an impartial observer is not something that can ever be achieved. I felt this idea to be deeply significant to me—as a person, therapist, and author/researcher. If an observer's expectations of the results of an experiment (in which they are making every attempt not to influence the situation being observed) nonetheless *still* have an ability to affect the results, surely it must be the case that a therapist (actively seeking to influence and help a client) must affect the conditions of the therapeutic result. Similarly, the client's own desired goals for themselves and the work must also inevitably affect the context and the outcome of the therapy.

The expectations of a client (as well as the expectations of their therapist) affect the client–art–therapist context (the triangular relationship).

A client's expectation that I may be able to help them itself becomes part of the intersubjective matrix within which the therapy is taking place. My client Christopher felt immobilised when he came to see me, but he also had an expectation that I was trying to help him. He was thus able to put his scepticism to one side for long enough to participate in the work (and choose objects from my practice-room shelves). Similarly, my own belief or expectation that a client has the resources and ability to help themselves can also influence their ability to find the therapeutic experience helpful. I had a belief that Christopher had the resources to find a way to overcome his block. I had a belief that Susan contained the resources within her to uncover the different Susans and reveal them to herself. According to the observer effect, these expectations I had for my clients would themselves partially influence the extent to which Christopher and Susan were able to overcome their difficulties. In this sense, two of the participating corners of the triangular relationship are actively influencing the success of the relationship itself, and of the work that takes place within it, whether they desire to do so or not. These therapist and client expectations are also influencing the art-images that are created and the ways they are interpreted.

For example, a client may imbue their chosen art-image with the power of a talisman to help them gain more mastery over their situation. This links directly to Schaverien's concept of the embodied image. My client Susan made the sculpture of Thin Susan that she brought to therapy. She seemed to be hoping, even *expecting*, this image to be of great benefit to her in the work. I believed that Thin Susan could "speak" for herself and that this would be helpful for Susan's development of a sense of feeling more like one person. These expectations of Susan's image were thus also an integral part of the intersubjective matrix in which we found ourselves and were highly likely to influence the outcome of the therapy in accordance with the observer effect.

A psychoanalyst traditionally attempts to provide as much of a "blank screen" as possible in their facial expression in an attempt to observe their client's projections and transference more objectively. The results of quantum experiments would appear to show that this is not possible. If a physicist cannot set up experiments that are entirely objective without affecting what is being observed, then a psychoanalyst surely cannot provide a stance towards their clients that eradicates the impact of their subjective presence—however neutral their facial expression. In fact, an attempted neutral facial expression from the analyst would itself contribute to (and affect) the psychoanalytic relationship and resulting work.

This idea of the participatory observer applies to my own research for this book. It is not possible to provide information that is devoid of my own subjective involvement however much I may aspire to do so. It is not a case of trying to eliminate bias. It is that I am an inseparable, contributory part of what it is that I observe; hence my choice to adopt a heuristic approach. A heuristic methodology requires me to clearly acknowledge my own involvement in all stages of the process. It allows for the fact that I am influencing what I am researching and not trying to achieve an (impossible) objective stance that attempts to eliminate bias.

Wave-particle duality

Classical physics has always maintained that matter consists of particles with simple properties, such as position, movement, mass, and charge (Zohar, 1990). In addition to this, there are waves. One of the most surprising and paradoxical discoveries of the double-slit experiment (which measures subatomic atoms) however is that all the constituents of matter and light are both wave-like and particle-like at the same time. Particles are localised at one point in space and time. When two particles meet they bump into each other and go their separate ways. Waves, on the other hand, are not localised. They can spread out across vast regions of space and time. This duality of matter and light is something entirely different to our Newtonian view of how things work. There is no consensus of agreement as to the implications of these findings for our everyday reality. This lack of agreement helps me feel entitled to entertain my own speculative ideas.

Roger Penrose (2005) believes that quantum mechanics might account for such diverse aspects of human thinking as insight, imagination, understanding, empathy, meaning-making, and free will. All of these aspects of thought are directly applicable to the world of arts-based psychotherapy and to my ever-growing understanding of breakthrough moments. I imagine the particle aspects of my clients' thoughts (and my own) being separate from one another whilst simultaneously the wave aspects might be merging. This is what it feels like to be in the room with a client. My phenomenological experience is frequently that I am actually stepping inside the client's imagination. Perhaps this newly created merged imagination fuels a client's creative process and supports them to arrive at a breakthrough moment.

Superposition and entanglement

Contrary to our experience in the macro-world, the undisputed facts of quantum physics show irrefutably that a submicroscopic entity can exist in a "superposition of two or more allowed states at the same time" until a measurement is made (Orzel, 2010). This strangeness arises because in classical mechanics all things are either waves (which can be superposed) or particles (which cannot). Nothing is ever *both*. Could this idea of superposition or entanglement be applied somehow to the therapy work with my clients?

Karl Pibram suggests that the brain of one individual might be seen to interconnect with something in the world (such as the brain of another individual) through the "language of wave interference" (Pibram, 1993). It seems this could be useful for understanding the relationship between client and therapist. Zohar suggests we can apply the wave-particle duality metaphor to human relationships. This supports my tentative idea that I could perhaps think of each of my clients (and myself as their therapist) as having our own space and time at the particle level, while at the wave level there could be an overlapping, superposition or entanglement of our thoughts and imagination. This would appear to fit with the theory of intersubjectivity (Stolorow & Attwood, 1992). And it certainly fits with my phenomenological experience of "wandering in the forest of ideas" with clients (a phrase coined by Lucy in her therapy). The client and I seem to come up with spontaneous and novel moments of inspiration from this wandering together in the forest. It is as if a creative, alchemical vessel has been formed—out of which new ideas and events arise, including breakthrough moments.

Mysticism

According to Fritjof Capra, the experimental results of modern physics lead us to a view of the world that is "very similar to the views held by mystics of all ages and traditions" (Capra, 1975). What is this view of the mystics? Two basic themes appear in mystics' view of reality—first, that there is a unity and interrelatedness of all phenomena (including consciousness), and second, that the universe has an intrinsically dynamic nature even where an object may appear to be stable or unchanging. These ideas invaded my thoughts and dreams and challenged my conception of what ultimately lies at the heart of reality: that everything is connected to everything else, in a never-ending dynamic dance of energy and influence (that also includes consciousness). I could almost *feel* myself changing as this new belief about the world began to take hold. In addition, I was learning that ultimate reality can never be an object of my own reasoning mind or anyone else's, nor can it ever be adequately described in words; whenever we use words to try and capture it, the concept that lies beyond those words is changed. Reality lies beyond the realm of the senses, and beyond the intellect from which our words and concepts are derived.

Mystics argue that it is only partially possible to ever know ultimate reality and that it can only be achieved via non-intellectual, intuitive experience—often known as a meditative or mystical state. When mystical experiences are expressed in words they are frequently accompanied by myths, symbols, images and paradoxical statements, because what they are attempting to describe is itself ineffable and inexplicable and beyond words. Quantum physicists have no choice but to employ images, metaphors and paradoxical statements to describe the bizarre and incomprehensible world at the quantum level. Clients frequently utilise myths, symbols and paradoxical statements in their therapeutic work to represent something that lies beyond their ordinary experience of the world.

Simon's story

One morning my client Simon was exploring his feelings about being watched. He had told me that an image he had drawn during the session represented a critical eye that was disapproving of him because it perceived he had been involved in sneaky and underhand behaviour (symbolised by his additional drawing of a snake) (see Figure 11.2). I felt Simon was perhaps feeling critical of me for not being able to help him more (and I was criticising myself for the same reason). However, I was experienced enough to recognise the occurrence of countertransferential feelings that arose from my client's view of himself, his world, and his art-image. As he continued his drawing, Simon added some rays of light emanating from the "all seeing eye" and tears began to form in the corners of his own eyes. He experienced an emotional breakthrough moment. His whole being softened and relaxed. Eventually he smiled

Figure 11.2. Simon's snake candle.

and looked at me. I wondered if this new, edited version of his drawing had made it possible for him to open up to the possibility of something beyond himself and beyond mere words (symbolised by the rays of light he had drawn around the eye).

He went on to tell me that the metamorphosis of his image had somehow presented a new experience of feeling that there was something beyond the literal. He explained that something about the eye suddenly felt supportive and compassionate, rather than critical and punitive. He felt it was showing him something beyond words and logic and opening him up to the possibility of a benign and caring energy— a presence that might support instead of judge him. This presence was beyond words and beyond his own artistic creation and it gave him a feeling of compassion, kindness, understanding, and warmth—feelings that he did not experience very often.

* * *

Working with arts media in psychotherapy provides a vehicle for clients to express and experience a reality beyond logic and their intellect. Clients' sand trays, pictures and sculptures frequently reveal a layer of experience that lies beyond words and leads them (and me) with a jolt of recognition to acknowledge something more than just the physical plane. This is the power of working with art. Art is language-less. Its meanings are intuitive and *felt*. Simon demonstrated that his image was able to reveal ineffable mysteries about the universe to him and that this gave him much comfort. Drawing rays of light around the eye seemed to herald a new way of viewing his image and it touched us both deeply.

Petruska Clarkson describes what she calls the transpersonal rela-tionship within the therapeutic relationship. She explains that this aspect of the multilayered therapeutic relationship includes qualities that presently transcend the limits of our understanding. It includes the aspects that are often described as spiritual, soulful, transcendent, numinous, sacred and unknowable (Clarkson, 1995). She also notes that many therapists make mention of an element of "mystery" in their work. Irvin Yalom, for example, refers to "throw-ins" that occur in a client's psychotherapy. These are the indefinable *somethings* that Yalom likens to the extra, unquantifiable *something* his mother used to throw in the pot when cooking her most delicious creations. Yalom believes that why and how therapy works is ultimately a mystery and that this "extra something" cannot be defined or manufactured (Yalom, 2001).

In my own case, the extra "something" I might bring unconsciously to the therapeutic relationship with my clients has undertaken a major shift since I began learning about the quantum world. My dizzying mus-ings about the quantum world seemed to have encouraged a transper-sonal element to enter the therapy. I cannot quite explain it in words, even to myself, but learning about the interconnectedness of everything seems to have provided me with a new way to experience a more spir-itual dimension of life that hitherto had not been accessible. As a result of this new way of viewing the world, I found myself better able to put my ego to one side and increasingly "trust the process!" (McNiff, 1998). Almost immediately I noticed that more breakthrough moments would arrive, as well as more frequent occasions when a client would enter a state of extended deep experiencing. Indeed, at around this time a remarkable session took place with my client Stephen.

Stephen's story (continued)

Whilst I was steeped in unfathomable quantum ideas, Stephen produced a multilevel image of a silhouette with arms reaching for the sky (see Figure 11.3). The image appeared to include a transpersonal dimension for him, as he returned to it many times and each time saw a new and alternative meaning. During one session he held his own arms up to match those of the figure in his image and gestured a silent connection he felt to something above and beyond the everyday. It was

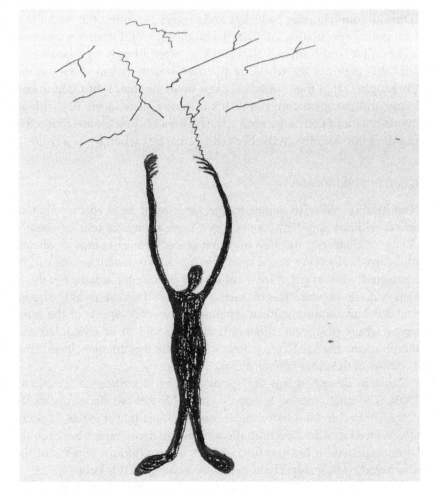

Figure 11.3. Stephen's arms-in-the-air drawing.

as though he connected with a feeling of something *more* than his own separate existence. His face softened and he smiled quietly to himself. His multilayered image had enabled him to connect with a spiritual or transpersonal aspect of his own reality (Clarkson, 1995). Something similar happened when the unexpected ray of sunlight appeared to emerge from my client Christine's image of the hand holding the orb. It was as though something bigger than Christine and myself was invoked in her therapeutic process.

* * *

If this all sounds rather New Age and esoteric, I remind the reader that I am purely speculating and that the quantum world itself is something inexplicable and hard to believe. It was after all only by discovering (and delving into) the world of quantum science (thanks to my client Christopher) that these mystical ideas awoke in me. It brought uncertainty and the cosmic mystery back to centre stage in my life with an intensity I hadn't felt since seeing the endless Mickey Mouse characters receding into infinity on the back of a cereal box when I was a child.

Quantum non-locality

Non-locality refers to action in the absence of local forces—that is, action without apparent connection. Classical physics tells us there is always a chain of causation and that some form of energy is always transferred. However at the quantum level, two distant events can be correlated without *any* transfer of energy or time-lapse between them. Danah Zohar explains this by saying that these two events at the quantum level are simultaneously separate events and aspects of the same larger whole (the wave function): they are said to be entangled and therefore any change to one automatically and instantaneously ensures a change in the other (Zohar, 1990).

Einstein described this as "spooky action at a distance" (Einstein, 1905). The phenomenon is deeply strange but it has been repeatedly demonstrated in laboratory experiments. Given that it exists, I speculate (with a large dose of dramatic and imaginative licence) that it could be an explanation for one (or more) of the mysterious aspects of the arts-based relationship I have been researching for this book.

Within supervision, for example, there are often experiences that might be considered analogous to spooky action at a distance.

A therapist may discuss with a supervisor a particular client in a supervision session and how they might help them with a particular difficulty or block in the therapy work. The therapist will then frequently go to the next session with this client and find the client has somehow resolved the very difficulty that was being discussed within the supervision. On such occasions the therapist has of course done nothing to alter the client's actual situation; they have merely discussed with their supervisor what they planned to do. And yet somehow in the intervening period, the client has resolved the problem. When this phenomenon occurs—and it does surprisingly often—it feels as though something like "spooky action at a distance" has occurred. As it happened, I attended a conference on supervision while writing this chapter, and one of the speakers presented a paper on this very phenomenon and linked it with ideas from the quantum world. Maybe we are all indeed more interconnected than we realise!

* * *

I had stumbled upon the quantum world because of my desire to be more helpful to Christopher. Once I began to read about this weird and uncertain micro-world, I found the ideas affected me deeply. In this chapter I have attempted to speculatively apply a few of these ideas to the subjects of this book. Later, I learned that Christopher had completed his essay on Quantum Physics and achieved a pass. Given the extreme difficulty he found in even approaching the subject at first, he was delighted with this outcome and I was delighted for him.

PART V

THE END OF THE JOURNEY

CHAPTER TWELVE

Stories and dreams

Elias' story (continued)

Elias was a personable young man in his early twenties. He had been struggling with his sense of identity and seeking to find purpose in his life. He had been raised in a strict, religious household and when he first came to see me, he was slowly trying to discard its prescriptive doctrines. At the same time, he was trying to maintain a sense of his core values. The reader may remember Elias' earlier session with the frog and baby. He had worked through many issues since then, although we had still not uncovered what lay behind his complex relationships with women. I first recognised Elias' conflicting attitudes towards women through countertransference. I had found myself feeling seduced by the charm of this young man and yet simultaneously pushed away by him. This gave me a better understanding of his tendency to feel drawn to women but later resent what they wanted from him.

About a year into his therapy Elias began a piece of work that spanned several weeks. Using miniature objects and art materials he started to recount and enact a metaphorical story called The Knight and The Baby (see Figure 12.1).

Figure 12.1. Elias' knight and baby scene.

Week after week, he told (and developed) this story of a knight who sets off on his horse to rescue a missing baby. The baby is imprisoned in a castle far away. As soon as the knight learns of this fact, he feels he must do something. But it occurs to him that he will be ill-equipped to care for the baby once it has been saved. The only person he can find to help him with the task is an old woman. A stray dog runs frantically back and forth along the path, enticing the old woman to join the rescue party. (There is also a blue elephant character, who just seems to be watching the story unfold without taking part in it directly—Elias and I frequently wondered aloud why this character was there.) Neither Elias nor I knew clearly what any of these characters represented or what his story symbolised—my client himself frequently seemed as surprised as I was to discover new developments in the tale he was telling.

On and on, for many months (and across many weeks of therapy), the strange rescue party travelled until finally they arrived at the foot of a mountain. They slowly began their ascent to rescue the baby (see Figure 12.2), although the knight had left them to it and was watching from a distant mountain top (Elias had moved the knight to a chair in the corner of the room). The dog was leading the way and the old woman kept looking down, to keep her attention away from how precarious their journey had become. There was a sheer drop to one side

Figure 12.2. Elias' baby in crib scene.

of the steep ridge. Much to my surprise at this point, Elias began to explain that the old woman was becoming younger and younger as she drew nearer to the baby—the dog was running back and forth between the two of them, as if to encourage their reunion. We were both taken by surprise at these new and unexpected twists and turns to the story.

With tears pouring down his face (and a lump in my own throat), Elias finally declared the baby had been rescued. It was to be cared for by the now-young woman—who it seems turns out to have been the baby's birth-mother. The knight, watching from a nearby mountaintop, was now released from the magic spell that had originally bound him to the role of caring for the baby. Both Elias and I had intuitively felt we should let his story evolve. Indeed, the development of the tale seemed to be outside of his own conscious steering and appeared to have a momentum and meaning all of its own.

* * *

In this chapter I will consider the use of story and dreams in arts-based therapy and the special role they can play in the arrival of breakthrough moments for my clients. I will describe how we eventually came to a possible understanding of the meaning of Elias' story and how this helped him understand that events from his past were affecting his current relationships.

Understanding Elias

When we talked some time later about what might have prompted Elias' story, it emerged that he had experienced an intergenerational saga in his own life that appeared to have unconsciously influenced his knight's tale. Although he was seemingly inventing a story—to all intents and purposes, a piece of imaginary fiction—and adding apparently random new characters and events as he went along, it seems nonetheless he was also slowly telling the story of his own family narrative. We did not make the link until after he had finished his story, but it transpired that Elias' mother had been adopted at birth, and in her thirties (following the death of her adoptive parents) had tried to track down her birth mother. Her birth mother was successfully contacted but chose not to meet with Elias' mother.

We thus uncovered one possible interpretation of Elias' story, although he had been unaware of it consciously at the time. Perhaps the knight symbolised Elias, and maybe he was going on an archetypal hero's journey to reunite the baby (his mother) with the old woman who became young (her birth mother). His mother had been relinquished at birth and perhaps Elias detected a sadness in her as a result. Elias then carried this sadness (and a strong desire to help his mother feel better) into his adult life. He explained to me that as a child he had felt compelled to make up for his mother's despair and these feelings had continued into adulthood. This made him feel as though he ought to be helping her more (and indeed helping others more). Though he felt drawn to help his mother, he simultaneously felt angry and rebellious at the perceived demand upon him, hence the resentment that came along with his protective feelings. He had never put together this feeling and his family history until the mythical story of the knight and baby revealed itself over many weeks of his therapy. It was as if he slowly uncovered (and revealed to himself) through symbol and metaphor his own family secret.

Elias had felt caught in a cycle of faith and doubt. It was as if his knight story was assisting him in explaining the unexplainable. Stories have been used this way traditionally—to capture and communicate otherwise ineffable aspects of our lives through symbol and metaphor. Telling the story seemed to induce a trance-like state in Elias—a period of extended deep experiencing. It also included several breakthrough moments—such as when the woman was reunited with her baby and Elias wept. The blue elephant remains a mystery. Towards the end of his therapy, Elias said he wondered if the elephant perhaps symbolised the spiritual aspect of his story.

Margot Sunderland makes the pertinent point that everyday language is not "the natural language of *feeling* for children". A child's natural language is that of "image and metaphor, as in stories and dreams" (Sunderland, 2000). This fits with my work with Elias. Everyday language was insufficient for him to access his childhood story. Neither could logical or common sense reasoning explain why he had such complex, powerful and ambivalent feelings towards his mother and other females (myself included). But once he let his imagination tell a mythical story about characters and situations with which he could identify, he began to make existential discoveries. This seemed to have an emotional impact for him that was archetypal, metaphorical, and illuminating. It did not lead him to any spontaneous (or ultimate) conclusions, but it enabled him to dwell temporarily in the world of his difficult feelings from a new and less intimidating vantage point. Expressing his feelings through the metaphor of story provided him with helpful distance from them and meant he did not need to fully understand what was troubling him. As Carl Jung has argued, for many clients "an archetypal experience is the only healing factor in therapy" (Jung, 1948).

Elias sensed he was a part of something bigger than himself and that his mother was inextricably linked somehow to his difficult feelings. He had previously struggled for years to make sense of complex feelings towards his mother, girlfriends, female friends, and me—his therapist. This involved feeling a strong pull towards the various women in his life, as well as a simultaneous desire to repel them. Within his sand tray images there would frequently be a baby—usually without a carer and often in a precarious situation, such as the baby that was eaten by a frog in his earlier therapy session (see Chapter Four). Once his story of the knight and the baby began to emerge, this unknown and unexpressed narrative of Elias' became a living experience for us both—one that unfolded in vivid colours as we sat enthralled cross-legged on the floor.

The hero's journey

Working with story in therapy can precipitate breakthrough moments and bring about client change. A story is almost always about the resolution of some kind of tension (Propp, 1968). Stories often feature archetypal characters. Aristotle was perhaps the first to recognise that characters who appear in stories might be identified as types. The knight of Elias' story might be seen as the hero archetype and the dog as the helper. The old woman (who later becomes the young mother of the rescued baby) might be seen as the wise authority figure. The mysterious blue elephant perhaps provides an objective and watchful God's-eye-perspective on events.

It seems the knight represented Elias and his hero's journey of self-discovery and self-development. But how is it that mythical, metaphorical and intergenerational archetypal stories can support clients in their therapeutic work? Erika Helm Meade speaks of the healing power of story in her book *Tell it By Heart* (Helm Meade, 1995). She suggests a number of different ways that stories can support an individual. For example, a story has the ability to arouse strong emotions and we tend to heal best when we are powerfully engaged in something. When genuine emotion comes to the surface, a person's psyche grows ripe for change. Elias' story was accompanied by strong emotion—sadness, anger, uncertainty, shame, and guilt—and perhaps this created the conditions whereby his psyche was "ripe for change".

Another key aspect to the healing power of story, according to Meade, is identification. Discovering and identifying a mythical character who shares our pain has the ability to decrease our feelings of shame and isolation. Elias created his own character—the knight, and this character shared many aspects of his own predicament. As Meade suggests, it may be that identifying with this knight character served to decrease Elias' own sense of shame and isolation. Additionally, as he was creating this story within the therapeutic relationship, his sense of feeling *alone* was also reduced.

Elias had the support and companionship of the dog in his story and the detached observance of the blue elephant. He said that both characters helped and comforted him in his pain. Meade says this is another example of the healing power of story—the internalisation of wise, helpful or comforting figures. She suggests that stories allow us to model alternative attitudes or stances and forge new paths to help us cope with hardships. By telling his story, Elias found a way to release the knight character from taking care of the baby. This knight left the other characters to continue their mission whilst watching on from a nearby mountain. This perhaps symbolised Elias' beginning to gain a more objective stance about the intergenerational story of his mother's sadness at having been abandoned as a baby.

Cheryl Neill explains the power of stories by saying that they are "mirrors in which we see facets of ourselves" (Neill, 1997). This might apply to stories we tell or stories we read (or hear)—such as fables, myths, and fairy tales. Neill says that stories, like our dreams, are filled with "symbolic images where different aspects of the psyche are highlighted". She believes our subconscious may recognise these symbols in some way even when our conscious mind does not. "The unconscious mind is very difficult to reach by rational argument alone," she argues (ibid.). Certainly this seemed to be the case with Elias. He had not even realised his mother's adoption could be relevant (let alone pivotal) to his complex feelings towards her and other women in his life. In telling his knight's tale, he began to teach his conscious mind the things he did not previously know he knew.

Bruno Bettelheim suggests that the imagery of fairy tales helps children "achieve a more mature consciousness to civilise the chaotic pressures of their unconscious" (Bettelheim, 1975). Archetypal stories and fairy tales often enable children and adults to recognise their shadow aspects and find new ways to acknowledge, make sense of, and begin to integrate them into their identity. Clients like Elias come to therapy with fragments of stories—excerpts and secrets that make up their personal narratives. One way a client can change is by changing the sort of stories they tell themselves and others about who they are (or who they believe themselves to be). Jung recognised that every human being has a personal story to tell. He suggested a "complex" can develop when a particular story is rejected or denied by a person. He believed that only in discovery (and rediscovery) of their stories could a client be healed.

In my own experience, stories that are told or created in arts-based therapy almost always lead to some sort of breakthrough moment and periods of extended deep experiencing for the client involved. The story also holds many embodied images that can be explored (such as the knight, elephant, baby and old/young woman of Elias' story).

Story and the brain

Louis Cozolino speaks of the importance of providing a specific kind of enriched environment in therapy. Such an environment is designed to "enhance the growth of neurones and the integration of neural networks" (Cozolino, 2002). Interventions (and approaches) can be of any theoretical (or practical) orientation but their success depends on the degree to which they are able to foster neural growth and integration. One of the ways Cozolino suggests a client might achieve new neural growth and integration is from "gaining new information and experiences across the domains of cognition, emotion, sensation and behaviour". For example, my client Elias created a story that moved between new ways of thinking, feeling, and sensing his body. This was achieved as he enacted the persona of each of the different characters in the story setting off to rescue the baby. The story included conscious and unconscious aspects of Elias' family history and his narrative took on many different twists, obstacles, and unexpected events. As the story unfolded, different aspects of his intergenerational story emerged and provided him with new information from his unconscious, enabling him to have new experiences that spanned the different domains.

The more a client visits these different areas of experience in their therapy, Cozolino believes, the greater the opportunity for integration of different aspects of their experience (across differing domains). Elias visited many different aspects, across a number of differing domains, in telling his story. According to Cozolino, this is likely to have supported the integration of multiple neural pathways for him. Cozolino recommends the "establishment of a safe and trusting relationship with empathic attunement" in order to maximise a client's potential to achieve new neural integration. In Elias' case, the inclusion of the arts in this triangular relationship (client–art–therapist) provided an additional layer of the "safe and trusting relationship" for him. The arts-based story he told provided an opportunity for Elias to visit difficult feelings and aspects of his family history that he had been denying for years. It also gave him some additional safety in the form of distance— enabled by the use of metaphor and symbolism within his story.

For Elias, telling a story seems to have helped him activate neural networks that were previously inhibited. These networks could only become available for inclusion into conscious processing through the telling of his story (Siegel, 1999). In particular, the story helped him navigate between his thoughts and feelings to establish new connections between the two (thus establishing some new left-right brain integration). The knight was able to watch from a nearby mountaintop as the old woman rescued the baby, which helped Elias to recognise that, in his own situation, looking after the baby was not his duty and responsibility but that of his mother's birth mother, who for unknown reasons was not able to look after her own child.

Elias' mother, it seems, had not found a way to work through the multiple losses she had experienced in her life, and these unintegrated and unprocessed feelings appeared to have been partly absorbed by Elias. He was now working through them in his own therapy so they could be integrated into his personal story. Along the way, Elias arrived at many breakthrough moments and was involved in extended deep experiencing throughout. He also utilised many embodied images, which served as a catalyst to his experience. None of this led him directly to finding a sense of purpose and identity, but provided the foundations for the integration of his previously lost and inexplicable feelings.

Dreams

Dreams are stories too, albeit stories that frequently involve surreal and confounding elements—they come from the depths of our subconscious. Take for example, a powerful dream experienced by my client Clive.

Clive's story

Clive first came for therapy when he was in his early seventies. He was struggling with retirement having left behind a fascinating and challenging job as the managing director of a global engineering firm. He had been pursuing various leisure activities in an attempt to fill the gap in his life, but no matter what he did he felt that nothing was as fulfilling as the career he had pursued since he was twenty-three. Towards the end of his first therapy session Clive told me he had had a vivid dream the previous night. I suggested that he recall the dream in the present tense as if he were experiencing it now.

"I am looking out to sea," he said. "My watch has fallen onto a breakwater that is covered in seaweed, mud, and water. I am thinking I can easily reach it but the more I stretch my arm out to collect it, the more the watch seems to move just out of my reach. Every time I almost grab hold of it, I feel it slipping further away until it's more and more submerged beneath the water. I have to give up—I have lost my watch!" Clive further explained that he had realised at that moment—still within the dream—that his watch was in fact safely on the bedside table and he had not lost it at all.

I asked Clive to speak as if he were the watch in his dream. He seemed to accept the strange invitation without difficulty. He closed his eyes and said:

> "I am Clive's watch. I am floating out to sea and yet I am simultaneously lying on his bedside table. Clive is desperately trying to hold on to me and I keep slipping through his fingers. I am all tangled up in seaweed and mud and submerging under the water and I am going out along the breakwater, further and further away from him ..."

As he completed this final sentence, Clive seemed to arrive at the edge of a breakthrough moment. He suddenly opened his eyes and looked across at me.

"That's it!" he said triumphantly. "It's not my watch that is slipping away from me. My watch is safely on the bedside table! It is time that is slipping away. I am losing time!"

I met his gaze and softly said back to him, "You can feel that time is slipping away from you".

Although this revelation was in some sense a cliché, it was nonetheless a profound realisation for Clive and suffused with deep feeling. A breakthrough moment had occurred that led to a deep connection between us; we had held each other's gaze and were full of emotion. We each felt a sense of awe too—at how apt his dream had been in expressing Clive's unacknowledged and unexpressed feelings about his life situation.

* * *

Carl Jung wrote that a dream "is the theatre where the dreamer is at once scene, actor, prompter, stage manager, author, audience and critic" (Jung, 1948). Dreams can be useful in therapy because they include conscious and unconscious elements in a similar way to stories. Clients frequently bring their dreams to therapy and often they can viscerally recreate the feel of such dreams in the present, as Clive did. Dreams often seem to provide the possibility for breakthrough moments and heightened awareness, as they tend to remain highly charged long after the dreamer has awoken. This makes dream material emotionally significant to a client even when frequently the content of the dream appears surreal and bewildering.

Jung believed that dreams contain "ineluctable truths, philosophical pronouncements, wild fantasies, memories, plans, irrational experiences and even telepathic visions" (ibid.). He suggested there are two basic ways to approach the analysis of a dream. In the objective approach, one considers that every character that appears in the dream refers to a real person in the dreamer's waking life. In the subjective approach, every character in the dream represents an unacknowledged aspect of the dreamer themselves.

Gestalt therapists extend this subjective approach to include inanimate objects and dream scenery (such as the seaweed in Clive's dream) as these too might represent aspects of the dreamer. The gestalt approach also suggests asking a client to speak as if they are the various different characters (or parts) of their dream, just as I suggested Clive might try to speak as the watch. This is to see whether free association around the inanimate objects (or landscapes) in the dream might prompt a client to express something that then resonates deeply and gets them closer to an understanding of the dream's meaning. This further illustrates why dreams are so powerful to work with in therapy and how they can frequently lead clients to a breakthrough moment.

In the case of arts-based psychotherapy, a client's dream is unique in that it is an example of an art-image that a client inadvertently (and unconsciously) creates outside the therapy room. The client may later enact the dream or create a physical image to bring it to life, but the dream itself has already served them with an image that is often accompanied by deep emotion and feelings of significance. In this sense, a client who arrives with a vivid dream they have had is a client who arrives with an art-image their unconscious has already prepared for psychotherapeutic work.

There is a lovely description of the power of dreams in Helen McLean's *The Dream Catcher's Handbook* (2001). Mclean suggests that during sleep, the mind relaxes and consciousness—our "window on the world"—closes its shutters. While our conscious mind rests, the other areas of the mind are given free rein. Worries, desires, hopes and fears do not disappear when we are asleep, Mclean says. They have the chance to bubble up to the surface and together with mundane details from everyday life become woven into a "weird and wonderful tapestry" that is our emotional and creative core. Our conscious mind (with its critical censoring filter) is absent during sleep and this gives it the ability to reach the very essence of a dilemma without being shut down or denied. This means that dreams frequently provide an authenticity and integrity that is deep and profound. Without the filter of the rational, conscious mind, our dream stories can be difficult to decipher but they contain "vital elements of truth and creativity" rarely available to us in our waking lives (ibid.).

Clive's dream contained his deep concern that meaningful life (and perhaps even life itself) was evading him. This fear seems to have been incorporated within the dream alongside his very real but irrational concern that he had lost his watch. The important thing for Clive about speaking as if he were the watch was that it enabled him to find a way to tell himself what the meaning of the dream was. It was not up to me (his therapist) to analyse or interpret this dream. My role was to enable him to find out what it meant *to him* and to be with him in the realisation of how he felt. Once he had gained the understanding, the task of processing these existential fears could begin to be integrated into Clive's conscious life.

Clients frequently tell me about recurring dreams they may have had over several months or even years. My client June, the reader may remember, had the same nightmare (about coffins in a graveyard) for many years. It is as if the unconscious mind in these cases is giving the dreamer a coded message of great importance and presenting it repeatedly (as well as in myriad variations) so the dreamer will pay attention and not ignore it. Such dreams can have the quality of nightmares and the dreamer will often wake up with a start.

Working therapeutically with clients' dreams frequently precipitates breakthrough moments and extended deep experiencing. Images from within a dream—such as Clive's watch—can become embodied images and provide a catalyst for change. As we have seen from Cozolino's discussion of neurobiology, it may also be that dreams and stories serve to support the integration of new neural pathways and foster integration.

CHAPTER THIRTEEN

Conclusion

Ali's story (continued)

There are many different ways for a client to end therapy. Some endings are planned in advance, others are more spontaneous. But however an ending occurs, it is individual to a particular client and the work they have explored. In general, we try to work with the ending in mind for around five to six sessions. During these sessions, the client and I will recall pivotal moments that have occurred along the way and look back at any images that have been created. On completing their therapy, ideally the client will leave with a new way of viewing themselves (or their issues) that can be practically incorporated into their everyday lives. There will hopefully be the potential for further change to take place in the future.

As my client Ali was approaching the end of her therapy, we discussed what she wished to do with her drawing of Eating Disorder Ali (that had been kept safely in my practice-room) (see Chapter Six, Figure 6.1). After much deliberation, Ali decided to create a ritual in which she would burn the image. The ritual was scheduled to take place five weeks before her final session. When the day in question arrived, she carefully and ceremoniously tore her drawing of Eating Disorder

Ali into tiny pieces. Then she placed these pieces in the sand tray, clearing an area of sand where the fire would take place (Figure 13.1). To ensure our safety, the pieces would be kept small and within the confines of a metal candle holder as they burned. Everything was ready for the ritual.

Ali sat staring at the torn pieces of Eating Disorder Ali. Was she going to be able to set fire to her image as planned? Could she really destroy this drawing that had served as a symbolic representation of part of her former self? Now the appointed day had arrived, she appeared less sure. The candle flame flickered. Its crackle reminded me of how Ali had described her stomach forever rumbling with hunger during the years she had deprived herself of food. I also found myself remembering the grumbling gremlin that had so shockingly appeared from within her image (when viewed upside down).

After about fifteen minutes of silent contemplation, Ali picked up one of the torn pieces of paper. Demonstrating how difficult the task clearly was for her, she slowly placed the first piece onto the candle flame. The fire leapt at this new type of fuel and together we watched as the first fragment of Eating Disorder Ali burned to ash. The ritual felt all the more remarkable as my practice-room was such an unusual

Figure 13.1. Ali's ritual.

place to be watching a fire. One by one, in an equally considered way, she proceeded to place each of the remaining torn pieces of her image onto the burning candle. The atmosphere in the room felt deeply reflective. The only noise was the gentle sound of the flame. The air smelled of smoke and my mind filled with recollections of Ali's previous therapy sessions. I sensed that she too was considering memories of the many weeks of deep, imaginative work that had led her to this powerful ritual. I wondered quite how the ritual would unfold. Would Ali say anything? Would she need or expect me to say anything? Perhaps surprisingly, she continued to burn the remaining pieces of her drawing without saying a word. I took my cue from her and remained silent.

The image of Eating Disorder Ali had served my client well throughout the previous months of therapy, as well as causing her much distress. Now it was time for her to move on. I understood this was painful for Ali but I hoped it would also be a relief for her to see such a destructive and challenging part of herself destroyed. She appeared to be enacting funereal behaviour with repetitive, ceremonial hand movements as she placed each piece of her drawing onto the flame. It was extremely moving to witness my brave client physically destroy an art-image that had come from her subconscious to teach her something. But having consciously explored and learned so many of its profound lessons, it was time now for the image to be burned to ashes.

* * *

The end of a client's therapy is a significant and often unsettling event—and not just for the client, but for the therapist too. In this concluding chapter, I will return to the key questions raised at the outset of my investigation and attempt to provide some final answers: What are breakthrough moments? What causes them? What is it about arts-based therapy that increases the potential for them to arise? And can they bring about lasting change? Along the way I will describe some poignant endings to the personal stories of clients presented in this book.

What is a Breakthrough Moment?

The reader should have a good idea by now of what I mean by a breakthrough moment. It is a pivotal moment that occurs within the therapy session in which a client has a sudden flash of insight and is able to understand or emotionally experience themselves (or their situation) in a striking new way. Such a moment frequently feels rewarding or pleasurable for the client and is usually accompanied by feelings of deep, wide-ranging emotion. The flow of a client's internal thoughts is halted and time becomes altered or distorted. When recalled by the client later, breakthrough moments are described as having had a sparkling and numinous quality. The experience is compared to a "golden elephant" having been revealed in the room—bringing with it an overwhelming sensation of awe and reverence, combined with a dramatically new way of looking at things. These moments frequently encourage a profound connection between client and therapist that is physically, emotionally and implicitly shared: a subjectively lived *happening*; a pure moment of present-ness. A breakthrough moment is irreversible, and after its arrival nothing in the therapy is ever quite the same again.

The astute reader will have noticed that the individual breakthrough moments described in this book have not been uniform in nature. In the following section, I have identified some of the different categories of breakthrough moments that might occur for a client. The reader should keep in mind it is not an exhaustive list—there may be more categories to discover, and these categories will not be mutually exclusive. One or more may be simultaneously present in a given breakthrough moment. It should also be remembered that breakthrough moments (regardless of which category or categories they involve) can vary in intensity.

Cognitive Breakthrough Moment

In a cognitive breakthrough moment, something new is learned by the client and they are flooded with satisfaction, relief and sometimes shock as a new way of configuring previous thoughts, ideas or understandings suddenly arrives. An example of a cognitive breakthrough might be my client Guy, who selected the Grim Reaper image. This image led Guy to a breakthrough moment in which he cognised for the first time that the shadow of his father's terminal illness had hung over his childhood and left him feeling too guilty to be happy.

Emotional Breakthrough Moment

In an emotional breakthrough moment, a client experiences a sudden rush of feeling or a dramatic change in their emotional state that is frequently expressed through tears; for example, my client Amy, who burst into tears when she realised her fear of having no curtains was linked to the fact she had been spied on by her mother's boyfriend. A client's emotional breakthrough can sometimes be precipitated by the therapist's own tears (a particular form of non-verbal self-disclosure): the therapist may be moved by their client's story and/or the art-image(s) they have created, as was the case with my tearful reaction to Henry's image of a little boy lost in the desert.

Laughter is another change in emotional state that has the power to trigger a breakthrough. In a humorous emotional breakthrough moment, shared laughter between therapist and client leads to a deep connection that heralds the breakthrough. An example might be Elias and his image of the baby-eating frog, or my own experience as a client—struggling to carry my red bicycle up the spiral staircase and ultimately bursting into laughter (with my therapist) at the futility of my imaginary task.

Relational Breakthrough Moment

In a relational breakthrough moment, a client and therapist meet in a dramatic moment of deep connection, similar to the "I–Thou" moment described by Martin Buber and Daniel Stern's Moment of Meeting. An example might be my client Ben. We locked eyes and connected in a profound way following his selection of (and extended deep experience with) the orangutan postcard.

Behavioural Breakthrough Moment

In a behavioural breakthrough moment, a client suddenly acts in a dramatically differently way than previously, and this shift in behaviour precipitates the breakthrough moment. An example might be when Martha suddenly sat up during her re-enactment of giving birth—it was this shift in her physicality that triggered a breakthrough.

Transpersonal Breakthrough Moment

In a transpersonal breakthrough moment, a client achieves a new layer of meaning, purpose or recognition that transcends their own plight or individuality and includes a sudden awareness of (or wonderment at) the bigger, spiritual picture. An example might be when the ray of sunlight was suddenly reflected under the orb of Christine's image, seeming to be the answer to her question, "is there *anything* that can help me?"

Artistic Breakthrough Moment

In an artistic breakthrough moment, it is the art medium itself that precipitates the breakthrough. My client Dave, who had felt immobilised and stuck, was suddenly able to speak in response to what his art-image (the piece of rope) was suggesting. Also, we can consider my client June, whose image of a graveyard led her to a profound awakening.

Synchronistic Breakthrough Moment

In a synchronistic breakthrough moment, the client achieves a breakthrough because of an accidental occurrence or coincidental event in the practice-room. For example, my client Betty slammed a plastic spider into the sand tray to depict her father's violent eruption of anger at the "dinner table". This inadvertently knocked over the table while the figures remained seated, in a synchronistic reconstruction of how the family would ignore her father's outbursts and carry on eating dinner.

Any combination of these categories may be present within the one breakthrough moment. For example, the breakthrough that arose for Ben with his orangutan image was first a sudden rush of emotion that he did not understand (emotional breakthrough). Then he made a connection between the influence of his historic, clingy relationship with his mother and his current relationship with his girlfriend (cognitive breakthrough) and then this brought with it an "I–Thou" moment of deep connection with me, his therapist (relational breakthrough).

Amy's story (continued)

Approximately six sessions before the end of my client Amy's therapy, she created a plasticine blob. This was intended to represent her mother's boyfriend when Amy had been a teenager (the man who had spied on her from a peephole in the attic). Having created her image of the man, I asked Amy where she now wanted to put "him". I imagined she might wish to bury him in the sand tray or toss him in the rubbish bin; maybe even throw him out of the window. But she chose to banish him to the corner of the room. I found myself concerned that the memory of this man could still be influencing her in many ways—particularly when he (in the form of a blob) was still sat in the corner of the practice-room and still watching her. I asked Amy if there was anything she wished to say or do to the plasticine blob. My thinking, in gestalt terms, was that there was clearly much unfinished business for Amy around this trauma. She seemed hesitant at my suggestion. The room was pregnant with possibility and heightened drama.

Amy looked pale and I guessed she might be feeling nauseous. I was surprised to find I felt desperate to get up and move around. This must have been countertransference, because as I had this thought, something seemed to rise up in Amy. She leapt up and towered over the plasticine blob in the corner of the room. It was as though her whole being was taken over with an urge that was outside of her control. She proceeded to stamp her feet furiously and flatten the blob whilst screaming and shouting. I sat and watched with (what I hoped was) an outward appearance of calm. I was in fact greatly affected by the suddenness and violence of her actions as she jumped up and down like a woman possessed. After she had finished stamping on the blob she screamed with unchecked rage for a moment, and then fell silent. It was clear I had witnessed something transformative take place. Towards the end of the session, when her rage had abated, I wrapped the flattened blob in a tissue. I said that in Amy's next session we would decide what to do with it—perhaps place it in the bin or bury it. My thought was that we needed to symbolically dispose of the image, because it still represented (and embodied) the horror of her past experience. Amy told me the following week that after the session she had stood beside a nearby stream and imagined the blob floating away out of her life.

To consider Amy's breakthrough moment using my own system of categories, it would seem that the first thing that occurred for her was a change in behaviour, accompanied by anger and tears (a behavioural breakthrough plus an emotional breakthrough). It felt like I was witnessing an outpouring of "grief-rage", as mentioned by my tutor Sue Fish during my training at the Institute for Arts in Therapy and Education (1999). As I sat watching the drama unfold, I was reminded of something Robert Akeret recounted was said to him during a supervision session with Eric Fromm: "we never *cure* anyone, Dr. Akeret … We just stand by and cheer whilst they cure *themselves*" (Akeret, 1995). I wanted to cheer as Amy stamped up and down on her plasticine blob. I was delighted she had found such an imaginative and emotional way to stamp on her own memories of this abusive man from her past.

I spoke to Amy three years after her therapy had finished and she told me that the breakthrough of jumping on the plasticine blob was the pivotal moment of her entire work. When I had first asked what she wished to do with the blob, she said she could vaguely remember thinking, "I don't want *anything* to do with him". But then a new feeling had overwhelmed her—a sudden fury and an "urge to annihilate him from my life". She told me that she now felt as if all the intervening years of frustration and anger had become channelled into that violent, explosive moment. I was astonished and moved at how clearly she could still describe the detail of what had taken place. It seems that this peak moment of her therapeutic work had made its way into the very fabric of her being.

What triggers a Breakthrough Moment?

Can we draw any conclusions about what triggers a breakthrough moment for a client? In my own opinion a great many different things contribute to the arrival of such a moment: the use of arts media, the client's mood (or frame of mind), a therapist's interventions and demeanour, arbitrary or synchronistic events (the weather, something randomly falling off a shelf). Any one of these things alone or in combination can trigger the breakthrough moment. In the case of my client Martin, his long-anticipated breakthrough finally arrived when he hastily selected two objects to describe his relationship with his mother.

Martin's story (continued)

Martin had been attending weekly therapy sessions for over a year now, during which time he had prolifically produced art-images that almost always contained claws somewhere in the picture. This long phase of his work seemed to be "moving [the therapy] along" (to use Stern's terminology) and we had no real understanding about what the claws in his images signified (although a few clues had recently suggested that anger might be involved).

It had always seemed important not to rush Martin and to allow his anger to remain contained within the metaphor of the claws until such a time as it revealed itself organically. However, Martin told me unexpectedly one day that he would have to end his course of therapy prematurely. His employer had relocated him to the north of England and travelling back for weekly therapy sessions was not going to be possible. I hoped having limited remaining time wouldn't prevent Martin from uncovering the true meaning of his claws; perhaps the meaning of the claws would be revealed precisely *because* his therapy was coming to an end. A client will often suddenly say something at the end of a session (or at the end of their therapy) that they have felt unable to say in the preceding time. This common phenomenon in therapy is known as the door handle effect, which has always reminded me of Peter Falk's Columbo from the 1970s TV series of the same name. Colombo, an unassuming detective, would frequently be about to leave the room having finished his questioning of a suspect when, with one hand on the door handle, he would turn back and say, "just one more thing"—the one more thing being some bombshell of skilled deduction.

The presence of claws in Martin's images seemed to have been leading us both to a moment in which they would finally reveal what they had been representing for him. One day, close to the end of his therapy, when he was using sand tray objects to describe his relationship with his mother, a strange thing occurred. Up until that point Martin had presented his childhood relationship with his mother as not exactly idyllic but not a cause of major anguish. But now, as he struggled to find words to describe it, he decided to show me rather than tell me what it felt like being around his mother when he was a child. With minimum apparent thought, he casually picked up two plastic objects from the practice-room shelves—a two-headed beast and a scorpion. After a few moments of hesitation, he put the beast on top of the scorpion (see Figure 13.2). He sat back on the floor cushion and studied the image he had made. He appeared to be in a trance-like state of extended deep experiencing. I found myself imagining this macabre, hybrid-beast as the mother he had turned to for comfort as a little boy. The thought filled me with new compassion for him.

It had not gone unnoticed by either of us that claws once again featured in this new image Martin had created. Something new however was that these claws featured in an image that was specifically intended to represent his relationship with his mother. After a while, Martin himself commented on the fact that there were claws in the new image. And

Figure 13.2. Martin's two-headed monster.

then suddenly he said, "my mother was like two people—one kind and one unkind". We were both spellbound as these words hung in the air.

What Martin thought he knew about his mother had reconfigured itself in a powerful breakthrough moment. He suddenly felt great anger towards her. He spoke of what he now recognised to be "the sting in her tail" (represented by the scorpion). He told me that his mother would pinch him to make him cry when he was a young boy.

"It seems the claws in your drawings have been holding the unspoken memory that your mother was sometimes unkind to you," I said. "And perhaps they also represent the anger you felt at being treated so badly." Martin became overwhelmed with emotion.

* * *

So what was it that finally broke the dam and triggered Martin's breakthrough moment? It seems that the premature ending of his planned therapy played a role, in that it may have accelerated the process. His art-image also clearly played a role—the two-headed beast and scorpion that he had seemingly absentmindedly created to symbolise his relationship with his mother. Perhaps the fact that his image this time was three-dimensional helped him to make a new neural connection. The "sloppiness" of improvisation and the importance of playfulness are identified by Stern as critical conditions for peak moments to occur in a client's therapy. It is my belief that a use of arts media makes it more likely that such sloppiness will occur and thus increases the opportunity for breakthrough moments to arise.

How do arts media encourage Breakthrough Moments?

The central argument of this book is that the use of arts media in a therapeutic relationship provides an increased opportunity for clients to achieve breakthrough moments. It is not the arts media in isolation that cause breakthrough moments, although we have seen examples where this was almost the case. Rather, the arts media expand the scope (and focus) of the therapeutic relationship, creating a triangular relationship (between client–art–therapist). I have argued that it is the chameleon-like ability of this triangular relationship to shift and tilt on many axes (from client–art to client–therapist) that offers a key explanation as to why arts-based therapies are so conducive to bringing about breakthrough moments.

There are a number of explanations for why the use of arts media can help facilitate breakthrough moments for a client. Art is a unique language to begin with, capable of making the hidden visible. We have seen many instances where a client has been unable to speak about something but is able to make a compelling art-image to "speak" about it instead. Clients are often held in trance-like periods of extended deep experiencing by the art-images they create—as if they intuitively know there is a secret message encoded within, waiting to be revealed. They are frequently able to develop skills of self-observation and self-analysis from viewing and considering their own art-images. Recurring symbols may appear (such as Martin's claws) and this can help a client make unconscious (and suppressed) material available to their conscious mind. In addition to all this, it is a relaxing activity for the client to make art, activating both hemispheres of their brain, decreasing anxiety and stress, and increasing focus. This can be a particularly conducive state for unconscious truths to flow unrestricted as the client plays and improvises with objects, drama, and art materials. The creative act can foster integration of their cognitive, emotional and sensory processes.

In any form of therapy a client must feel safe and able to trust their therapist. Preferably they will experience the therapist as warm, empathically attuned, flexible, receptive, and open to possibilities. I have argued that with arts-based therapies, these qualities of attunement, flexibility and receptivity must also be extended to the art-image, as well as to the client. Art-images can trigger breakthrough moments for a client because they are able to contain, conceal, reveal and support the expression (and exploration) of emotion. They can help a client gain insight, understand behavioural patterns, improve relationships, gain a stronger sense of self, precipitate change, practise new ways of relating, and manage difficult situations. The use of arts media can lead a client to breakthrough moments and instigate the beginnings of desired change.

My study of neurobiology has provided me with additional ideas as to how the use of arts media might support the arrival of breakthrough moments for my clients. Working with arts media gives a client the opportunity to work with deeper emotions in the form of symbolic images and these are predominantly held within the right hemisphere of the brain. We have seen that Bessel van der Kolk's research shows that the the Broca's area (one of the language centres of the brain) shuts down during trauma and also when an individual is thinking about (or reliving) past traumatic experiences. This means that for a client who has experienced trauma, working with images—symbols and metaphor, spontaneous improvisation, and unconscious play—provides them with an opportunity to bypass the language area of their brain and work directly and therapeutically on the hidden unconscious feelings that may be too difficult to acknowledge or address directly.

My client Betty, for example, had experienced decades of trauma and had no words for her experience. She had been unable to access her pain and was unable to begin the task of reintegrating the splintered pieces of her fractured memories—*until* she began creating the mask of the Vigilant Cockerel. We have seen how aspects of a client's trauma can become "locked" (with inaccessible feelings of terror, pain, and shame) and that working with arts media often helps the client access these feelings in a meaningful way without words—through the power of the image. This can facilitate the reintegration of previously split-off neural pathways.

* * *

In preparing this book for publication, I had the valuable opportunity of interviewing many of the clients whose stories feature within its pages. I wanted to see how they remembered the pivotal moments of their own therapeutic experience and how much they considered the various uses of arts media to have contributed to the work. I asked each of them three simple questions: What part of your therapy stood out the most? Have you experienced any significant changes in your life since the therapy finished? What role did the use of arts media play in your therapeutic process?

All of the clients I interviewed said that they felt their most significant moments could not have taken place if arts media had not been included in the therapy. My client Ali said, for example, that working with art materials had been "absolutely key" and "the way in" for her. "I would have had a very different experience with just *speaking*," she told me. My client Amy recalled that when she first entered the practice-room she had thought cynically, "Oh no! What's this nonsense? I don't need pipe cleaners and little figures to work out what's wrong with me!" But she went on to say, "How wrong I was! In the end, I found it hugely helpful. It was a massive event in my life to have experienced arts-based psychotherapy and I now recommend it to people I meet through my work".

My client Elias said that working with the sand tray had enabled him to visit feelings that felt "split off". He told me that his fable of the knight and the baby had been so important and that at no point in the course of telling it did he feel the need to know exactly what the story symbolised. He feels now that it was important we did not try to make complete sense of the story until the end. It was a childlike fairy tale that we simply allowed to play out. Elias learned firsthand the need to trust the process and to let the story tell *him* what it was about.

My client Susan explained that she had previously tried many types of counselling. She had "talked around in circles and danced a stupid dance" for years and not discovered there were other Susans. For the therapy to have successfully brought her to this realisation, she believed, it was crucial that there had been a visual element—something beyond words. Indeed, this appears to be a critical element in most of my clients' testimonies (and another key to understanding why breakthrough moments occur more frequently in arts-based therapies): art is a wordless language, rich with untranslatable meaning. It can be seductive, provocative and emotionally impactful, but it has the power to do all these things *without* any linguistic content or fixed definition. Susan had been "talking around in circles" in her previous therapy experiences and felt as though she had "got nowhere". But the wordless power of the art she created had a lightning-bolt ability to bypass her patterns of destructive thought and strike through to something insightful and revelatory.

Here is a non-exhaustive list of some of the many ways an art-image (or related art-experience) might enable the arrival of a breakthrough moment for a client:

1. It encourages extended deep experiencing

The art-image has the power to arrest the attention of the client who has created it and put them in a trance-like state. I have called this extended deep experiencing and argued that it almost always leads to some sort of breakthrough moment. For example, when Susan brought Thin Susan to therapy, or Ali created her ritual for Eating Disorder Ali; or when Elias was telling his story of the knight and the baby—in each of these cases the client appeared to enter a state of altered consciousness for an extended period.

2. It can become embodied

The art-image can encourage change by becoming a lucky mascot for a client or a "talisman". Alternatively, it might become the container for their unwanted feelings or "a scapegoat" (Schaverien, 1999). All the characters in Elias' knight's tale seemed to be embodied images, as was Amy's (model) house, Susan's basket of tipped stones, and Ben's orangutan postcard. Betty explored her metaphor of the Vigilant Cockerel variously through the use of music, drama, mask-making, mask-wearing, poetry, and dance. Another example might be my client Barbara, who switched between song, dramatisation and sand tray making as she explored her relationship with her boyfriend.

3. It can act as a catalyst

We have seen that Tessa Dalley describes how the art-image can act as a catalyst to bring about small or large changes for a client. Elias' image (his knight's tale) became the catalyst for several breakthrough moments. For virtually all the clients' stories presented in this book, their self-created images acted as a catalyst to bring about the deepening of their therapy, their breakthrough moment, and change. I have argued that sometimes an image may provide a latent catalyst—that is, it may be seen as possessing a dormant power to bring about change at a later date (rather like a riddle set by the unconscious that is only slowly solved by the conscious). Martin's claws were a latent catalyst and did not reveal their meaning until the end of his therapy when he created the representation of his mother made out of a two-headed beast and a scorpion.

4. It can provide "holding"

The art-image can help a client control unwanted and unmanageable feelings. For example, Susan's stones held aspects of herself that were hidden and inaccessible. My client Lucy created an image of a scribbled mess to depict what she felt unable to speak about. The art-image can also hold negative and positive transference. My client Brenda lined up miniature figures to defend herself against a perceived attack from me (when she flipped into negative transference). Prior to this, she had imbued her image with positive transference when she used a superheroine figure to represent me in her sand tray.

5. It can reveal the transpersonal

The art-image often has potential to reveal a transpersonal dimension to a client's experience. For example, when my client Stephen lifted up his arms to mimic the drawing he had made, it led him to a transpersonal breakthrough moment. The art-image can also provide an element of surprise or synchronicity. The surprise of something unplanned arising during the creation of an image—such as the ray of light that emerged from Christine's orb or Ali's grumbling gremlin that "appeared" in her drawing—can seem so shocking to a client that they are led to a breakthrough moment.

6. It can encourage "full contact"

The art-image can bring a client and therapist abruptly and fully into the present moment achieving "full contact" (Mann, 2010). This full contact might be with the therapist, an aspect of the client's self, memories, events, or even objects. When a client is involved in extended deep experiencing or a breakthrough moment both client and therapist tend to be dramatically pulled into the present and the potential for full contact is increased. Gestalt theory suggests that it is this full contact that brings about client change (Polster & Polster, 1974). Elias' telling of his knight's story placed him and me in the here and now, watching in awe as the elaborate tale unfolded.

Can breakthrough moments bring about lasting change?

I frequently wondered if breakthrough moments had the ability to bring about lasting change for my clients. These moments always feel so powerful when they arrive in the course of a session, but at the beginning of my research I had no way of knowing if they could bring about permanent change. After interviewing former clients for this book, I realised just how long a pivotal moment can remain etched in a client's mind after the work has ended—in one case as long as a decade. Each client spoke of the significance of their respective breakthrough moment and said that they believed their breakthrough had enabled them to change in positive ways since the end of their therapy. For the first time I was provided with numerous firsthand accounts of the ways in which my clients felt breakthrough moments had precipitated lasting change in their lives. It was immensely exciting. I present some of their remarks here.

My client Amy spoke about her breakthrough moment when she jumped on the plasticine blob (symbolising her mother's voyeuristic boyfriend). She said, "I think it was all part of that moment. That was the keystone—the deep frustration that was blocking me in so many parts of my life. I seemed to have lost myself. Other people thought I was happily living my life but really I was just *functioning*. It had a massive impact on my moods in general and now I just feel that I am able to cope much better with life. My relationships with my husband, mother and career have all improved beyond measure". "From a neurophysiological standpoint," she added, "being able to visualise something in a new way [using arts media] helped me to change the way that this childhood trauma was stored in my brain". Amy said that when dealing with current issues in her life she would remind herself of various aspects of her arts-based therapeutic work and this supported her in dealing with the situation more positively.

Amy frequently imagined the flattened blob leaving her forever (and with it the memory of the man who had abused her). She said this had enabled her to move forwards in a number of areas in her life where previously she had felt stuck. This included improvements in her mood and improvements in the kind of relationship she had with her mother and husband; she also felt less insecure in her work abilities. Amy would inevitably find herself thinking about the former abuse on occasions, but she told me that when this happened she would remember the session in which she crushed the plasticine blob and would imagine it floating away upstream, almost as if it were a flattened carcass. This image (in her mind) helped her to feel less caught up in horrific feelings and to maintain a more objective stance about her past trauma. Amy provides a wonderful illustration of the fact that in at least some cases clients are still able to imaginatively interact with their art-images beyond therapy. This is yet another powerful argument for the use of arts media in psychotherapy: that long after the therapy has ended the memory of the images can retain a healing, therapeutic role.

When asked whether his arts-based therapy experience had provided him with any lasting change in his life, my client Elias explained that, "in some ways you feel like you always did—as if nothing has changed. And yet I *do* think a lot has changed. How I *feel* about things has changed—I'm more in touch with that now". He said that a close friend had informed him that the way he expressed himself had positively changed. "Things are still settling down," Elias told me. "It's a life-long process but I feel happier about the fact it's a life-long process now. I don't feel the old, urgent need to know. I can sit more comfortably in the not-knowing and in the joy of finding things out about myself". He said he went through some very "dark times" while he was in therapy but that now he could make choices "that feel right" for him: "I have stopped thinking the world will hate me for it!" Elias had abandoned formal religion and said that he felt more liberated as a result. He still found himself seeking, however, and felt clear that his new-found freedom did not preclude the possibility of a spiritual element at some point in the future. He was still looking for a bigger context; still searching and wondering.

Ali told me that the work she had done with Eating Disorder Ali had been a deeply significant part of her therapy. "It has changed things forever," she told me, particularly with regards to her past trauma. And my client Martha, who returned to see me some ten years after her therapy had finished, said that taking part in the re-enactment of her daughter's birth had enabled her to "make peace with it" so that now a decade later it was "not a trauma any more". Martha explained that whenever she remembers an art-image or arts-based exercise from her therapy, it helps her to "manage situations" in her current life. She felt that her arts-based therapy sessions had given her a "bank of memories" that were still actively useful to her today.

Susan said that she felt her life had changed irrevocably since her therapy. Now she listens to the quieter Susans, she told me. She assesses which Susan is currently at the forefront and no longer allows the "verbal, eloquent" Susan to dominate as she used to. Now she said she feels able to spot that particular Susan starting to take over and no longer has to simply accept the fact. She is able to say, "Budge over! Another Susan has something to say about this!" She said she feels more confident in herself and better able to give others her time and attention. She believes this is directly due to the fact that she now gives the other Susans more respect than she used to before her therapy.

To my delight, each of the former clients I interviewed described how their respective breakthrough moments were still very much at the forefront of their memories. They said that these vivid and profound memories still actively enabled them to manage their everyday lives.

Nothing will ever be the same

I feel it is important to end this book with a reminder of my sense of wonder at the world. This sense of wonder was first awoken many decades ago as I sat at breakfast, staring at a seemingly infinite series of Mickey Mouses on the back of a cereal box. My wonderment and appetite for existential mysteries has been reawakened and redoubled by my quest to discover more about breakthrough moments. As a result, I now find myself putting uncertainty, indeterminism, creativity and personal and cosmic meaning centre stage in my life—as a therapist, a writer/researcher, and as a human being. I have greater recognition of the importance of psychic energy and the impact this has in human connections and relationships, creativity and imagination, personal health and spirituality. I also have a new way of thinking about the transpersonal or inexplicable elements that creep (and sometimes *leap*) into my practice-room.

My understanding of breakthrough moments (and of the therapeutic process) has expanded in the course of writing this book and my thinking has consequently changed. There was always a mysterious and inexplicable aspect to a breakthrough moment long before I embarked upon researching the subject, and this mysterious element remains today. It is beyond me to fully understand what happens in a breakthrough moment, but my confidence has grown considerably as a therapist. The arrival of breakthrough moments with my clients is not such an unusual occurrence these days but it still *feels* as extraordinary as it ever did.

I have all these theoretical ideas and conjectures about breakthrough moments now, but I realise I must put them to one side and be present with my clients. I need to trust the process and not think too consciously about the ideas in this book—a bit like an actor who studies her role and learns the lines, but once she has stepped onto the stage must let all conscious thought of these elements go and listen and respond in the moment. This is what I try to do with my clients and it is something I stress is important to therapists who come to me for supervision. As well as trusting the process with my clients and trusting the process with the art-images they create, I have had to trust the process with my research. I have had to trust that this book was worth writing and that after many years of preparation I was in fact ready to present answers to some of my questions.

If I have stimulated the reader's imagination regarding breakthrough moments and the power of using arts media in psychotherapy then I will feel satisfied. I realised from the start that definitive answers were going to be elusive. I do feel, on the other hand, that I have gained some new insight into these powerful moments and I hope the reader has at least some idea of the magical way they can arise and change the course of a client's life forever. As nine-year-old client Joe said to his therapist Craig (my supervisee), "Everything can change in a moment."

The story ends …

Susan's story (continued)

During a session a few weeks before the end of her therapy, Susan and I were looking back at the many art-images she had made during the course of her work. Susan told me that "all the Susans" we had uncovered in the previous weeks were now hanging on an imaginary mobile (a kinetic sculpture that she imagined was suspended between us). She said the Susans were not exactly in harmony but that they were now co-existing on this hanging mobile without any one particular Susan being completely in charge. She told me that this meant none of the Susans had to be totally silenced or banished. She described the mobile as making a tinkling noise as the Susans moved around. This was because each of the Susans was symbolised, in her mind, by a tiny bottle. I could vividly picture this mobile and imagined hearing the tinkling of all the Susans. We sat together for a long time just visualising the hanging sculpture she had described.

"Can the Susans change position on this mobile or are they fixed?" I asked. This was based on my genuine curiosity as to whether each Susan remained in the same place or if the Susans could vie for different positions on the sculpture. I obviously had not read the situation well.

233

I should have waited longer before posing any questions, because a few seconds after I said these words Susan gasped in horror and sat staring at the floor. She had gone very pale and all her excitement about the visualisation had disappeared. "It's collapsed!" she said. "It's all tangled up now on the ground!" Her imaginary mobile was now imaginarily broken. She was crestfallen.

I had to stifle a gasp of horror at this new information. I was frustrated with myself. My premature intervention had spoiled a deeply important visualisation involving a new-found integration of all the Susans. It felt momentously important that I make an appropriate response. How could I rescue this beautiful visualisation my client had begun?

I pictured the collapsed mobile as a tangled-up string puppet on the floor. I was visited by a clear memory of the frustration I felt as a child when my own string puppet would get all tangled up. I vividly remembered the accompanying panicky feeling that it might never be untangled. I wondered if Susan thought that her imaginary mobile could not be untangled and how devastating this would surely feel for her. "What can we do to put it back together again?" I found myself saying. "It seems far too important to be left all muddled up on the floor."

About five minutes of tense silence followed. This time I was determined not to spoil it by saying or asking anything of her. Suddenly, Susan made the unexpected remark that the mobile had reassembled itself. I wondered if she had said this simply to please me. But it didn't seem like it and it would not have been in keeping with her character from the preceding weeks of therapy. I felt convinced that she really could *see* the reassembled mobile when she added that the light was now shining through the glass and the colour of the little bottles was glinting. She was busy describing which Susan was next to which Susan on this mobile when suddenly she experienced a powerful breakthrough moment. We met eyes (it felt like we did so through the structure of the fictional mobile hanging between us). I felt a flood of relief—the whole mobile seemed to have been restored as quickly as it had collapsed. It was almost as though Susan had pressed a rewind button and gone back to the beginning of her visualisation.

* * *

The creation of this mobile—where all the Susans could be together—was deeply important for my client and despite the near-calamity caused by my clumsy intervention, it had been put back together again. Susan's trauma surrounding the death of her mother when she was a teenager seemed to have caused different parts of her to become dissociated and as a result she felt like many Susans. It seems that her visualisation of the mobile represented the beginnings of her tentatively putting the Susans back together and feeling like a single person once again.

Eight years after her therapy had ended, I asked Susan about this experience with her collapsed, imaginary mobile. She remembered it vividly and explained that the mobile had collapsed because it felt as though by asking a question of it, I was crushing it before it had had a chance to fully come into being. On the other hand, she felt that the respect I had shown for the importance of her imaginary mobile may have enabled her to restore the visualisation intact.

In attempting to describe her therapeutic work, Susan spoke of the "out of body experience" she would have at times during her sessions. She said she felt hyper-alert and had a sense of being out of control. It was as though something "very real was happening and neither of us knew where it was going to go—we could only be in the moment and see what happened". She also spoke about how complicated it would feel at times when we used to *talk* in the therapy. She said that whenever I said something—even something trivial, she would hear a plethora of voices from the different Susans all jockeying to respond in conflicting ways. She said that having tried various forms of "talking therapy" in the past, she could finally understand why it had never been of any use to her—it was because the dominant Susans would simply "take over, and anyway many of the Susans were completely incapable of speaking".

Susan felt that her image of the mobile allowed some of the quieter, less verbal Susans to come forth without being overpowered by the central, more vocal Susans. She said the image had stayed with her throughout the passing years. "On separate occasions," she said, "different Susans are in the foreground and others are in the shadows".

By the time she ended her therapy it seems she felt the Susans were in harmony and none were banished or silenced. On the day of her last session she handed me a card that she had drawn herself. Inside she had written simply, "thank you from all the Susans".

* * *

My life is filled with the stories and artworks of clients who have climbed the stairs and entered the sacred, mysterious world of my practice-room. We spend time together every week for months or even years. It is a place outside the ordinary world filled with fantastical toys, objects and art materials; a place that welcomes and receives pain, anxiety, laughter, and hope. It is a place where breakthrough moments, gentle, momentous, moving and shocking continue to arrive at the most unexpected times, conjured into being by the amazing and often multifaceted art creations of my courageous clients.

A shelf in my practice-room.

REFERENCES

Akeret, R. U. (1995). *The Man Who Loved a Polar Bear.* London: Penguin.

Badenoch, B. (2008). *Being a Brain-Wise Therapist.* New York: W. W. Norton.

Baugh, M. (2010). *Strange Attractors in a Fractal Psyche: Chaos Theory Non-dual Wisdom & Psychotherapy.* Third Wave Behavioural Centre of Issaquah.

Bettelheim, B. (1975). *The Uses of Enchantment: The Meaning and Importance of Fairy Tales.* New York: Vintage.

Bloch, S. (1982). *What is Psychotherapy?* New York: Oxford University Press.

Böhm, T. (1992). Turning point and change in psychoanalysis. *International Journal Psycho-Analytic, 73:* 675–684.

Bohr, N. (1958). On atoms and human knowledge. *Daedalus, 87* (2).

Boroson, M. (2007). *The One Moment Master.* London: Rider.

Bowlby, J. (2006). *The Making and Breaking of Affectional Bonds.* London: Routledge.

Bradway, K., & McCoard, B. (1997). *Sandplay—Silent Workshop of the Psyche.* London: Routledge.

Braud, W., & Anderson, R. (1998). *Transpersonal Research Methods for the Social Sciences.* London: Sage.

Buber, M. (1958). *I and Thou.* New York: Philosophical Library.

Butz, M. R. (1997). *Chaos and Complexity.* London: Taylor & Francis.

Capra, F. (1975). *The Tao of Physics.* London: Flamingo-Harper Collins.

Case, C., & Dalley, T. (1992). *The Handbook of Art Therapy.* London: Routledge.

Chopra, D. (2003). *Synchro Destiny.* London: Random House.

Clarkson, P. (1995). *The Therapeutic Relationship.* London: Whurr.

Clarkson, P. (2002). *The Transpersonal Relationship in Psychotherapy.* London: Whurr.

Coburn, W. J. (2014). *Psychoanalytic Complexity: Clinical Attitudes for Therapeutic Change.* London: Routledge.

Combs, G., & Freedman, J. (1990). *Symbol Story & Ceremony: Using Metaphor in Individual and Family Therapy.* New York: W. W. Norton.

Cozolino, L. (2002). *The Neuroscience of Psychotherapy.* New York: W. W. Norton.

Dalley, T., et al. (1993). *3 Voices of Art Therapy: Image, Client, Therapist.* London: Routledge.

Dayton, T. (1994). *The Drama Within: Psychodrama and Experiential Therapy.* Deerfield Beach, FL: Health Communications.

DeWitt, R. (2010). *Worldviews: An Introduction to the History and Philosophy of Science 2nd edition.* Oxford: Wiley-Blackwell.

Doidge, M. D. (2007). *The Brain That Changes Itself.* London: Penguin.

Duvall, J., et al. (2007). Research as retelling: Capturing pivotal moments in therapy and training. In: S. Madigan (Ed.), *Therapeutic Conversations.* New York: W. W. Norton.

Edelman, G. (1987). *Neural Darwinism.* New York: Basic.

Einstein, A. (1905). On the electrodynamics of moving bodies. Based on the English translation of the original 1905 German-language paper (published as Zur Elektrodynamik bewegter Körper, in Annalen der Physik. 17: 891, 1905). In: *The Principle of Relativity.* London: Methuen, 1923.

Ellenberger, H. F. (1970). *The Discovery of the Unconscious: The History and Evolution of Dynamic Psychiatry.* New York: Basic.

Erikson, E. H. (1994). *Identity and the Life Cycle.* New York: W. W. Norton.

Eysenck, M. W. (2004). *Psychology: An International Perspective.* Hove: Psychology Press.

Freier, M. (2006). *Time Measured by Kairos and Kronos.* Whatif Enterprises LLC, 2007.

Gilroy, A., & McNeilly, G. (2000). *The Changing Shape of Art Therapy: New Developments in Theory and Practice.* London: Jessica Kingsley.

Gladwell, M. (2000). *The Tipping Point: How Little Things Can Make a Big Difference.* London: Abacus.

Gotswami, A., Reed, R. E., & Gotswami, M. (1993). *The Self-Aware Universe.* London: Penguin-Putman.

Greer Essex, J. Arts in Therapy Network. www.artsintherapy.com (retrieved on 03.03.2005).

Haneberg, L. (2006). *Coaching Basics.* Alexandria, VA: American Society for Training & Development (ASTD) Press.

Harris, B. (2007). *Thresholds of the Mind.* Beaverton, OR: Centrepointe Research.

Hass-Cohen, N. (Ed.) (2008). *Art Therapy and Clinical Neuroscience.* London: Jessica Kingsley.

Hebb, D. O. (1949). *The Organisation of Behaviour.* New York: Wiley.

Helm Meade, E. (1995). *Tell it by Heart: Women and the Healing Power of Story.* Chicago IL: Open Court.

Henley, D. (2002). *Clayworks in Art Therapy: Plying the Sacred Circle.* London: Jessica Kingsley.

Hiles, D. (2000). *Defining the paradigm of humanistic-existential psychology.* Paper for Conference at University of West Georgia, US, 11–14 May.

Hughes, D. A. (2006). *Building the Bonds of Attachment: Awakening Love in Deeply Troubled Children.* Oxford: Rowan & Littlefield.

Hycner, R., & Jacobs, L. (1995). *The Healing Relationship in Gestalt Therapy.* Gouldsboro, ME: Gestalt Journal Press.

Johnson, S. (2001). *Emergence*. New York: Penguin.

Jones, P. (2010). *Drama as Therapy. Vol 2*. London: Routledge.

Jung, C. G. (1916). *The Structure of the Unconscious*. In: C. G. Jung, *Collected Works*, Vol 7 437–507 (pp. 263–292). London: Routledge, 1953.

Jung, C. G. (1948). General aspects of dream psychology. In: R. Hull (Trans.) *Dreams* (pp. 23–66). Princeton, NJ: Princeton University Press [reprinted, 1974].

Jung, C. G. (1997). *Jung on Active Imagination*. London: Routledge.

Knill, P. J., Levine, E. G., & Levine, S. K. (2005). *Principles and Practice of Expressive Arts Therapy: Toward a Therapeutic Aesthetics*. London: Jessica Kingsley.

Kottler, J. A. (2014). *Change*. New York: Oxford University Press.

Lapworth, P., Sills, C., & Fish, S. (2001). *Integration in Counselling & Psychotherapy*. London: Sage.

LeDoux, J. (2002). *Synaptic Self*. New York: Penguin.

Lewis, P. (1993). *Creative Transformation: The Healing Power of the Arts*. Asheville, NC: Chiron.

Lorenz, E. N. (1963). The predictability of hydrodynamic flow. *Transactions of the New York Academy of Sciences*. 25 (4): 409–432. Available at: onlinelibrary.wiley.com/doi/10.1111/j.2164-0947.1963.tb01464.x/abstract [last accessed 1 September 2014].

Mahoney, M. J. (1991). *Human Change Processes*. New York: Basic.

Mahrer, A. R. (1986). *Therapeutic Experiencing: The Process of Change*. Toronto, ON: W. W. Norton.

Malchiodi, C. A. (2005). *Expressive Therapies*. New York: Guilford Press.

Mandelbrot, B. B. (1997). *Fractals, Form, Chance, and Dimension*. San Francisco, CA: W. H. Freeman.

Mann, D. (2010). *Gestalt Therapy: 100 Key points & Techniques*. London: Routledge.

Marks-Tarlow, T. (2008). *Psyche's Veil*. London: Routledge.

Maslow, A. H. (1971). *The Farther Reaches of Human Nature*. London: Arkana-Penguin.

Mazza, N. (2003). *Poetry Therapy: Theory and Practice*. New York: Brunner-Routledge.

McGilchrist, I. (2009). *The Master and His Emissary: The Divided Brain and the Making of the Western World*. New Haven, CT: Yale University Press.

McLaughlin C., & Holliday, C. (2014). *Therapy with Children and Young People: Integrative Counselling in Schools and Other Places*. London: Sage.

McLean, H., & Cole, A. (2001). *The Dream Catchers Handbook: Learn to Understand the Personal Significance of Your Dreams*. London: Carlton Books.

McNiff, S. (1998). *Trust the Process*. Boston, MA: Shambhala.

McTaggart, L. (2004). *The Field*. London: Element-Harper Collins.

Meadows, D. H. (1993). *Thinking in Systems*, eBook. Hartford, VT: Chelsea Green.

Mendelsohn, G. A. (1976). Associative and attentional processes in creative performance, *Journal of Personality, 44*(2): 179–369.

Moustakas, C. (1990). *Heuristic Research*. London: Sage.

Natterson, I. (1993). Turning points and intersubjectivity. *Clinical Social Work Journal, 21* (1): 45–56.

Nauert, R. (2015). *Insights on the "A-ha" moment.* Weizmann Institute of Science: Psych Central.

Neill, C. (1997). Story making and storytelling: Weaving the fabric that creates our lives. In: B. Warren (Ed.), *Using the Creative Arts in Therapy: A Practical Introduction.* London: Routledge.

O'Connell, C. (1986). *Amplification in context: The interactional significance of amplification in the secured-symbolising context-plus field.* Unpublished PhD dissertation. California Institute for Clinical Social Work.

Orzel, C. (2010). *How to Teach Quantum Physics to your Dog.* London: Oneworld.

Penrose, R. (2005). *The Road to Reality: A Complete Guide to the Laws of the Universe.* London: Vintage.

Perls, F. (1973). *The Gestalt Approach & Eye Witness to Therapy.* Palo Alto, CA: Science & Behavior.

Pert, C. B. (1997). *Molecules of Emotion.* New York: Scribner.

Philippson, P. (2009). *The Emergent Self.* London: Karnac.

Pibram, K. (Ed). (1993). *Rethinking Neural Networks: Quantum Fields and Biological Data.* New York: Erbaum.

Polster, E., & Polster, M. (1974). *Gestalt Therapy Integrated.* New York: Vintage.

Prigogine, I. (1984). *Order Out of Chaos.* New York: Oxford University Press.

Propp, V. (1968). *Morphology of the Folktale.* Bloomington, In: Publications of the American Folklore Society.

Rogers, C. R. (1961). *On Becoming a Person: A Therapist's View of Psychotherapy.* London: Constable.

Rowan, J., & Jacobs, M. (2003). *The Therapist's Use of Self.* London: Open University Press.

Ruelle, D. (1993). *Chance & Chaos.* New York: Oxford University Press.

Sacks, O. (2007). *Musicophilia: Tales of Music and the Brain.* New York: Random House.

Salzberg, S. *"Life is like an ever shifting kaleidoscope: a slight change and all patterns alter".* Motivational quotation www.quotationspage.com (retrieved on 13.09.10).

Schaverien, J. (1999). *The Revealing Image.* London: Jessica Kingsley.

Schwartz-Salent, N. (1998). *The Mystery of Human Relationship: Alchemy and the Transformation of the Self.* London: Routledge.

Siegel, D. J. (1999). *The Developing Mind.* New York: The Guilford Press.

Siegel, D. J. (2010). *The Mindful Therapist.* London: W. W. Norton.

Siegel, D. J., & Payne Bryson, T. (2012). *The Whole-Brain Child.* London: Constable & Robinson.

Siegel, D. J., & Solomon, M. (2013). *Healing Moments in Psychotherapy.* New York: W. W. Norton.

Stanislavski, C. (1990). *An Actor's Handbook.* London: Methuen.

Stern, D. N. (1998). *The Interpersonal World of the Infant.* London: Karnac.

Stern, D. N. (2004). *The Present Moment.* London: W. W. Norton.

Stolorow, R. D., & Atwood, G. E. (1987). *Psychoanalytic Treatment: An Inter-subjective Approach.* Hillsdale, NJ: The Analytic Press.

Stolorow, R. D., & Atwood, G. E. (1992). *Contexts of Being.* London: Routledge.

Sunderland, M. (2000). *Using Story Telling as a Therapeutic Tool with Children.* Milton Keynes: Speechmark.

The Code of Ethics and Practice Guidance for Professional Conduct from The Diploma in Wellbeing Practice for Children and Young People Course at The Institute for Arts and Education (IATE), Islington, London.

Tolkein, J. R. R. (1954). *The Fellowship of the Ring.* London: Harper-Collins.

Van Der Kolk, B. (2015). *The Body Keeps the Score: Mind, Brain and Body in the Transformation of Trauma.* London: Penguin.

Van Lommell, P. (2010). *Consciousness Beyond Life.* London: Harper Collins.

Waller, D., & Gilroy. A. (Ed.). (2000). *Psychotherapy Handbooks.* London: Open University Press.

Welch, M. (2005). Pivotal moments in the therapeutic relationship. *International Journal of Mental Health Nursing, 14*(3): 161–165.

Wheeler, J. A., & Zurek, W. H. (Eds.) (1983). *Quantum Theory and Measurement.* Princeton, NJ: Princeton University Press.

Wieland-Burston, J. (1992). *Chaos & Order in the World of the Psyche: Or Chaos & Order in the Inner and Outer World.* London: Routledge.

Wilber, K. (2001). *No Boundary.* Boston, MA: Shambhala.

Winnicott, D. W. (1965). *Maturational Processes and the Facilitating Environment Studies in the Theory and Emotional Development.* London: Karnac.

Wolf, F. A. (1989). *Taking the Quantum Leap: The New Physics for Non-Scientists.* New York: Harper & Row.

Yalom, I. (2001). *The Gift of Therapy.* London: Piatkus.

Zinker, J. (1977). *The Creative Process in Gestalt.* New York: Vintage.

Zohar, D. (1991). *The Quantum Self.* New York: Quill.

INDEX

Individual stories can be found under the entry: client stories